THE UNITED STATES
AND ISRAEL

STUDIES OF INFLUENCE IN INTERNATIONAL RELATIONS
Alvin Z. Rubinstein, *General Editor*

SOUTH AFRICA AND THE UNITED STATES
The Erosion of an Influence Relationship
  Richard E. Bissell

SOVIET-INDIAN RELATIONS
Issues and Influence
  Robert C. Horn

SOVIET INFLUENCE IN EASTERN EUROPE
Political Autonomy and the Warsaw Pact
  Christopher D. Jones

U.S. POLICY TOWARD JAPAN AND KOREA
A Changing Influence
  Chae-Jin Lee and Hideo Sato

SOVIET AND AMERICAN INFLUENCE IN THE HORN OF AFRICA
  Marina S. Ottaway

THE UNITED STATES AND IRAN
The Patterns of Influence
  R. K. Ramazani

SOVIET POLICY TOWARD TURKEY, IRAN AND AFGHANISTAN
The Dynamics of Influence
  Alvin Z. Rubinstein

THE UNITED STATES AND PAKISTAN
The Evolution of an Influence Relationship
  Shirin Tahir-Kheli

THE UNITED STATES AND BRAZIL
Limits of Influence
  Robert Wesson

THE UNITED STATES, GREECE AND TURKEY
The Troubled Triangle
  Theodore A. Couloumbis

THE UNITED STATES AND MEXICO
Patterns of Influence
  George W. Grayson

THE UNITED STATES AND ISRAEL

Influence in the Special Relationship

Bernard Reich

PRAEGER SPECIAL STUDIES • PRAEGER SCIENTIFIC

New York • Philadelphia • Eastbourne, UK
Toronto • Hong Kong • Tokyo • Sydney

Library of Congress Cataloging in Publication Data

Reich, Bernard.
    The United States and Israel.

    (Studies of influence in international relations)
    Bibliography: p.
    Includes index.
    1. United States—Foreign relations—Israel.
    2. Israel—Foreign relations—United States. I. Title.
    II. Series.
    E183.8.I7R45   1984   327.7305694   83-24795
    ISBN 0-03-060566-0 (alk. paper)
    ISBN 0-03-060564-4 (pbk. : alk. paper)

Published in 1984 by Praeger Publishers
CBS Educational and Professional Publishing
a Division of CBS Inc.
521 Fifth Avenue, New York, New York 10175 U.S.A.

456789   052   987654321

Printed in the United States of America
on acid-free paper

EDITOR'S PREFACE

Over the years the United States and Israel have developed a special relationship that is closer than that between the United States and most of its allies, even though there is no formal treaty of alliance; that is more extensive than that between the United States and most developed countries, even though Israel is a tiny country of less than 4 million with no strategically valuable resources; and that is more beset with perennial tugs and pulls across a wide range of political, military, economic, and technological issues, even though they share essentially the same values, aims, and conceptions of the world. It is a multifaceted relationship that is at one and the same time strategic, military, political, and moral in character.

At the heart of U.S.-Israeli relations is a vexing paradox: the more economically and militarily dependent Israel becomes on the United States, the more it seems able to frustrate U.S. policy makers; conversely, the more assistance and support the United States provides Israel, the less it seems able to affect Israel on issues that it considers important. This paradox—increasingly evident since the late 1960s—has become a major source of tension. From 1948 to 1967 government-to-government relations were good but not particularly close. Notwithstanding President Truman's de facto recognition of the new state of Israel minutes after it proclaimed independence on May 15, 1948, U.S. policy kept Israel at arm's length as it sought to accommodate and court Arab nationalism. For Washington, Israel was more an embarrassment than a commitment. Had Stalin not permitted arms and immigrants to flow from eastern Europe, it would not have survived the first Arab-Israeli war of 1948-49. During the Eisenhower and Kennedy administrations, France provided the wherewithal that ensured Israeli security. Not until after the 1967 June War, when the Soviet Union emerged as a lavish supplier of arms to the Arabs and U.S.-Soviet rivalry intensified and expanded throughout the Middle East, did the United States gradually assume its preeminent position in Israeli policy.

Professor Bernard Reich's study analyzes the evolution and dynamics of the "new" relationship between the United States and Israel since 1967. It focuses on the peace process, on the quest for a lasting settlement of the Arab-Israeli conflict as it has developed in the Johnson, Nixon, Ford, Carter, and Reagan presidencies. Rich in detail and attention to the changing regional and international environment within which the United States and Israel have fashioned their cooperation and carried on their disagreements, the study examines key policy issues and determinants. It provides an expert guide to the complexities that both cement and buffet their special relationship; explores the limits of the ability of each to influence the other; and with sensitivity and insight assesses the domestic factors that greatly condition the determination of U.S. policy toward Israel.

This study is a timely contribution to our understanding of an important bilateral relationship, and a welcome addition to the Praeger series Studies of Influence in International Relations.

Alvin Z. Rubinstein
Series Editor

PREFACE

The United States and Israel have been linked in a "special relationship" that existed prior to the establishment of the Jewish state in 1948 and has focused on the continuing U.S. support for the survival, security, and well-being of Israel as an independent state in the Middle East. Israel and the United States each occupy special positions in the other's foreign policy, which are more than the sum of the tangible factors that can be readily enumerated. The relationship has been the subject of extensive discussion and much speculation since the independence of the Jewish state in 1948. The politics and foreign policy of Israel have been examined in numerous studies and writings, much of which has been polemical in nature. The relationship has been analyzed from diverse perspectives, but few have illuminated it in terms of the influences that each has had on the policies of the other.

The United States has been active in the political life of the Middle East since World War II and has been the main extraregional power in that area for much of the time. Since the 1967 war it has been the dominant power in the Arab-Israeli sector and the efforts to resolve the Arab-Israeli conflict have relied almost exclusively on the United States for much of what has been achieved. Israel was a creation of the international community, more precisely the United Nations, but the United States has been its main benefactor, particularly in the period since 1967. Today, and for the foreseeable future, the United States is essential for the survival, security, and well-being of the Jewish state. The ties between one of the largest and most powerful states and one of the smallest have attracted much attention but little concrete explanation of the nature of the influence relationship. Some assume that it is one-sided or should be, given the disproportionate size and power of the two states. Others argue that the flow of influence is reversed; that Israel has a disproportionate influence on the nature and content of U.S. policy. In fact, each state at different times has been successful in influencing the behavior of the other through a multiplicity of techniques.

The purpose of this study is to assess the interaction of the two states, with emphasis on the period since the advent of the Carter and Begin tenures in 1977 and on the issue areas relating to the peace process, which has been central to the policies and activities of both. The United States and Israel share a number of concerns, of which the goal of peace in the Arab-Israeli conflict remains significant.

The discussion of U.S.-Israeli relations seeks to illuminate the nature of the influence relationship, and in so doing to contribute to a better understanding of their relationship and of the concept of influence in international relations. Professor Alvin Rubinstein has suggested a useful definition, which will be employed in this study. "Influence is manifested when country A affects, through nonmilitary means, directly or indirectly, the behavior of country B so that it rebounds to the advantage of A."[1] This alteration may occur in many ways and may be achieved through numerous techniques, some of them imperceptible. States engage in multifaceted efforts to affect the policies of others, both friends and adversaries, with varying degrees of success at different times. Influence is rarely forceful and open in nature but more often is exercised through subtle means. It is not proportionate to power, in the narrow sense of that term, but is an element of the relations of two states. We will seek to identify the alterations in policy outcomes and the mechanisms by which they were achieved.

We will illustrate the areas in which the policies and activities of both Israel and the United States have altered or modified the policies and activities of the other. We identify the extent to which economic and military assistance and political and diplomatic support may have influenced the decisions of the recipient and how the behavior of the recipient may have affected the activities of the donor. In the case of the United States and Israel, however, the issue is complicated by the nature of their respective political systems and by the complexity of the issues they have faced and of the regional environment in which they have had to operate. Thus, while policy outcomes can be identified and while activities often can be enumerated, evaluation of a cause and effect relationship may not always be obvious. The link between attempts at influence and resultant actions is at best tenuous and cannot be measured in a precise way or quantified with any ease. Our goal is, therefore, modest: we hope to shed light on the complex nature of the influence relationship between the United States and Israel.

The U.S.-Israeli relationship is a special case for a number of reasons, not the least of which is that Israel is the only Jewish state in the modern world, and while of the Third World in many respects, it is clearly different from that grouping of states, from which it has been formally excluded. Its unique position, regionally and globally, has defined foreign

---

[1] Alvin Z. Rubinstein, *Soviet Policy Toward Turkey, Iran and Afghanistan: The Dynamics of Influence* (New York: Praeger, 1982), page viii.

policy parameters unlike those which exist for other states. Israel's Jewishness has been an element of its special situation and an important factor in its links with the United States. It is neither large nor rich, and its power, while impressive regionally, is highly circumscribed in extent and in potential effect.

It has been suggested that influence is a function of both time and issue; thus we will seek to examine this proposition in the specific instances of the relationship to identify variances over time and with regard to issue. Similarly, because states are not the sole actors in contemporary international relations, we will examine the role of non-state actors, particularly the Jewish organizations, which influence the relationship on both sides. There is also the domestic political factor and particularly the special role of the legislative branch in the United States. Throughout the discussion we must keep sight of the question of whether or not the U.S.-Israeli relationship is special to the extent that broader generalizations about influence cannot result.

This manuscript was completed in the summer of 1983, while the influence relationship continued to revolve around many of the themes discussed in this volume. No doubt the study would have been enriched by detailed consideration of those interactions but a book must end somewhere and a dramatic shift in the relationship is unlikely.

ACKNOWLEDGMENTS

Any study results from a substantial effort over an extended period during which numerous people make contributions that often cannot be acknowledged. This volume has benefitted from my numerous visits to Israel and the Arab world where its subject matter has been discussed at length with academics, journalists, and government officials, as well as the "man in the street." It has gained insight from substantial connection with the U.S. policy machinery, including many of the participants in the decision-making process, and with the Washington "rumor mill." I am indebted as well to extensive discussion of many of these themes in universities, public forums, and foreign ministries in numerous countries, worldwide, which has helped to shape the presentation found in this volume.

A number of U.S. and Israeli officials, academic and other colleagues and friends, have reviewed all or part of the manuscript and offered suggestions that have improved its accuracy and contributed to its interpretations.

To avoid embarrassment to any they shall all remain nameless. Several of my students at The George Washington University, which has provided a congenial atmosphere for the preparation of this study, have been able to reverse roles and provide valuable critiques of portions of the study. All deserve some of the credit, while the errors are mine.

The primary debt is owed, and this book is dedicated, to those who contributed the most in time and energy: Suzie, Barry, Norman, Michael, and Jennifer.

CONTENTS

the United States began to display a major concern for the political and security aspects of the Palestine issue.

The initial U.S. involvement was prompted by a humanitarian concern that centered on the emigration of displaced persons from Europe to Palestine. Truman saw a need to aid the remnants of European Jewry, and while Britain severely restricted the influx of Jews to Palestine, the United States pressed for increased immigration quotas. Truman seemed to believe in the need to redeem the Balfour Declaration pledges concerning the establishment of a Jewish homeland in Palestine, which the United States had endorsed. He also considered the advantages to be gained in the domestic political arena by adopting a course of action aiding the Jews of Europe. The establishment of the Anglo-American Commission of Inquiry in the fall of 1945 did little to alter the divergent approaches of the two allies to the problems associated with the future of Palestine.

The matter took on a different coloration when the British decided, in the spring of 1947, to terminate their responsibility for Palestine and to turn the question over to the United Nations for ultimate resolution. The U.N. Special Committee on Palestine (UNSCOP) was created and eventually proposed a plan for partition of Palestine that recommended the creation of an Arab state and a Jewish state in Palestine that would be linked in an economic union. This proposal was adopted by the U.N. General Assembly on November 29, 1947, by a vote of 33 to 13, with 10 abstentions. The United States supported the proposals of UNSCOP and worked for the adoption of the partition resolution. By so doing it made its most significant decision to that date with regard to the Palestine problem.

U.S. support for the resolution went beyond its single vote in the U.N. General Assembly; it was active in seeking the support of other governments and was the party most instrumental in assuring its adoption. Truman summed up American policy in these terms:

> My purpose was then and later to help bring about the redemption of the pledge of the Balfour Declaration and the rescue of at least some of the victims of Nazism. I was not committed to any particular formula of statehood in Palestine or to any particular time schedule for its accomplishment. The American policy was designed to bring about, by peaceful means, the establishment of the promised Jewish homeland and easy access to it for the displaced Jews of Europe.[1]

After partition the conflict between the communities in Palestine escalated to new, higher, and more dangerous levels than had existed previously. Sporadic and limited episodes of violence now became more constant and damaging. Observers noted that the accelerating conflict might prevent the implementation of the U.N. resolution, and the United Nations Palestine Commission reported that violence and chaos would follow termination of the mandate unless the United Nations was prepared to provide the force necessary to implement partition. A number of governments suggested that partition be postponed and an alternative be identified. It was in this context that the U.S. representative to the United Nations, Warren R. Austin, proposed, on March 19, 1948, a U.N. trusteeship as a temporary and emergency measure to restore public order. The plan had little support and was soon overshadowed by developments in the region. Despite the apparent vacillation in U.S. policy, when Israel declared its independence on May 14, 1948, the United States was the first to accord it recognition (albeit de facto and not de jure).

The lack of an overall approach that would guide the making of specific decisions was an obvious attribute of U.S. policy. The vacillation was a result of the disagreement within the executive branch concerning the advisability of supporting the creation of a Jewish state. There was no clear determination to support that creation "no matter what." Truman's decisions were taken against the advice of some of his advisers and the overwhelmingly negative view of the professionals of the Department of State and Department of War (later, Defense), who were concerned that a decision in support of a Jewish state would be harmful to American strategic and political interests in the Arab world, particularly with respect to access to Arab oil.

Truman's motives remain a matter of some controversy, but it is clear that humanitarian and moral factors played a significant part in influencing him. He was genuinely moved by the plight of the Jews of Europe and by the need to honor earlier pledges, such as those of the Balfour Declaration. There were, no doubt, also domestic political considerations, but it appears that these were of a lesser order of magnitude in influencing his decisions.

The independence of Israel and the Arab-Israeli war that followed set the stage for the continuing Arab-Israeli conflict and the parameters for the evolving U.S.-Israeli relationship.

TRIALS AND TRIBULATIONS, 1948-67

The ongoing Arab-Israeli conflict provides the focal point of the U.S.-Israel relationship, at the heart of which has been the mutually agreed goal of resolving the conflict in such a manner as to assure the survival and security of Israel. From the outset they have agreed on the goal but not always on the method to achieve it.

The first Arab-Israeli war precipitated a U.S. policy that had not been carefully determined in advance. Throughout the first conflict the United States maintained a posture of nonparticipation and favored U.N. efforts at resolution. As early as May 14, 1948, the United States had supported a General Assembly resolution calling for the appointment of a mediator; subsequently it endorsed the resolution of December 11, 1948, establishing the Palestine Conciliation Commission (PCC), of which it became a member. It also supported the creation of the U.N. Truce Supervision Organization. In December 1947 the United States embargoed arms shipments to the region in an effort to prevent conflict or, in the event of conflict, to reduce its scope. This proved far more damaging to Israel than to the Arab states, which obtained arms from Britain.

Ever since the Truman administration the United States has focused its attention, in the broadest sense, on the need to terminate the Arab-Israeli conflict—an objective that continues to be regarded as essential for the achievement of regional stability and the advancement of other U.S. interests. During the Truman years the United States channeled many of its efforts to resolve that conflict through the PCC, which submitted proposals to Israel and the Arab states for a political, territorial, and economic settlement.

There was some change in the early Eisenhower years because the focal point of the Dulles stewardship of foreign policy was an intensification of concern about the Soviet Union and international Communism, and the desire to contain them. In the Arab-Israeli sector the stress was on the concept of "impartial friendship," and Eisenhower often spoke of remaining neutral in the conflict. Israel's importance was diminished as increased weight was given to other elements in the formulation of U.S. policy. The oil and political "value" of the Arab states became key considerations in the struggle against Soviet penetration of the Middle East, although resolving the Arab-Israeli conflict remained an element in the overall objective of strengthening the region against Soviet encroachment.

The United States sought an Arab-Israeli rapprochement through diverse approaches, including increased economic aid to the Arab states in order to spur economic development and thereby secure a more reasonable perspective, an effort to deal with the Palestinian refugee problem, and an attempt to allay Arab fears of Israel. Dulles's visit to the region in May 1953 set the tone, and the policies to support his perspective were soon inaugurated. Israel became concerned about a perceived "pro-Arab trend" in U.S. policy, but no serious rupture characterized those early years.

Amelioration of economic and social conditions was identified as a means to achieve an Arab-Israeli settlement. Eisenhower's personal representative, Eric Johnston, explored steps that might lead to an improvement of the general situation in the region through development and utilization of the water resources of the Jordan River. It was believed that a comprehensive Jordan Valley development plan would contribute to regional stability and economic progress, and thus help to reduce tension and perhaps promote accommodation between Israel and the Arabs. But, despite some agreement at the technical level, there was no overall accord among the riparian states.

In August 1955 the Eisenhower administration took a more direct approach. In a speech before the Council on Foreign Relations, Secretary of State John Foster Dulles noted the need to deal with three problems—the refugee issue, the "pall of fear," and the lack of "fixed permanent boundaries"—and suggested that they "seem capable of solution." He proposed a multifaceted approach: resettlement and repatriation, with additional arable land created to facilitate the effort, and projects for development of water resources with U.S. funds and an international loan that would enable Israel to pay compensation to the refugees. To promote security and to alleviate the fear prevalent in the region, the United States would join in formal treaty arrangements to help guarantee and preserve the permanent borders between Israel and its neighbors that would replace the 1949 armistice lines. These suggestions and related efforts had no practical result.

These efforts were soon overshadowed by developments that led to the 1956 Suez War. Israel's decision to go to war, with Britain and France, against Egypt conflicted with Dulles's view of the need to seek a settlement of the problem by peaceful means, and was made despite American entreaties not to take forcible action. Israel saw the war as a defensive action against a hostile and dedicated foe, and as a result of its fear that Egypt would become too powerful after the Czech-Egyptian arms deal, despite Israel's arms supply arrangement with France. After the commencement of hostilities the United States took a leading role in bringing about a cease-fire and the eventual withdrawal of Israeli, British, and French troops from Egyptian territory. U.S. pressure, as well as reassurances, eventually proved decisive in securing Israel's full withdrawal from the Sinai and Gaza.

The Suez episode was a major irritant in U.S.-Israeli relations and involved a number of elements. There was a crisis of confidence involving the secretive nature of the tripartite effort, the exclusion of the United States from the councils of the planners, and the responses to U.S. queries with less than full candor. There was also the ignoring of U.S. entreaties not to go to war and the moral dilemma resulting from the use of force as a means of implementing national policy. Israel was dismayed by the U.S. position, particularly the heavy pressure to force its withdrawal from Egyptian territory. At the same time Israel secured some gains with the opening of the Strait of Tiran to its shipping and the placement of the U.N. Emergency Force in Sinai to help guarantee the arrangement and the tranquillity of the Egypt-Israel frontier. A U.S. pledge of support for Israel's right to sail in the Gulf of Aqaba proved significant. Thus, even in this early case U.S. influence was crucial in modifying Israeli policy. Urgent demands combined with reassurances led Israel to acquiesce in the U.S. request for its withdrawal from Egyptian territory. This pattern of entreaty/ reassurance has been utilized often in the continuing relationship.

The withdrawal of foreign troops from Egypt in 1957 terminated the Suez crisis and ushered in a new period in U.S. policy. It ended the U.S.-Israel confrontation that followed Israel's invasion, and inaugurated a period of relative tranquillity in the bilateral relationship. The substantial British and French roles in the politics of the post-World War II Middle East came to an end, and the two superpowers emerged as the major external forces in the region. The new U.S. role lent further credence to its articulated interest in resolving the Arab-Israeli conflict.

There also seemed to emerge a U.S. understanding of the fact that termination of the dispute was a complex and long-term process and that, in the short term, efforts to move in the direction of an interim settlement would have to take precedence over efforts to achieve a comprehensive settlement. The interim approach was that of maintaining security and stability in the region while trying to create conditions that would serve to ameliorate the long-term situation. Henry Cabot Lodge articulated this perspective in a statement at the U.N. General Assembly in March 1957:

> The United States would like to see as rapidly as is practical a definitive settlement of the Palestine problem—such a peace as is contemplated by the Armistice Agreements. Realistically we must accept the fact that this cannot be attained at the present.[2]

Efforts to resolve the conflict received a lessened priority because of this realism as well as because of the shift of attention to the Soviet initiative in the region. The Eisenhower Doctrine, which focused on Communist threats to the independence and integrity of Middle Eastern states, was the major element of U.S. policy in the latter part of the 1950s and reflected that administration's views of the priorities. The administration believed that efforts to counter the Soviet threat, which it perceived as more dangerous, might also contribute to long-term resolution of the conflict between Israel and the Arabs. However, the Eisenhower Doctrine had little direct applicability to the Arab-Israeli problem because its primary direction was against Communist penetration and radical Arab influences.

By the end of the Eisenhower administration, U.S. efforts to encourage a permanent and lasting settlement of the Arab-Israeli conflict had achieved no significant gains. The United States seemed to prefer efforts to maintain the status quo rather than the launching of new peace initiatives. The disagreement between Israel and the Arabs seemed to be fundamental, with frequent small-scale military encounters and vitriolic verbal exchanges characteristic of the situation. The United States focused on the prevention of war, the maintenance of stability, and the promotion of economic and social development. During this period Israeli and U.S. interests were in basic consonance, and the relations between the two states more nearly resembled the ones prevailing during the Truman administration than those during the first years of the Eisenhower tenure. The United States sought to avoid becoming a major arms supplier in the Arab-Israeli sector and to avoid an arms imbalance that might lead to conflict. It also assisted in economic and social development through grants and loans as well as technical assistance.

The 1960 presidential campaign suggested that relations between the United States and Israel might be different with Eisenhower's successor, inasmuch as both major candidates pledged a renewed effort to achieve an Arab-Israeli settlement. Senator John F. Kennedy proposed the convening of a conference of Israeli and Arab leaders, while Vice-President Richard M. Nixon said he would assign vice-presidential candidate Ambassador Henry Cabot Lodge responsibility for directing negotiations. Kennedy's election indicated the possibility of a change in U.S. policy. Certainly his style was different from that of his predecessors, and he also seemed to have a somewhat different point of departure in his decision making. He was more of an activist in foreign policy. Kennedy sought to open a dialogue with the leaders of the Arab world and to improve ties through various moves (such as the choice of John Badeau, former president of the American University in Cairo and of the Near East Foundation, for the crucial post of ambassador to Cairo).

These overtures concerned Israel, which envisioned a negative effect on the bilateral U.S.-Israel relationship. But Kennedy reiterated past policies in support of U.N. resolutions concerning the Palestine problem and pledged the use of U.S. influence to help establish a just and peaceful solution to the Arab-Israeli conflict. This helped to reassure Israel. The refugee issue was given increased attention primarily through the PCC, of which the United States was a member. Joseph E. Johnson was dispatched to the region to see what might be done on a practical level to deal with the refugee issue. The end result was a report and some optimistic projections but, ultimately, no tangible accomplishments. The United States also became involved in efforts to maintain the arms balance and made its first important sale of military equipment to Israel (the Hawk missile) in 1962. The remainder of the Kennedy administration saw no significant effort to deal with resolution of the Arab-Israeli issue, and no dramatic shifts in the bilateral relationship.

Prior to the 1967 War, and despite a small increase in the U.S. involvement in the region, the Johnson administration refrained from engaging in any major effort to resolve the Arab-Israeli conflict. U.S. policies sought to maintain the military balance as a means of preventing hostilities. The U.S. position could be characterized as seeking to prevent an Arab-Israeli war while promoting regional security, stability, and socioeconomic improvement. In general, Israel concurred in this approach because, at that time, it also seemed to believe that resolution of the conflict was not an achievable objective. The maintenance of the military balance, the consequent supply of military equipment to Israel to ensure security, and the improvement of social and economic conditions received a high priority in Israeli decision making as well.

This congruence of perspective was reflected in the bilateral relationship. While U.S. relations with Egypt were deteriorating, the ties between the United States and Israel seemed to be constantly improving. The improved relationship seemd to reach a plateau in June 1964, when Prime Minister Levi Eshkol visited the United States and met with President Lyndon Johnson and other senior officials. Although former Prime Minister David Ben-Gurion had visited the United States on several occasions and had met with senior U.S. officials, this was the first official visit by an Israeli prime minister to the United States. In a joint communiqué issued in Washington on June 2, 1964, it was noted that Johnson "reiterated to Prime Minister Eshkol United States support for the territorial integrity and political independence of all countries in the Near East" and emphasized U.S. opposition to the threat or use of force. This reassured Israel in the face of continued Arab threats to overwhelm the Jewish state.

THE AFTERMATH OF THE JUNE WAR

The June War of 1967 was a major watershed in U.S. relations with Israel and in the U.S. approach to the Arab-Israeli sector of the Middle East. The war suggested the failure of the previous approach to the Arab-Israeli conflict and radically changed the political climate of the Middle East by creating new circumstances—such as the Israeli occupation of substantial amounts of Arab territory through its dramatic victory over the Arab armies—thought to be more conducive to a settlement of the conflict. The links between the United States and Israel became more obvious in the weeks before the war and during the six days of hostilities. The congruence of perspective and policy in the aftermath of the hostilities provided a solid base for the development of the new bilateral relationship.

The United States actively sought a settlement of the conflict instead of pursuing stability, which had been the effective operational approach during the preceding decade. President Lyndon B. Johnson said:

> We achieved a cease-fire, but it was clear that the road to peace would be long and hard. Nevertheless, a true peace in the Middle East was the only appropriate objective for us to pursue. Twenty years of fragile truce, of hatred and anxiety, had yielded three dangerous armed conflicts. This time, I was convinced, we could not afford to repeat the temporary and hasty arrangements of 1957.[3]

The shift in the U.S. perspective was crucial. Before the war the United States had spoken of peace but apparently had not believed it to be a viable objective. After the war it established peace as an operational goal. Between the 1967 and 1973 wars, and under both the Johnson and the Nixon administrations, the United States sought to achieve an effective and durable Arab-Israeli peace (not simply a cease-fire arrangement) arrived at by the parties and not imposed by the superpowers.

The June War of 1967 seemed to have a comparable effect on Israeli thinking. For several years before the conflict, Israel had focused on internal development, and peace had receded as an operational goal of its foreign policy. That is, while Israel hoped for and sought peace, it was not considered to be an achievable short-term objective, and the relatively stable situation allowed it to focus on domestic developments. The main thrust of Israel's foreign and security policy was the acquisition of military equipment and support for its security, in the absence of a viable option for peace.

The war was neither launched nor waged with peace as the objective; Israel's goals were limited and tactical, primarily to relieve the military threat posed by the actions of Egyptian President Nasser and his military forces. But once the magnitude of the Israeli accomplishment in the June War became clear, there was hope that the military gains might be converted into political achievements. Peace suddenly loomed as an operational and practical objective of Israeli policy. In an important statement to the Knesset on June 12, 1967, Prime Minister Eshkol stated:

> To the nations of the world I want to say: be under no illusion that the State of Israel is prepared to return to the situation that reigned up to a week ago. The State of Israel arose and continued to exist as a matter of right, and this nation has been compelled to fight and fight again for that right. . . . The position that existed up till now shall never again return. . . .
>
> We have already explained to the nations of the world that we look, not backward, but forward—to peace. . . .
>
> A new situation has been created, which can serve as a starting point in direct negotiations for a peace settlement with the Arab countries.[4]

Eshkol's perspective was subsequently endorsed by the cabinet, which decided unanimously on July 30 that there would be no withdrawal from the occupied territories unless there were direct negotiations with the Arabs to achieve peace.[5] On August 1 the Knesset supported the government's policy.[6] Israel did not believe that peace was imminent or that it was achievable in the short term. But the changed circumstances, particularly the fact that Israel had acquired negotiating cards by occupying territories that the Arabs wanted to reclaim, shaped a hope that a negotiated peace, in which one could envision peace and security for Israel in exchange for territories restored to the Arab states, was possible.

Israel was not thinking in terms of total withdrawal, but only of a partial return of territory in exchange for peace, which would permit retention of some areas in order to achieve secure and permanent borders for the Jewish state. Eshkol elaborated these themes in a public statement on June 27, 1967:

> So long as our neighbors will persist in their policy of belligerence and will make plans for our destruction, we will not relinquish the areas that are now under our control and that we deem necessary for our security and self-defense. If, on the other hand, the Arabs will forego

their war against us, there is no problem I hope that will not be able to [be solved] in direct negotiations, for the benefit of all parties concerned.

The prospects of direct negotiations are better today, I would say, than they have been at any time in the last twenty years, because the Arab states should be closer than ever to recognizing the need to face realities in the Middle East. . . .[7]

The U.S. perspective was predicated on the view that the magnitude of the changes caused by the war created conditions favorable to resolution of the overall problem, and that the situation was too dangerous not to make an attempt at a settlement.

Although they shared the perspective of the improved prospects for peace, the two states did not underestimate the obstacles and the extensive efforts that would be required to convert prospects into realities. At the same time there was concern in Israel about the precise nature of the U.S. role.

Despite the fears of some Israelis, the United States decided after the June War not to repeat the approach utilized in 1957, which had forced an Israeli withdrawal from Sinai in exchange for no significant concessions by the Egyptians. Instead, believing that Israel would exchange territory (albeit not "every square inch") for peace, the United States sought to use the captured territories as bargaining chips to secure meaningful Arab concessions for a genuine peace. There were two important indicators of the U.S. position: Johnson's "Principles of Peace" and the interaction between the United States and the Soviet Union during and after the conflict.

Johnson foreshadowed the U.S. approach in a speech on June 19, 1967, in which he committed the United States to an Arab-Israeli peace based on five principles: "every nation in the area has a fundamental right to live and to have this right respected by its neighbors," justice for the refugees, the right of innocent maritime passage, limits on the arms race, and "respect for political independence and territorial integrity of all the states of the area."[8] The goal was a lasting peace reached through a negotiated settlement that rejected a return to the situation of June 4, 1967. He argued: "Clearly the parties to the conflict must be the parties to the peace. . . . It is hard to see how it is possible for nations to live together in peace if they cannot learn to reason together." This general approach was reiterated on numerous occasions by Johnson and other senior members of the administration, and provided the framework for U.S. peace efforts until the end of Johnson's tenure. This general perspective comported well with the Israeli concept, which focused on a permanent peace reached through direct negotiations and with territorial withdrawals in the context of an overall settlement.

Soviet-U.S. exchanges seemed to substantiate the U.S. approach. In the immediate postwar period the superpowers came into direct conflict concerning the appropriate goals of diplomatic activity. While the United States sought to exploit the new circumstances to move toward a genuine settlement, the Soviet Union sought a return to the status quo ante and focused on total Israeli withdrawal from the territories occupied during the war. The Soviets sought to negate the Arab defeat and to salvage their position in the region. This approach took a number of forms and utilized various forums, but the basic theme was similar in all—total Israeli withdrawal from occupied Arab territory, followed by condemnation of Israel and the requirement that it pay reparations to the Arabs. Among various actions was a Soviet request for an emergency special session of the U.N. General Assembly. The United States opposed the session, on the grounds that it would hinder rather than assist the quest for peace and that its primary purpose was propagandistic in nature. The session took place, but the United Nations did not follow the preferred Soviet course and there were no conclusive results.

The leaders of the two superpowers met at a summit conference in Glassboro, New Jersey, at the end of June 1967; there Johnson and Soviet Premier Alexei Kosygin discussed the Middle East and other issues. No substantive agreement emerged from these meetings or from the special General Assembly session, and in the end the matter was returned to the attention of the Security Council. Soviet efforts in the General Assembly to condemn Israel and achieve its withdrawal from Arab territory, as well as to gain compensation for the Arabs, were unsuccessful. The meetings were characterized by debate, statement, and consultation, but ultimately had no substantive effect. Israel and the United States viewed the end of the session with a degree of relief and as something of a vindication of their positions. Meanwhile, the Soviet and Arab perspectives were becoming more congruent.

In the wake of the June War, the Arab and Soviet views focused on the "liquidation of the consequences of the Israeli aggression." The Arab view was clearly articulated at the summit conference held in Khartoum, Sudan, at the end of the summer, at which the Arab leaders reassessed their position in the wake of the June War debacle. They agreed to unite their political efforts ". . . to eliminate the effects of the aggression and to ensure the withdrawal of the aggressive Israeli forces from the Arab lands which have been occupied since the aggression of 5 June." Furthermore, they noted that this "will be done within the framework of the main principles by which the Arab states abide, namely no peace with Israel, no recognition of Israel, no negotiations with it, and insistence on the rights of the Palestinian people in their own country."[9] This decision, and the perspective it reflected, clearly indicated the Arab view that negotiations for peace with Israel were not possible.

Given the contrasting positions of the main antagonists, it is not surprising that efforts to achieve peace and implement the Johnson formula were unsuccessful in the months immediately following the war. Although the United States continued to believe that the region was dangerous and that the prospects for peace had improved, the lack of progress made it more willing to consider a wide range of alternative approaches. This led to some uneasiness in Israel, which believed that the pressures generated by its June victory would facilitate a change in the Arab position in the direction of a settlement, and that there was no pressing need to move ahead. On the other hand, Israel was concerned that U.S. impatience might lead to precipitous moves that Israel could not accept. Israel believed that this would result not from bad faith but from other U.S. concerns, such as the desire to resolve disputes with a high conflict potential, an interest in resuming relations with those Arab states that had broken them at the time of the June War, pressure from domestic commercial (especially oil) interests to restore relations with the Arab states, and a desire to reach an accommodation with the Soviet Union on some issue (almost without concern as to its nature).

The regular fall meetings of the U.N. General Assembly and the sessions of the Security Council provided a test of the perspectives that had developed in the wake of the war. Israel sought to ensure that the General Assembly would not allow the Arab states to avoid direct negotiations, and thus worked to prevent third-party intervention in the situation. It pressed for direct negotiations to help foster the move from war to peace. The United States worked to develop some momentum for the peace process. The General Assembly allowed private negotiations and the superpowers met to consider the situation, but nothing substantial emerged from their efforts.

The United States pressed a number of proposals (based on Johnson's five "principles of peace") to achieve momentum. Israel expressed reservations about U.S. proposals that did not emphasize the need for direct negotiations between the parties. It also sought and focused on the need for direct negotiations between the parties, and for a situation that would not prejudice its positions or policies. Ultimately the U.N. Security Council adopted a resolution offered by the British representative, Lord Caradon, on November 22, 1967. This resolution was the result of intensive bargaining and negotiation among the members of the Council, and other U.N. members, and included what were generally believed to be the essential ingredients of a solution.

Resolution 242 called for a "just and lasting peace" based on "the application of both the following principles":

> (i) Withdrawal of Israeli armed forces from territories occupied in the recent conflict;

> (ii) Termination of all claims or states of belligerency and respect for and acknowledgement of the sovereignty, territorial integrity and political independence of every State in the area and their right to live in peace within secure and recognized boundaries free from threats or acts of force.

It also affirmed the following necessities:

> (a) For guaranteeing freedom of navigation through international waterways in the area;

> (b) For achieving a just settlement of the refugee problem;

> (c) For guaranteeing the territorial inviolability and political independence of every State in the area, through measures including the establishment of demilitarized zones;

The resolution also provided for the appointment of a U.N. special representative; Ambassador Gunnar Jarring of Sweden was chosen. The resolution contained most of the principles articulated by Johnson in June and seemed to be an acceptable basis for negotiations between the parties to achieve a settlement.

U.N. Security Council Resolution 242 has continued to be the focus of the Arab-Israeli peace process. All significant subsequent efforts to achieve a settlement, particularly those of the United States, have been based on, or at least have paid homage to, this document. The United States has suggested that the resolution contains the basic principles that must be incorporated in a settlement if it is to be effective, and has continued to support it in its entirety ("in all its parts")—clearly indicating that the entire resolution is essential, not simply the sections preferred by either side.

Jarring's initial efforts were accorded the support, or at least were spared the opposition, of the superpowers. During the initial year after his appointment he was especially active and his continuing efforts were allowed to be central. The United States was particularly supportive, since the goals comported well with its policy and particularly with the principles articulated by the president and reflected in Resolution 242. Despite Jarring's extensive efforts and great-power support, the mission made no substantial progress toward a settlement, despite some other achievements of note (for instance, an exchange of prisoners of war).

During the final year of the Johnson administration, the United States and Israel viewed the overall situation in essentially parallel terms, although disagreements on specific issues, such as the return of Arab refugees to Israeli-occupied territory, the status of Jerusalem, and the modality of peace negotiations, occurred from time to time. These were relatively minor and occasioned no significant tensions between the two states. The broad area of concord was exemplified by the visit of Prime Minister Levi Eshkol to the United States in January 1968 and the harmonious nature of his visit with Johnson at the LBJ Ranch in Texas. The two leaders reiterated their commitment to peace based on Johnson's five principles and Resolution 242, and their mutual concern about such matters as Soviet military supply to the Arab states. Their similarity of perspective on the need for peace and the appropriate bases for its achievement allowed them to note "the traditionally close, friendly, and cooperative ties which link the peoples of Israel and the United States."[10]

The president's perspective was rearticulated by U.S. representatives in a number of forums, and Johnson reaffirmed and elaborated his approach in a speech to B'nai B'rith on September 10, 1968. He indicated strong U.S. support for Israel, but while the two states were in broad accord on the need for and content of peace, there were also areas of discord and potential disagreement. Johnson criticized both the Arab states and Israel for impeding Jarring's work, and suggested that all parties had to share in the blame for the continuing conflict. He favored frontier adjustments for security (but not expansion) and focused on the need for Jerusalem to be united and whole (but noted the international aspects of the problem). Overall, Johnson emphasized the goal of peace: "the time has come for real peace in the area—a peace of justice and reconciliation, not a cease-fire, not a temporary truce, not a renewal of the fragile armistice."[11]

In the fall of 1968 the Soviet Union offered a proposal to the United States for resolution of the dispute that included a four-power guarantee and stressed Israeli withdrawal to the pre-June War frontiers. The Soviet proposal seemed designed to divert attention from the invasion of Czecho-slovakia and to produce tension between the United States and Israel by seeking to emphasize their divergence on specifics of the peace process. By promoting a pro-Arab formula, the Soviets (the United States believed) sought to strengthen the polarization and identification of the United States with the Israeli position. Although there were superpower contacts on the proposal, the United States seemed to stress the need for the involved par-ties to deal directly with one another, and expressed reservations about the wisdom of a settlement by powers outside the region. It also reiterated its support for Jarring. Secretary of State Dean Rusk rehearsed the U.S. posi-tion concerning the centrality of Resolution 242 and the Jarring mission, and did not even mention the Soviet plan, in his U.N. General Assembly address in October 1968. While Israel was generally pleased with the U.S. position, there was some concern that it might erode, owing to the desire for improved superpower relations.

The United States sought to have Israel adopt a more flexible attitude toward negotiations. This effort was based on the view that Israel had placed an unwarranted obstacle in the way of the Jarring mission by insist-ing on direct negotiations with its Arab antagonists. The United States maintained that the question of direct negotiations was "procedural," while Israel regarded it as substantive.

When Israeli Foreign Minister Abba Eban addressed the U.N. Gen-eral Assembly on October 8, 1968, and outlined a nine-point framework for peace, it was partly in deference to the U.S. urging for an Israeli initia-tive. The Israeli framework included withdrawal from occupied territory in the context of peace, but also the need for a negotiated, just, and lasting peace; permanent, secure, and recognized boundaries; security arrange-ments; open frontiers; freedom of navigation; resolution of the refugee issue; and arrangements for Christian and Muslim holy places in Jerusalem. Eban also suggested a modification of the requirement for direct negotiations by noting the possibility of exchanging ideas through Jarring "with any Arab Government willing to establish a just and lasting peace with Israel." The United States was generally receptive to Eban's points, and a State Department spokesman called the statement "constructive" be-cause its flexibility might facilitate negotiations.

During the 1968 presidential campaign, both major candidates—Richard Nixon and Hubert Humphrey—supported the Johnson administra-tion's position but went further in recognizing Israel's security needs and the necessity to maintain an arms balance in the Middle East, and in em-phasizing that peace was the goal of U.S. policy. But despite these similarities of statement and viewpoint, there were adumbrations of change. The fact-finding mission to the region of former Governor William Scranton and his statement concerning an evenhandedness of U.S. policy conjured up images of the pre-June War formula, which, to Israel, suggested a move away from the close ties of the United States and Israel. At a press conference on his return, Scranton said:

> America would do well to have a more even-handed policy. We are interested, very interested, in Israel and its security, and we should be. But it is important to point out to the Middle East and to people around the world that we are interested in other countries in the area and we have friends among them.[12]

This seemed to foreshadow an "evenhandedness" in the U.S. approach. Israeli concerns were heightened by an exchange of messages between Nixon and Nasser and by the postponement of a projected visit by Eshkol to Washington. There was also an article by Charles Yost, appointed as Nixon's U.N. ambassador, in which he noted that if the parties could not reach a settlement, it would be time for a U.N. initiative with great-power backing. This seemed to suggest some thinking about an imposed solution, which Israel believed would be inappropriate, counter to existing U.S. assurances, and not in keeping with the preferred means of achieving peace through direct negotiations of the parties.

As these factors were troubling Israel and raising questions about the U.S. role, the Soviet Union came forward with a "plan" that elaborated a series of previously identified positions but focused on the need for the United States to exert its influence on Israel to achieve total Israeli withdrawal from the occupied territories. Apparently the Soviets had timed their proposal to take advantage of the change in the U.S. government and the sense of urgency generated by the apparently deteriorating circumstances in the Middle East (most notably the Israeli raid at the Beirut airport in December 1968, in response to an attack on an Israeli airliner in Athens by the Popular Front for the Liberation of Palestine). The U.S. reaction took the form of reiteration of support for the Jarring mission and a request for clarification—measures designed to leave the detailed response for the incoming Nixon administration.

The Soviet plan was accompanied by a French proposal, reiterated by Charles de Gaulle and made partly in response to the Israeli raid on Beirut, to engage in four-power talks concerning the Middle East as a means of implementing Resolution 242. The United States generally had not supported

Israel's retaliation policy and there was a feeling that the Beirut raid, in particular, was far out of proportion to the Athens attack that had generated it. In addition, the United States generally supported Lebanon's special position in the Arab-Israeli conflict. The timing also was unfortunate because it came shortly after the U.S. announcement of the sale of Phantom jets to Israel, and thus would affect the Arab view of the sale and, more generally, of their relations with the United States. The United States protested the Israeli raid and later joined in a unanimous Security council censure of Israel.

THE NIXON ADMINISTRATION: THE EARLY YEARS

The advent of the Nixon administration raised questions about the nature of U.S. policy, especially its approach to the Arab-Israeli peace process and its relations with Israel. The transition period had been marked by a number of events that suggested a need to reconsider the Middle East situation, and the region was high on the administration's agenda. There were the international reverberations of the Beirut raid, and the Soviet and French proposals were awaiting a detailed U.S. response. Clearly the president was concerned. In his first press conference, on January 27, 1969, Nixon said:

> I believe we need new initiatives and new leadership on the part of the United States in order to cool off the situation in the Mideast. I consider it a powder keg, very explosive. It needs to be defused. I am open to any suggestions that may cool it off and reduce the possibility of another explosion, because the next explosion in the Mideast, I think, could involve very well a confrontation between the nuclear powers, which we want to avoid.[13]

The administration soon began considering proposals for dealing with the Arab-Israeli conflict. The National Security Council met and discussed the situation at length, and in a press conference on February 6, Nixon spelled out his "new initiatives" for the Middle East:

> What we see now is a new policy on the part of the United States in assuming the initiative. We are not going to stand back and . . . wait for something else to happen. We are going to assume it on . . . five fronts: We are going to continue to give our all-out support to the Jarring Mission. We are going to have bilateral talks at the United Nations, preparatory to the talks [among] the four powers. We shall have four-

power talks at the United Nations. We shall also have talks with the countries in the area, with the Israelis and their neighbors, and in addition, we want to go forward on some of the very grave economic problems in that area.[14]

In an apparent effort to implement the president's policy, the United States began to work on bilateral and four-power talks. In a departure from previous U.S. policy, which had been cool to the post-1967 proposals by de Gaulle for great-power discussions, the United States agreed to the French call for four-power (United States, Soviet Union, England, France) talks. Bilateral U.S.-Soviet talks were also initiated. These efforts were described by the United States as a means of facilitating the Jarring mission and the efforts of the regional states, and not as a prelude to imposition of a great-power settlement.

The U.S. position was affected not only by a desire to ameliorate the situation in the Middle East but also by broader global considerations. There was the hope for an improvement in the U.S.-Soviet relationship and a desire to please de Gaulle as part of a Europe-oriented perspective of the new president. Tensions and dangers in the Middle East contributed to the perspective, and this combination suggested the methods outlined by Nixon.

Israel was clearly concerned. Foreign Minister Eban visited the United States to articulate Israel's case and to assess the situation. Israel recognized the U.S. needs, but its views reflected a different perspective. Israel's ultimate concern was whether the approach would serve its interest in peace and security, and it was unclear whether this new approach would serve Israeli interests as well as it might serve U.S. goals. Israel feared an imposed solution. Nixon's meeting with de Gaulle and obvious efforts to improve relations between the United States and France seemed likely to move the United States in the direction of four-power participation in the peace process, which Israel opposed. Eban also sought to allay U.S. fears concerning the regional situation, which might otherwise impel the United States to act in support of the president's powder keg theory. A war of attrition had already begun along the Suez Canal, and Israel's view was that it would not escalate to a more generalized level of conflict because the Arab armies were not prepared for such a confrontation. It believed the war had numerous political motivations, including the creation of a sense of urgency designed to stimulate the concern and involvement of the United States and other great powers.

Israel was pleased with the basic content of U.S. policy, including the stress on agreement between the parties, but expressed worry over the prospects for increased great-power involvement, which it believed might well become an imposed settlement that would work to its disadvantage. What emerged as the real issue between the United States and Israel was not the question of an imposed settlement, which both probably recognized as unrealistic, but the nature and extent of great-power participation in the peace process. Israel sought to have the great powers play virtually no role, preferring that the parties to the conflict be the parties involved in the peace negotiations. The Nixon administration seemed to believe that the great powers could prove useful, through Jarring, in breaking the deadlock between Israel and the Arabs in the dealings. On matters of substance the United States and Israel seemed to be in basic accord, but there was disagreement on the matter of procedure (although Israel regarded this as bordering on substance). They remained in agreement on the need for a durable peace, reached by Israel and the Arabs and assuring Israel's security within negotiated and recognized boundaries.

As in other areas of concern, the United States sought to allay Israel's fears. Among other means, it suggested that the great powers were not in accord on what might be done, and thus the talks were designed to help bring them closer together, thereby facilitating the Jarring mission.

The four powers began their efforts to contribute to a peaceful political settlement by meeting in early April 1969. Their approach was based on Resolution 242 and on the Jarring mission, for which they reaffirmed their support.

Israel opposed the talks on a number of grounds. It believed that peace should be negotiated between the parties directly concerned, and it opposed any effort to which they had not agreed. In a statement on March 30, 1969, the cabinet noted that "Israel is not, and will not become, the object of power politics, or intrapower politics, and will not accept any recommendation which is in conflict with her vital interests, her rights, and her security." Israel disagreed with some of the assumptions underlying the process, including Nixon's "powder keg" perspective, and the view that the parties could not reach agreement on their own. Its opposition also was a result of the involvement of hostile powers (the Soviet Union and France) in a process affecting its future.

Israel saw the effort as a preemption of the possibility of direct, bilateral talks, since the Arabs could now wait to see what might be accomplished for them, thus allowing them to forgo direct dealings with

Israel, which they opposed. Israel also believed that, while a great-power settlement might not be imposed, it would be very difficult for it to resist a proposal put forward by those powers. Furthermore, Israel was convinced that such a settlement would favor the Arabs. In an interview in the summer of 1969, Prime Minister Golda Meir illustrated her concerns about such a process (and revealed a good deal about the U.S. role as Israel's advocate):

> Supposing the United States reached an agreement with Russia and all sorts of other nations on a peace settlement, we say, so what? Where do we come in? I don't ask where Egypt comes in, not that I regard her sovereignty [as] second-class to ours—but because she is already in. The Russians are not just Egypt's friends in the way America is our friend. But they are Egypt's lawyer and will not compromise their client's demands. There is no doubt that the Soviets will not agree to anything without Nasser's consent.[15]

In the final analysis Israel's concern was practical—it feared that the great powers would not give its security problems the same priority it did, and therefore the best four-power attempts would not be the same as its own efforts to secure its best interests and ensure its security. Israel's fears proved to be unfounded because the four-power talks produced no identifiable progress that could be translated into a viable agreement to resolve the conflict. Bilateral talks took place between the United States and the Soviet Union during much of the period of the four-power talks. But little was accomplished at that level either.

By the fall of 1969, the mood seemed to have changed, and when Nixon addressed the United Nations in September, few new ideas were put forward. He reiterated that a settlement had to be based "on respect for the sovereign right of each nation in the area to exist within secure and recognized boundaries," and that "peace cannot be achieved on the basis of substantial alterations in the map of the Middle East. And we are equally convinced that peace cannot be achieved on the basis of anything less than a binding, irrevocable commitment by the parties to live together in peace."[16] The Arabs were disappointed but Israel welcomed the Nixon approach, with its apparent return to the onus for negotiations being placed on the parties and not the great powers. The address demonstrated the continuity of U.S. policy and the fact that Israel and the United States shared a view on the need for a permanent peace based on secure and recognized borders. Nevertheless, there were indications that they did not agree on such matters as direct negotiations and the precise definition of what constituted secure and recognized borders.

Golda Meir visited Nixon in September 1969 and reiterated Israel's skepticism concerning the bilateral superpower talks and its preference for direct negotiations between Israel and the Arabs. Other issues were discussed, but no movement concerning the peace process was achieved.

Bilateral U.S.-Soviet discussions continued in the fall of 1969, and the United States brought various proposals for use in negotiations between Israel and Egypt to the table. In early December the four-power talks were resumed. However, the major item for discussion was a proposal by Secretary of State William Rogers.

On December 9, 1969, Rogers outlined U.S. Middle East policy and articulated specific proposals for peace between the United Arab Republic (Egypt) and Israel. In a lengthy and detailed statement he suggested that an agreement among the great powers could not be substituted for an agreement among the parties, and that the agreement must be in accordance with the entire text of Resolution 242. He noted that the United States would pursue a "balanced" policy "to encourage the Arabs to accept a permanent peace based on a binding agreement and to urge the Israelis to withdraw from occupied territory when their territorial integrity is assured as envisaged by the Security Council resolution." He supported the concept of Israeli withdrawal from occupied Arab territory and stated that while there should be changes in boundaries, they "should not reflect the weight of conquest and should be confined to insubstantial alterations required for mutual security."

The refugee problem had to be resolved, and a "just settlement must take into account the desires and aspirations of the refugees and the legitimate concerns of the governments in the area." Resolution of the problem of Jerusalem was an issue of some magnitude, and Rogers said that the United States opposed "unilateral actions by any party to decide the final status of the city."

> . . . [we] believe Jerusalem should be a unified city within which there would no longer be restrictions on the movement of persons and goods. There should be open access to the unified city for all persons of all faiths and nationalities. Arrangements for the administration of the unified city should take into account the interests of all its inhabitants and of the Jewish, Islamic, and Christian communities. And there should be roles for both Israel and Jordan in the civic, economic, and religious life of the city.[17]

The Rogers Plan was the most detailed proposal dealing with the Arab-Israeli conflict the United States had advanced to that time.

Israel's response was strongly negative, and critical of both the procedural and the substantive aspects of the plan. Israel seemed to prefer a U.S. role designed to bring the parties together; Rogers believed in the utility of a broader U.S. role and a more detailed posture. Israel focused on the desirability of direct negotiations to achieve a durable peace based on a treaty arrived at without prior conditions. Rogers saw the United States playing a role because of its international responsibilities; and while it would not impose a settlement, it would seek to achieve peace, because that would be in the national interest of the United States.[18] Israeli concerns were specific: "The Cabinet rejects these American proposals in that they: Prejudice the chances of establishing peace, disregard the essential need to determine and secure agreed borders through the signing of peace treaties by direct negotiations, affect Israel's sovereign rights and security in the drafting of the resolutions concerning refugees and the status of Jerusalem."[19] Israel also spoke of appeasement of the Arabs at Israel's expense. Mrs. Meir articulated in detail her opposition to the plan in the Knesset on December 29, 1969:

> The proposals do not obligate the Arab states expressly to recognize Israel's sovereignty, they do not advocate the delineation of secure, recognized, and agreed borders by free negotiations between the parties, they do not obligate the Arab states effectively to put an end to terrorist activities from their territories. On the other hand, they involve a violation of Israel's sovereign rights in regard to Jerusalem and a danger to Israel's security in the proposed arrangement about the Arab refugees.

The deterioration of the bilateral relationship was apparent:

> We have never demanded of the U.S. that the friendly relations existing between us be exclusive. We have never expected that power, which has interests throughout the world, to refrain from maintaining friendly relations with our neighbors. Nevertheless we have the right to demand that the policy of the U.S. should not be conducted at the expense of our essential interests.

Israel's objections also were directed to the procedure by which the proposals were formulated and publicized. Lack of prior consultation was disturbing, particularly when contrasted with the experience of close cooperation Israel had enjoyed during the Johnson administration. There seemed to be a consensus that U.S.-Israel relations had reached their lowest point since the Eisenhower administration and the 1956-57 Suez crisis.

The Rogers Plan did not generate immediate momentum in the peace process and was, to a significant degree, overshadowed by the war of attrition that Nasser had initiated in the spring of 1969. That war was designed, as Nasser indicated, to wear down the Israeli forces on the eastern bank of the Suez Canal, to effect a change in Israeli strategic thinking, and ultimately to secure an Israeli withdrawal from the canal area because of the increased cost of maintaining that military position. Israel's initial reaction was to dig in deeper along the canal, to respond with its artillery, and to launch an occasional commando raid. The air force was not used in the earlier phases of the war, and Israel's casualties increased. By the summer Israel had begun to reverse the situation by utilizing its air force to advantage, first along the canal and later with deep penetration raids into Egypt's heartland. The latter were made possible by Israel's acquisition of Phantom F-4 aircraft, which possessed the supersonic speed, range, maneuverability, versatility, and load capability for such operations.

Israel's concerns about the Rogers Plan, and other developments that seemed to affect its security, became more significant. In late January 1970, Nixon sought to influence Israeli thinking by reassuring it concerning American policy. He sent a message to the National Emergency Conference on Peace in the Middle East in which he reaffirmed U.S. friendship for Israel. Nixon stated that the United States wanted to help the people of the region to achieve peace, which could be based only "on agreement between the parties and that agreement can be achieved only through negotiations between them." The United States would neither negotiate nor impose the terms of peace. He also affirmed U.S. willingness to supply military equipment to support friendly governments, such as Israel, and that the United States would maintain a careful watch on the situation in the region. Nixon's statement seemed to deal with virtually all the significant points of Israeli concern about the Rogers Plan and the regional military balance.

Regional developments generated growing concern as it became clear that the Soviet Union increasingly was participating in the air defense of Egypt, posing the danger of a direct Soviet clash with Israel and possibly with the United States as well. By the end of June, the United States sought once again to ameliorate the situation by utilizing the direct involvement of the secretary of state.

On June 25, 1970, Rogers announced that the United States had undertaken a political initiative to encourage the parties "to stop shooting and start talking under the auspices of Ambassador Jarring." The importance of the initiative, in light of the increased Soviet presence and involvement and the growing potential for superpower conflict, was highlighted by Nixon and National Security Adviser Henry Kissinger in public and private statements and comments. On July 1, 1970, in a nationally televised interview, Nixon said: "I think the Middle East now is terribly dangerous. It is like the Balkans before World War I where the two superpowers, the United States and the Soviet Union, could be drawn into a confrontation that neither of them wants because of the differences there."[20]

After considerable internal debate after Egypt's positive response and U.S. pressures and reassurances, the Israeli cabinet, on July 31, 1970, accepted the initiative. Its communiqué was explicit in its desire to be responsive to the United States following its appeals and clarifications. Further disagreements developed, however, concerning the specific language of the Israeli acceptance and the method by which the United States announced it.

The cease-fire called for in the initiative went into effect, but soon afterward was violated by Egypt and the Soviet Union. This led to further disagreements between the United States and Israel. Israel complained of violations of the agreement, in that Egypt deployed missiles in the "standstill" zone. The initial U.S. response was to downplay the violation and to suggest that discussion was more significant. Despite the controversy, and the differing U.S. and Israeli assessments, the talks began under Jarring's auspices in late August 1970, but the violations and the response eroded Israeli confidence in the United States.

In early September, Israel announced that it would not participate in the talks with Jarring as long as the agreement was not respected in its entirety and unless a missile rollback restoring the original situation was achieved. This decision marked the beginning of a period of intense negotiation between the United States and Israel to clarify the military and political support Israel could expect from the United States in light of the Egyptian violations. When removal of the missiles became unrealistic, Israel sought assurances and guarantees of U.S. military and political support as its condition for resuming discussions. The United States sought "rectification" of the situation.

Ultimately the United States was able to reassure Israel with pledges of military, economic, and political support, and Israel agreed to return to the negotiations. The talks were resumed in early January 1971.

Jarring took several initiatives to try to secure some form of agreement between the parties, but ultimately his mission foundered on the matter of divergent views with respect to withdrawal; it ceased to be a viable option for the attainment of peace by the spring of 1971. At that juncture the

United States, reflecting its view that an impasse had been reached and that perhaps a partial step could be taken that might achieve some progress, launched an effort to achieve an "interim" agreement on the reopening of the Suez Canal and a partial withdrawal of Israeli troops from Sinai. This was a departure from previous efforts that focused on a comprehensive accord—this new process was to be step-by-step—and it was based on suggestions by both Israeli Defense Minister Moshe Dayan and Egyptian President Anwar Sadat. The shift also reflected a U.S. view that movement toward a settlement was more significant than the gains achieved by keeping the Suez Canal closed and denying its use to the Soviet navy, which would gain significantly from its reopening.

Exchanges of views between Egypt and Israel through the United States were complemented in early May 1971 by a visit to the Middle East by Rogers, the first by a secretary of state since Dulles in 1953. The exchanges, and U.S. pressures (primarily on Israel), generated a degree of optimism that the dialogue (indirect though it was) would continue. But despite the initial optimism, the Rogers visit ultimately did not achieve tangible results.

On October 4, 1971, Rogers outlined the U.S. position to the U.N. General Assembly. He stressed the need for an overall settlement and a lasting peace, and endorsed the Jarring mission. He appealed to Israel and Egypt to enter into an interim agreement on the Suez Canal as a practical and attainable step toward implementation of Resoloution 242. Rogers saw this latest proposal as a compromise between the positions of Israel and Egypt, but Israel saw it as an acceptance of the Egyptian perspective. Israel was concerned that this represented yet another erosion in U.S. policy, and its opposition centered on the United States taking an independent and substantive stand. Israel maintained the view that the problem must be solved in discussions between the parties and that the United States should confine its efforts to those of an intermediary. It also insisted that any withdrawal would be part of a special agreement, not linked to Resolution 242, and reiterated its opposition to Egyptian troops crossing the Suez Canal.

In a formal statement to the Knesset on October 26, Mrs. Meir articulated the main elements of Israel's objections. A central theme was that instead of an Egyptian-Israeli dialogue, there was "a discussion with the Americans about their recommendations for concessions on our part on some of the points we regard as most vital." Other changes in the U.S. position were regarded as having moved closer to the Egyptian perspective in the period between March and October 1971.

Despite the extensive criticism, the United States designated Joseph Sisco to conduct "proximity talks" or "hotel talks" as a form of "shuttle diplomacy," to see if he might be able to catalyze the parties to reach some form of agreement. Further clarifications of the situation were needed, and part of the discussion focused on the United States providing Israel with additional equipment to ensure that the military balance would not tilt to its disfavor. Continuing discussions ultimately led to an Israeli decision, in early February 1972, to participate in the proximity talks. The United States then pressed for support of the talks by Egypt, but Egypt balked. The failure of this effort shifted the policy focus from Rogers and Sisco to Nixon and Kissinger.

The Middle East remained uncharacteristically quiet, with no crises dominating the attention of the media. U.S.-Soviet summit meetings soon preempted the process, but they achieved little. Various consultations, meetings, and discussions in the region and elsewhere failed to generate any real momentum, and the process seemed to reflect the complacency of many of the participants—with the exception of Egypt. U.S.-Israel relations remained cordial and their policies congruent.

Reflecting the changed circumstances and the existing situation was Golda Meir's visit to Washington in March 1973. It came at a time when U.S.-Israel relations had retained a positive tone for more than a year and there was a similar perspective concerning the region in Washington and in Jerusalem. At the same time there had been Israeli agreement, after clarifications and reassurances, to participate in the U.S.-proposed close proximity talks for an interim settlement. Egypt had consistently refused to participate in such a process. The administration believed that the military balance had to be maintained. Thus, with regard to the peace process and to the military balance essential for Israeli security, the two states were in general accord. During her visit to Washington, Prime Minister Meir was assured by Nixon of continuing U.S. support, including economic aid and military supply.

U.S. efforts to promote proximity talks for an interim settlement continued throughout the spring and summer, and into the fall, of 1973 while regional developments were moving, apparently unknown at the time, in a different direction. By the end of the summer, the question of oil and its potential importance in the Arab-Israeli equation came under increased scrutiny and gained additional attention. Henry Kissinger became secretary of state. In a press conference at the beginning of September 1973, Nixon noted that "we have put at the highest priority moving toward making some progress toward settlement of that dispute."[21] It seemed likely that the

United States would make additional efforts to deal with the issue, but there appeared to be no sense of urgency. There was an air of confidence that events would not force the situation, and that there was adequate time to pursue the process in a deliberate and orderly way. The October War changed this thinking and provided a markedly altered environment for the peace process and for the U.S.-Israel relationship.

THE PEACE PROCESS AFTER THE OCTOBER WAR

The October War, which began on October 6, 1973, erupted suddenly when the armies of Egypt and Syria launched attacks on Israeli positions along the Suez Canal and in the Golan Heights.

Israel knew of the prospective Arab strike in advance and the chief of staff, General David Elazar, prepared the Israel Defense Forces (particularly the air force) to launch a preemptive strike. It was clear to Israel's decision makers that war was inevitable, and the question was whether Israel should strike first or absorb the Arab attack. When presented with the choice, Prime Minister Golda Meir responded: "I know all the arguments in favor of a preemptive strike, but I am against it. We don't know now, any of us, what the future will hold, but there is always the possibility that we will need help, and if we strike first, we will get nothing from anyone." Later, after the Arab attack and when the American resupply airlift began, she reacted with these words: "Thank God I was right to reject the idea of a preemptive strike! It might have saved lives in the beginning, but I am sure that we would not have had that airlift, which is now saving so many lives."[22] Clearly she was concerned with the political repercussions of an Israeli first strike, particularly the potential U.S. reaction.

Israel was under strong pressure not to launch a preemptive strike as a result of U.S. entreaties and warnings. In their study of Kissinger, Marvin and Bernard Kalb stress his strong injunctions given to Israel over an extended period, and repeated in the hours preceding the conflict, that Israel should not take any preemptive action. The clear implication was that such a strike would make it more difficult for Israel to receive American support.[23] There was also an effort to court world public opinion by making it clear that Israel was attacked. In its April 1974 report Israel's Agranat Commission of Inquiry noted that the prime minister decided "for political reasons" not to launch a preemptive strike.

The United States was surprised by the outbreak of hostilities, but reacted quickly to try to end the conflict and to create circumstances that would facilitate postwar negotiations to achieve a just and lasting peace. It was important for each side to achieve a victory, and Kissinger's efforts were utilized to ensure a war of "double victory and no defeat." In the latter days of the conflict, when the tide of battle had turned significantly to Israel's advantage, this meant preventing Israel from humiliating Sadat. The establishment of the cease-fire before Israel could achieve a decisive victory and the resupply of the trapped Egyptian Third Army thus became issues of controversy between the United States and Israel.

While Kissinger often claimed that by going to Moscow he would gain additional time for the Israeli military to act, his primary purpose was to ensure a cease-fire at the appropriate moment in order to facilitate the postwar peace efforts. Once agreement was reached in Moscow, the United States pressed Israel for its assent. Both Nixon and Kissinger were involved in the effort, and stressed its significance to Israel and to the United States. Kissinger was concerned that Israel might seek to destroy the Third Army or force its surrender, thereby humiliating Egypt and upsetting Kissinger's plans for a postwar peace initiative. He made it clear to Israel that the issue was one of consequence, and eventually he secured its agreement to allow medical and food supplies to reach the Third Army. U.S. pressures included a reported threat, attributed by Dayan to Kissinger, that the United States would provide the supplies if Israel did not allow their provision through other means.

In the wake of the war there was considerable popular opinion in Israel that it had been pressured by the United States to act in a manner contrary to its best interests.[24] The United States and Israel viewed the cease-fire and the supply of the Third Army differently, and the U.S. position prevailed. These matters were among the topics discussed during Mrs. Meir's visit to Washington at the beginning of November 1973. Following meetings with Nixon and Kissinger, she stated publicly that "there is no pressure" and that the United States would not pressure Israel to make one-sided concessions to the Arabs in order to achieve peace. At a press conference she said that she had come to "find out there was no pressure."[25] Despite these comments there was a chill in the relationship occasioned by considerable Israeli concern about U.S. actions during and immediately after the war and potential activities in the envigorated U.S. peace initiative.

Ultimately the United States and the Soviet Union reached agreement on U.N. Security Council Resolution 338 of October 22, 1973, which called for a cease-fire, negotiations for peace, and implementation of Resolution 242. From the Israeli perspective the most noteworthy item was the call for direct negotiations between the parties, a major element of Israeli policy that hitherto had not been a requirement of the peace process. The Arabs focused on the reiteration of Resolution 242, with its call for Israeli withdrawal from occupied territory. The cease-fire proved successful after an initial breakdown, accompanied by considerable confusion, and the passage of Security Council Resolution 339 to supplement and endorse it.

For both the Arabs and Israel the war and its aftermath generated significant changes, especially psychological, that provided the basis for the Kissinger initiative. The potential danger of the Arab-Israeli conflict widening to involve the superpowers was particularly obvious with the use of the U.S.-Soviet hotline, the placing of U.S. troops worldwide on a precautionary alert status (DEFCON III), and various ambiguous moves by the Soviet Union. The war also highlighted the effects of an oil embargo on the prosperity of the industrialized world (and some of the Third World), as well as the differences in U.S. and European approaches to Israel and the conflict that generated tension and discord within the Western alliance.

Among the changes wrought by the war and its immediate aftermath were those that occurred in the U.S.-Israel relationship, particularly in Israeli perceptions of the altered nature of the links between the two states.

After the termination of hostilities, the stage was set for an effort to achieve a settlement. For Israel the primary goal was to achieve peace with security. U.S. postwar policy was to achieve a settlement, and it was prepared to play the various roles necessary to expedite it. Kissinger also set out to reduce the possibility of a major Soviet role, and his concept of keeping the Soviets "informed but not involved" remained a cardinal feature of the approach. However, the process first required an attempt to deal with the results of the conflict. This meant a disengagement of forces along the Suez Canal and in the Golan Heights, and it was to achieve these goals that Kissinger turned initially. He sought to rearrange the existing deployment of forces into a more stable pattern and, as a result, to achieve a first step toward an overall agreement. Discussions between Egypt and Israel at Kilometer 101 on the Cairo-Suez road at the end of October began the process. A conference at Geneva in December, chaired by the United States and the Soviet Union, marked an important second phase. Neither the talks at Kilometer 101 nor the Geneva conference yielded an overall agreement because a number of significant differences divided the parties. After further consultations Kissinger decided to visit the Middle East in an effort to develop a proposal that might be dealt with at Geneva.

Kissinger secured disengagement agreements between Israel and Egypt in January 1974 and between Israel and Syria in May 1974. They involved significant activity by the secretary of state, strongly backed by the president, and important commitments by each of the participants. These were the beginnings of a "step-by-step" approach designed not only to deal with specific "minor" issues but also to build confidence to permit the parties to approach the central issues in dispute. The achievement of the two disengagement agreements, which resulted directly from the efforts of Henry Kissinger, produced a euphoric mood and engendered expectations of future achievements. This concluded the first phase of postwar diplomacy. To cap it and take advantage of its benefits, Nixon visited the Middle East in June 1974. During this period the United States saw the need for disengagement agreements and, subsequent to those agreements, further step-by-step diplomacy.

After a brief respite Kissinger sought to identify the next round of potential negotiations. Various alternatives were investigated during visits by regional leaders to Washington and a Kissinger visit to the Middle East in October 1974. But the matter was soon overshadowed by the decision of the Arab summit meeting in Rabat, Morocco ("the Palestine summit"), at the end of October, which designated the Palestine Liberation Organization (PLO) as "the sole legitimate representative of the Palestinian people in all liberated Palestinian territory." This decision clouded the prospects for further Arab-Israeli negotiations, since Israel had said it would not negotiate with the PLO, and the PLO had consistently refused to recognize Israel's right to exist. It also raised doubts about the viability of Kissinger's step-by-step negotiating aproach. With the adoption of the Rabat decisions by the Arab states, Israel and the United States faced the dilemma of dealing with this new reality if they were to make progress toward a settlement.

Kissinger returned to the Middle East in early November to explore possible "next steps" in light of the Rabat decisions and the probability that Jordan-Israel negotiations were unattainable. The overall accomplishment of the November trip was to avert a collapse of the Kissinger effort. The "Jordan option" (that is, negotiations between Israel and Jordan) and Israel-PLO negotiations were ruled out as unacceptable to Israel (and the PLO) and unrealistic, but the Egypt-Israel focus seemed to be reaffirmed because both appeared prepared to negotiate. Consultations and discussions concerning the next phase of negotiations and a next-step agreement continued over the following months. Israel and Egypt focused on the exchange of political concessions by Egypt for territorial withdrawals by Israel. Israel sought to minimize its territorial withdrawals while attaining political concessions and a time period of sufficient duration to provide a breathing spell. Egypt sought to have Israel withdraw from the Mitla and Gidi passes and the Abu Rudeis oil fields, while keeping Egyptian "political concessions" to a minimum.

Despite these gaps between the parties, Kissinger was buoyed by various contacts and believed that an exploratory trip to the region would be beneficial. He hoped to identify a framework for negotiations and believed that there was some prospect for reconciling the positions of the parties. Kissinger visited the Middle East again in February but, despite some expressions of optimism, the positions of Israel and Egypt did not undergo substantial change. Kissinger apparently felt he had uncovered sufficient nuances to indicate that the gap between the parties might be bridged and that a return to the region in March was justified.

Kissinger was optimistic on the eve of his March 1975 shuttle. He apparently believed that both parties would make concessions modifying their seemingly irreconcilable positions, and that he could thereby secure an agreement. There also appeared to be some assumption that tacit support from Saudi Arabia and the Soviet Union would be helpful. He began his diplomatic shuttle early in the month and made a considerable effort to narrow the gap between the parties. However, neither party moved very far from its original position; Egypt wanted substantial Israeli withdrawals and Israel sought substantial political concessions from Egypt.

During these extensive discussions, it was reported that Israel recieved a firm letter from President Gerald Ford urging additional concessions. No major alterations occurred in the Israeli or the Egyptian position and, despite the areas of accord and the apparent desires of all concerned to reach some form of settlement, the differences proved irreconcilable. Israel would not give up the strategic passes and the valuable oil fields in return for a short-term, essentially nonpolitical agreement; Egypt would not accept less than the passes and the oil fields, and sought to minimize its political concessions. Kissinger's shuttle had failed.

On March 23, 1975, Ford ordered a reassessment of U.S. Middle East policy. The announced reassessment and related efforts to determine "next steps" were devised in response to the failure of shuttle diplomacy and the general disarray in U.S. policy following the fall of Vietnam. They were also to serve a second purpose—to pressure Israel, despite official denials, by using the reassessment as a lever to influence and modify Israel's policy so that it would be closer to that of Egypt and make possible a U.S. (that is, Kissinger) effort to bridge the gap. The United States clearly saw Israel as the party primarily responsible for the failure of the shuttle because it had not been sufficiently forthcoming by taking appropriate risks.

Notwithstanding the discord and pressures associated with the reassessment, Israel acted with circumspection and chose not to engage in a direct public confrontation with the Ford administration. The main focus of the discussions in the wake of the shuttle failure was on identifying a procedure for resuming the negotiations—there was some discussion of a return to the Geneva conference format, but Kissinger clearly seemed to prefer the step-by-step approach. The United States spoke of a setback rather than a failure of the March shuttle, thus indicating its preference for restarting the step-by-step procedure. In the U.S. view the earlier effort had been suspended not terminated.

It was during this reassessment that 76 senators wrote to Ford, on May 21, 1975, urging him to be "responsive to Israel's economic and security needs." This seemed to reflect lack of support for continued pressures on Israel, and suggested to Kissinger and Ford that resumption of the step-by-step approach was the most viable option available.

The cooling-off period allowed for a reassessment of the positions of the parties. Israel apparently weighed the costs and benefits of the Kissinger failure and the subsequent reassessment, then decided to modify its position, primarily to improve its relationship with the United States. Ultimately Israel made significant concessions concerning its positions in Sinai, and gained important U.S. assurances and aid, in order for Kissinger to achieve Sinai II. Consultations for renewed negotiations soon gained momentum, and substantial discussions took place in Washington, the Middle East, and elsewhere over the following months. These discussions focused on the extent of both Israeli withdrawal and Egyptian political concessions, and proposed changes in the U.S. role to bridge the gap between the positions of the parties.

To complete the arrangements, Kissinger embarked on a new shuttle, arriving in Israel on August 21, 1975. The visit was noteworthy, in part, for provoking substantial demonstrations against inordinately generous concessions in the negotiations. Kissinger sought to assuage these fears with a statement in which he pointed out the "steadfastness of the American-Israeli relationship—a steadfastness which has helped protect Israel's security for over a quarter of a century—a steadfastness on which Israel can rely in the future."[26] He also stated that Ford had sent him to "provide the strongest possible United States support for progress toward peace and to consult with Israeli leaders on how best to do this in a manner which will protect Israel's security and maintain the closeness of U.S.-Israeli relations."[27] Shuttle diplomacy was needed and was successful in narrowing the gap between the two parties. An agreement was initialed on September

1, 1975, in Jerusalem and in Alexandria, and was signed in Geneva on September 4, by Egypt and Israel.

Sinai II was qualitatively different from the previous Arab-Israeli agreements, and contrasted with the 1974 military disengagements by providing the first steps toward political accommodation between the parties that were indispensable for an overall settlement. The Egypt-Israel agreement provided that "the conflict between them and in the Middle East shall not be resolved by military force but by peaceful means," and stated that although this was not a final peace agreement, it was "a significant step toward a just and lasting peace" and that the parties "shall continue their efforts to negotiate a final peace agreement within the framework of the Geneva Peace Conference in accordance with Security Council Resolution 338." As part of the withdrawal arrangements, a new buffer zone was established in which the U.N. Emergency Force would continue to function. It was also agreed that "nonmilitary cargoes destined for or coming from Israel shall be permitted through the Suez Canal."

Sinai II clearly engaged U.S. prestige, participation, and expenditure in the continuing effort to achieve a settlement. It thus formalized the increased U.S. involvement that had characterized the period following the October War, and further defined the nature of the conflict and subsequent peace efforts that had become central in the U.S.-Israel relationship. The United States remained the central and indispensable power, the one state to which all parties interested in resolution of the problem could turn. No other actor played any substantial role in the 1974 and 1975 agreements. The Soviet Union was "informed but not involved," and was prevented both from claiming credit for accomplishments and from playing the role of "spoiler." The final agreement would not have been possible without substantial U.S. efforts to "bridge the gap" during the negotiations and to provide various "guarantees," including assurances and undertakings (particularly to Israel), a direct American presence, and aid (both economic and military). The United States agreed to provide a staff of up to 200 civilians for an early-warning system to be placed between Egypt and Israel in Sinai.

The assurances and undertakings provided Israel by Kissinger at the time of the Sinai II agreement included a pledge that "The United States Government will make every effort to be fully responsive, within the limits of its resources and Congressional authorization and appropriation, on an on-going and long-term basis to Israel's military equipment and other defense requirements, to its energy requirements and to its economic needs." An important U.S. political-diplomatic assurance to Israel was as follows:

The United States will continue to adhere to its present policy with respect to the Palestine Liberation Organization, whereby it will not recognize or negotiate with the Palestine Liberation Organization so long
as the Palestine Liberation Organization does not recognize Israel's
right to exist and does not accept Security Council Resolutions 242
and 338.

After the conclusion of Sinai II the problem was to identify an appropriate next step, given the realities of the situation in the region. Neither
Syria nor Jordan was an appropriate choice, the former being unwilling to
negotiate with Israel on the basis of Resolution 242 and the latter having
lost its mandate as a result of the Rabat Arab summit decisions of 1974. In
this milieu, and despite the reiteration of U.S. policy concerning the PLO
in the Sinai II agreement, there were signs (albeit somewhat unclear and
contradictory) in November and December 1975 of a reevaluation of the
Palestinian factor among the senior ranks of the Department of State, as
suggested by Assistant Secretary of State Harold Saunders in testimony before Congress—the "Saunders document"—in November. Saunders called
for a "diplomatic process which will help bring forth a reasonable definition of Palestinian interests." Although disowned by Kissinger, it was a
harbinger of future policies. In any event, the Kissinger step-by-step approach was soon overshadowed by the Lebanese civil war and associated
developments. No meaningful achievement followed Sinai II in the final
year of the Ford-Kissinger tenure, and the U.S.-Israel relationship was
characterized by relative tranquillity.

SOME OBSERVATIONS ON THE FIRST THREE DECADES

Between 1947 and 1977 the United States and Israel developed a
complex relationship, which fluctuated from relative indifference to closeness and from an essentially humanitarian focus to a multifaceted relationship. At the outset the United States based its policy on the humanitarian
considerations associated with the plight of European Jews, but by the late
1970s political and strategic considerations dominated the situation. The
arms supply relationship (discussed in further detail in chapter 4) evolved
from embargo to principal supplier, and arms became a major tool of U.S.
policy to reassure Israel and to achieve policy modification.

The two states developed a diplomatic-political relationship that focused on the need to resolve the Arab-Israeli dispute. But while they agreed
on the general concept, they often differed on the precise means of achiev-

ing the desired result. The relationship became especially close after the June War of 1967, and a congruence of policy prevailed on many of the salient concerns of the two states. An exclusivity seemed to develop as the Arab states broke ties with Washington and the Soviet bloc did the same with Israel. Despite general concord there were also significant disputes. The two nations often held differing perspectives on regional developments, on the dangers and opportunities, and on the appropriate modalities of response.

The United States and Israel often sought to influence each other's thinking and policies, especially after 1967. This generally took the form of visits by senior Israeli officials to the United States in an effort to "clarify" the situation—that is, to influence thinking and policy. Israel sought, through persuasion and argument, and the United States sought, through entreaties and reassurances, to alter and modify the policies of the other. No major ruptures took place, although significant tensions were generated at various junctures, especially at the time of the 1956-57 Sinai war.

Policy differences were reconciled through dialogue and discussion, although some "threats" were occasionally included in the dialogue. Influence was exerted through discussion, entreaty, and reassurance; rarely through blatant threat. Only in 1957 was there a general and public perception of American "pressure" to force an Israeli decision contrary to its preferred position—and that, too, was accompanied by American reassurances. Subsequent episodes of conflict were of lesser magnitude and less public in their nature. The American approach, tempered by reassurance, was successful in achieving modification of Israeli policy, such as returning to negotiations and agreeing to modify policy positions to facilitate an agreement. A pattern of consultation also developed, but primarily after the 1967 war. Israel was concerned about the lack of consultation during this early period, especially during the 1956-57 episode and at the time of the first Rogers Plan in 1969. In each instance, however, the U.S. administration soon sought to reassure Israel about its decisions and policies.

NOTES

1. Harry S. Truman, *Memoirs,* II, *Years of Trial and Hope* (Garden City, N.Y.: Doubleday, 1956), p. 157.

2. Henry Cabot Lodge, "Israeli Withdrawal from Egyptian Territory," *Department of State Bulletin,* Mar. 18, 1957, p. 433.

3. Lyndon Baines Johnson, *The Vantage Point: Perspectives of the Presidency, 1963-1969* (New York: Holt, Rinehart, and Winston, 1971), p. 303.

4. Henry M. Christman, ed., *The State Papers of Levi Eshkol* (New York: Funk and Wagnalls, 1969), pp. 131-32.

5. See *Haaretz,* July 31, 1967.

6. See *Divrei ha-Knesset,* Aug. 1, 1967.

7. Christman, ed., *The State Papers of Levi Eshkol,* pp. 137-38.

8. Lyndon B. Johnson, "Principles for Peace in the Middle East," *Department of State Bulletin,* July 10, 1967, pp. 31-34.

9. Text of the resolutions as published in *Arab Report and Record,* Sept. 1-15, 1967, p. 286.

10. "U.S. and Israel Reaffirm Dedication to Peace in the Middle East," *Department of State Bulletin,* Feb. 5, 1968, p. 174.

11. *Weekly Compilation of Presidential Documents,* Sept. 16, 1968, p. 1341.

12. *New York Times,* Dec. 14, 1968.

13. *Weekly Compilation of Presidential Documents,* Feb. 3, 1969, p. 177.

14. *Weekly Compilation of Presidential Documents,* Feb. 10, 1969, p. 227.

15. Interview with Golda Meir, *Washington Post,* Aug. 7, 1969.

16. *Department of State Bulletin,* Oct. 6, 1969, pp. 299-300.

17. Department of State press release no. 371, Dec. 9, 1969.

18. See *Department of State Bulletin,* Jan. 12, 1970, esp. p. 23.

19. Full text in *Jerusalem Post,* Dec. 23, 1969.

20. *Weekly Compilation of Presidential Documents,* July 6, 1970, p. 869.

21. *Department of State Bulletin,* Sept. 24, 1973, p. 387.

22. Golda Meir, *My Life* (New York: G. P. Putnam's Sons, 1975), pp. 426, 427, 431.

23. Marvin Kalb and Bernard Kalb, *Kissinger* (Boston: Little, Brown, 1974), esp. pp. 459-61.

24. See testimony of Bernard Reich, May 23, 1974, "The Middle East, 1974: The Political Mood in Israel," in U.S. House of Representatives, Committee on Foreign Affairs, Subcommittee on the Near East and South Asia, *Hearings, the Middle East, 1974: New Hopes, New Challenges* (Washington, D.C.: U.S. Government Printing Office, 1974), pp. 103-30.

25. Transcript, press conference of Prime Minister Golda Meir, Washington, D.C., Nov. 1, 1973.

26. Department of State press release no. 424, Aug. 21, 1975.

27. Ibid.

2

THE CARTER ADMINISTRATION

The administration of Jimmy Carter sought a comprehensive settlement and attempted to reconvene the Geneva conference, which had first met in December 1973, in contrast with the preference for Kissinger's step-by-step techniques and a U.S. monopoly on the peace process. This approach developed early in the new administration, which accorded a high priority to the settlement of the Arab-Israeli conflict, and occasioned sharp clashes with Israel.

In the 1976 election campaign Carter focused on many of the traditional themes with regard to Israel and the Arab-Israeli conflict. He emphasized his religious perspective, Israel's rights, and the affinity between two democratic states. He saw the significance of Resolution 242 and of direct negotiations between the parties, and suggested that the "heart of the matter" was the need for a basic change in the Arab attitude toward Israel—including recognition, diplomatic relations, a peace treaty, open frontiers, and the end of boycotts and hostile propaganda. He suggested that a settlement proceed in stages and that the Soviet Union be prevented from undermining it. The pro-Israel pronouncements of Carter as candidate did not presage significant policy changes when he secured the presidency.

Despite the campaign, there were Israeli apprehensions about the substantive issues of a settlement, compounded by an apparent U.S. move in the direction of the Arab states because of oil and the strategic value attributed to Egypt. U.S. military sales to Egypt and Saudi Arabia to encourage their pro-U.S. attitudes seemed to raise the possibility of an erosion of Israel's military position vis-à-vis the Arab states and in the U.S.-Israel bilateral relationship.

Although there were expectations that the new administration would wait some months before becoming fully engaged in Middle East diplomacy, there were early expressions of interest and concern by Carter and Secretary of State Cyrus Vance. In a statement one week prior to his inauguration, Carter expressed optimism, based on Israel's positions, "moderation of Arab leaders," the deescalation of the civil war in Lebanon, and the fact that all parties had indicated a willingness to go to Geneva: "There is a fine opportunity for dramatic improvements there."[1] Underlying the Carter approach was the view that the time had never been more propitious to work for peace, and to lose the opportunity could be disastrous for the region as well as the international political and economic order. A just and lasting settlement was seen as essential for a more peaceful world, since "conflict there carries the threat of a global confrontation and runs the risk of nuclear war."[2]

The need for peace and the advancement of U.S. interests suggest part of the rationale for involvement, but the United States assumed the central role also because of its special relationship with Israel and its developing links with the Arab states.

> It is precisely because of our close ties with both Israel and her Arab neighbors that we are uniquely placed to promote the search for peace, to work for an improved understanding of each side's legitimate concerns, and to help them work out what we hope will be a basis for negotiation leading to a final peace in the Middle East.[3]

The administration's view of its role, the negotiations process, and the substance of a settlement emerged in statements and "signals" over time. The administration believed that a new approach was needed. At the base was Resolution 242, but it was not deemed sufficient. "We, therefore, decided to work with the parties concerned to outline the overall framework for an enduring peace."[4] A comprehensive approach for an overall settlement was to replace the Kissinger-style step-by-step limited accords.

From the outset there was a realization that a settlement would come only at the end of long and complicated negotiations, and Vance continually cautioned about underestimating the difficulties the process would face. The year 1977 was considered crucial and the administration was hopeful that it could achieve an overall settlement that would be implemented through a step-by-step process. Reconvening the Geneva conference seemed to be an appropriate mechanism although it would mean Soviet participation. The self-identified U.S. role was to act as a catalyst to

bring about negotiations between the parties and to establish a set of principles (but not details) that might serve as a basis for successfully negotiating
a settlement. Clearly the parties would need to negotiate directly with each
other, since "we cannot conceive of genuine peace existing between countries who will not talk to one another."[5] A logical consequence of this perspective, reiterated numerous times, was that the United States could not
seek to impose a settlement. However, the United States viewed the issue
as sufficiently important and intractable for it to act as more than a mediator
bringing the parties together; therefore, U.S. views and suggestions "to
stimulate fresh thought" became an element of the process.[6]

Despite protestations that it would not impose a settlement, the administration increasingly began to identify its views, to suggest that their
adoption would facilitate movement toward peace, and to think in terms of
persuasion (and even leverage) to secure support for them. In an interview
in May 1977 Carter said:

> I would not hesitate if I saw clearly a fair and equitable solution to use
> the full strength of our own country and its persuasive powers to bring
> those nations to agreement. I recognize, though, that we cannot im-
> pose our will on others, and unless the countries involved agree, there
> is no way for us to make progress.[7]

By October the position had become more precise, and Zbigniew
Brzezinski, Carter's national security adviser, stated:

> . . . the United States has a legitimate right to exercise its own lever-
> age, peaceful and constructive, to obtain a settlement. And that's
> exactly what we will be doing.[8]

THE FRAMEWORK

As a part of their effort to assist the parties in outlining a framework
for a lasting peace, Carter and Vance identified three elements as central
and indispensable: definition and assurance of permanent peace, definition
and establishment of territory and borders, and the Palestinian issue.

The "intellectual" origin of Carter's approach lay in several sources.
In a coauthored article Brzezinski argued the need for resolution of the
Arab-Israeli conflict so that it would not affect the interests, especially the
oil supply, of other states. It advocated an overt U.S. initiative "outlining
both the substance of an eventual settlement and the required international

framework for it," which implied Soviet participation.[9] There was also the "Brookings Report" *(Toward Peace in the Middle East),* in which a diverse group of Americans (including Brzezinski) sought to develop a consensus on a framework for an Arab-Israeli settlement and a U.S. role in the effort. It suggested several perspectives that later appeared as elements in the Carter approach.[10]

During the spring of 1977, as Carter received leaders from the Middle East in Washington, he began to articulate his views on a solution.

The definition of peace involved a comprehensive approach that went beyond the end of war. It was most fully expressed by Carter at Clinton, Massachusetts, in March 1977:

> . . . the first prerequisite of a lasting peace is the recognition of Israel by her neighbors, Israel's right to exist, Israel's right to exist permanently, Israel's right to exist in peace. That means that over a period of months or years . . . the borders between Israel and Syria, Israel and Lebanon, Israel and Jordan, Israel and Egypt must be opened up to travel, to tourism, to cultural exchange, to trade, so that no matter who the leaders might be in those countries the people themselves will have formed a mutual understanding and comprehension and a sense of a common purpose to avoid the repetitive wars and death that have afflicted that region so long.[11]

A second central element was territory, withdrawal, and borders. The crucial problem was to provide permanent borders that were secure, acceptable, and recognized by all the parties. Resolution 242 refers to "secure and recognized" borders, while Israel has talked in terms of "defensible" borders. The United States has generally relied upon the words of Resolution 242. However, on March 7, during welcoming ceremonies for Israeli Prime Minister Yitzhak Rabin, Carter spoke of Israel having "defensible" borders. Carter mentioned Vance's recent trip, during which he had tried "to explore some common ground for future permanent peace there, so that Israel might have defensible borders, so that the peace commitments would never be violated, and that there could be a sense of security about this young country in the future." This statement, which seemed to embrace Israel's position, set off an immediate protest in the Arab world and the terminology was not repeated. Subsequently U.S. officials sought to convey that no policy change was intended, and Vance told reporters later that day that "there is no change in position by the use of the words 'defensible borders.' "

The United States did not identify precise lines for the future borders between Israel and the Arab states, but substantial Israeli withdrawal from occupied territories and negotiated minor adjustments or modifications in the pre-1967 lines were the main elements.[12] Although it believed that major changes in the 1967 lines were not consistent with Resolution 242, there was a suggestion that defense lines, and Israeli defense capability, might go beyond the legal borders.[13] In the final analysis, negotiation and agreement between Israel and the Arabs would have to decide the situation.

The Palestinian element increasingly emerged as significant and the most controversial. The traditional U.S. approach, which concentrated on the refugee and humanitarian aspects of the problem and, after the June war of 1967, also on terrorism, was given a political component by the Carter administration. Terrorism receded, and while refugees were still a concern, the issue was seen as broader in scope. The administration sought to include provisions for the legitimate interests of the Palestinian people in any settlement.[14] The idea of a homeland appeared publicly for the first time on March 16, 1977, at Clinton, Massachusetts, when Carter said that the solution required some form of homeland for the Palestinians: "The third ultimate requirement for peace is to deal with the Palestinian problem. The Palestinians claim up 'til this moment that Israel has no right to be there, that the land belongs to the Palestinians, and they've never yet given up their publicly professed commitment to destroy Israel. That has to be overcome. *There has to be a homeland provided for the Palestinian refugees who have suffered for many, many years.*"[15]

Carter believed that the boundaries, nature, and political status of the "homeland" would have to be negotiated, and his preference was that the Palestinian entity (not an independent country) be linked with Jordan.[16] To gain the benefits of such a settlement, he felt the Palestinians should be expected to demonstrate their willingness to exist in peace. This perspective caused an immediate uproar in Israel and among Israel's supporters in the United States, because the phrase "Palestinian homeland" had come to symbolize an independent Palestinian state in the West Bank and Gaza Strip, which Israel strongly opposed.

Underlying the administration's approach was the view that for peace to endure, the Palestinians must have a stake in it. Increasingly this meant that they must be involved in the peacemaking process and must be represented at Geneva, although exactly how or by whom remained unclear.[17] One of the proposed alternatives was for the PLO to represent the Palestinians at Geneva, but underlying the U.S. approach was the Sinai II pledge to Israel that the United States "will not recognize or negotiate with the Palestine Liberation Organization" until the PLO accepted Israel's right to exist and U.N. Resolutions 242 and 338. In the U.S. view PLO representation was only one of the possible alternatives. In an interview on September 16, 1977, Carter said, "We have never called on the PLO to be part of the future negotiations."[18] In a September 29, 1977, press conference Carter stated:

> Obviously they [the PLO] don't represent a nation. It is a group that represents certainly a substantial part of the Palestinians. I certainly don't think they're the exclusive representatives of the Palestinians. Obviously there are mayors, for instance, and local officials in the West Bank area who represent Palestinians. They may or may not be members of the PLO.

On July 28, 1977, Carter spelled out the conditions for a PLO role in these terms: they need to "forego their commitment presently publicly espoused that Israel should be destroyed." In Plains, Georgia, on August 8 he elaborated: "If the Palestinians will recognize the applicability of the United Nations Resolution 242, then it would open up a new opportunity for us to start discussions with them and also open up an avenue that they might participate in the Geneva conference." He also said that there was a need for "the Palestinians and their leaders [to] recognize Israel's right to exist . . . ."[19] However, on September 29, 1977, Carter restated the pledge to Israel "that we will not negotiate with nor deal directly with the PLO until they adopt United Nations Resolution 242 as a basis for their involvement, which includes a recognition of the right of Israel to exist." He went on to say: "If the PLO should go ahead and say 'we endorse UN Resolution 242—we don't think it adequately addresses the Palestinian issue because it only refers to refugees and we think we have a further interest than that,' that would suit us okay. We would then begin to meet with and to work with the PLO. . . . If they accept UN 242 and the right of Israel to exist, then we will begin discussions with the leaders of the PLO."

The Carter administration's perspective was more specific than that of its predecessors and reflected a departure in procedure and substance. Israel was concerned by these developments, and the two states clashed as the process to implement the Carter views got under way.

THE PROCESS

By early February 1977 the Carter administration's interest and concern were articulated by Vance:

> Let me say that we do attach the highest priority to progress in the Middle East and to progress in 1977. There is no issue, insofar as the United States is concerned, which has higher priority; and the fact that President Carter has asked me to undertake this mission [his visit to the Middle East in February] as the first major diplomatic effort of this country I think is an indication of the importance which this Administration and President Carter attach to the peaceful solution of the Middle East problem.[20]

In mid-February Vance traveled to Israel, Egypt, Lebanon, Jordan, Syria, and Saudi Arabia to lay the groundwork for the administration's efforts. The White House spokesman said Vance would convey to regional leaders "the importance the President attaches to making significant progress this year toward a just and lasting peace in the Middle East."[21] The trip also enabled the secretary of state to get a better understanding of the issues, to learn the views of the parties on procedure, and to achieve a firsthand familiarity with regional leaders. At the conclusion of his tour Vance stated that Arabs and Israelis remained "deeply divided" on how to reach a settlement, and that he didn't want to underestimate the complexity of the situation.

Vance's visit was followed by a round of exploratory conversations in which regional leaders met with Carter and other senior U.S. officials. The first was Israeli Prime Minister Yitzhak Rabin, who came to Washington in March. For Rabin the trip had dimensions beyond those relating to a settlement. He sought to bolster his image at home, in anticipation of the forthcoming parliamentary elections, and to get positive responses from Carter on a number of specific issues, including the proposed Israeli sale of Kfir jets to Ecuador, the sale by the United States of concussion bombs to Israel, and the coproduction of F-16 jet aircraft. There was also the matter of Israeli drilling for oil in the Red Sea, which had occasioned public discord. The visit did not reassure Israel; and, on his return home, Rabin noted that there were "strong differences" between the two states on the elements of an Arab-Israeli solution as advanced by Carter, thus foreshadowing the clashes that were to follow over the succeeding months. It was during the Rabin visit that Carter began to articulate publicly the procedural and substantive elements of an Arab-Israeli settlement.

President Anwar Sadat of Egypt arrived in Washington on April 3. He sought economic assistance and arms (particularly TOW antitank missiles and F-5E aircraft). Sadat stressed the Palestinian factor and told Carter that is "the core and crux" of the Arab-Israeli dispute, and that "no progress whatsoever can be achieved so long as this problem remains unsolved."[22] He praised Carter's comments about a Palestinian homeland. The consultations continued with the visit of King Hussein of Jordan to Washington in late April, during which all aspects of the Arab-Israeli conflict were reviewed. Carter's meeting with President Hafez Assad of Syria took place in Geneva on May 9. They focused on the question of a Palestinian homeland and Palestinian participation in negotiations for a settlement. Carter generally appeared pleased and subsequently told newsmen, with Assad at his side: "There must be a resolution of the Palestine problem and a homeland for the Palestinians."[23] Vance met with Israeli Foreign Minister Yigal Allon in London on May 11 to brief him on the meeting. Israel also sought reassurances about U.S. pressure for a settlement and its exclusion from a preferred list of countries eligible to receive advanced military technology, weapons, and coproduction agreements. Vance was reasonably successful in reassuring Allon that Israel's special position and its concerns would receive the administration's attention.

The process of presidential consultation with regional leaders continued with the visit to Washington of Crown Prince Fahd of Saudi Arabia in late May. Following their review of the situation, Carter and Fahd agreed that "the major effort should continue toward trying to reconvene the Geneva conference in the second half of 1977."[24]

The Israeli election in May interrupted the process. Menachem Begin's views, articulated again after the election, conflicted with the positions advanced by Carter, portending problems in the bilateral relationship. The Carter administration was surprised and dismayed by Begin's victory; no plans for a reaction to it had been formulated, and it was believed his election would slow the timetable for a Geneva conference and a settlement because his views were radically different from those of Rabin and Shimon Peres. The administration's approach had been based, in part, on an assumption of a Labor Party victory (and Rabin or Peres as prime minister, both of whom were considered to be moderates), and the ascendency of Begin and the Likud seemed to put it in jeopardy and presaged continuing clashes between the two states.

The U.S. response was cautious—a "wait and see" attitude was adopted and a hiatus in diplomacy was assumed—although the administration sought to put the best face on the victory and spoke in somewhat optimistic terms about the results. Carter said he hoped ". . . that the election of Mr. Begin will not be a step backward toward the achievement of peace."[25] To bolster the administration's position, Carter stressed the importance of movement toward a settlement. At the same time the United States sought to undermine the new Israeli government, which was seen as being weak because of its small majority in the Knesset. Efforts were made to separate it from its supporters at home and abroad, particularly among those American Jews who supported Israel, but not necessarily Begin and the Likud. These efforts soon proved fruitless, and eventually had a counterproductive effect as support for Begin grew at home and abroad, partly in response to this perceived strategy.

The initial U.S. dismay promoted the view that the Likud victory under Begin's leadership would slow the peace process just when the administration believed the time was propitious and movement was needed. The U.S. media reaction mirrored the administration's concern and generally pessimistic outlook. It was also reported that U.S. Jewish leaders had misgivings about what would be seen as the outspoken "intransigence" of Begin. This view was articulated by Carter and others on a number of occasions, and set the tone for the relationship between the two states and their leaders.

U.S. unease at Begin's victory and Israel's anxiety about Carter's policy revolved around a number of issues in dispute between the two states. There was the apparent U.S. support for a Palestinian entity in the West Bank and Gaza. Begin's cabinet, more than any previous Israeli government, was committed to Israeli control of the West Bank for ideological and religious reasons, not only because of security considerations. Israel objected to a role for the PLO in the negotiations, not only because it perceived it to be a terrorist organization but also because PLO participation would imply acceptance of a Palestinian entity in the West Bank. Israel was suspicious of the Soviet Union, and had misgivings about U.S. efforts to bring it into the peace process. Israel feared that the reconvening of the Geneva conference would leave it isolated as the superpowers vied for the sympathy of the Arab states.

Israel seemed increasingly anxious about the nature of specific U.S. policies and potential U.S. "pressures," and the United States seemed concerned that a propitious moment for peace would be lost. As the new administration moved toward reconvening the Geneva peace conference and articulated some of the specifics of its conception of peace, and the Begin administration defined its positions and policies, clashes between the two powers became more obvious and more vocal.

A series of decisions by Carter soon after his inauguration helped to engender Israeli concern with the new administration. In February 1977 the administration called Israeli oil drilling in the Gulf of Suez illegal and not helpful to the peace process. Carter canceled the sale of CBU-72 concussion bombs to Israel that had been pledged by Ford. The Carter-Rabin meetings at Washington, in March 1977, were partially characterized by discord on the extent of Israeli withdrawal from territory occupied in the June War (1967) and changes in the pre-1967 frontiers. In May 1977 the administration's presidential review memorandum on limiting U.S. arms supply to foreign states (PRM 12) suggested possible alteration of Israel's preferred access to U.S. arms. Israel's sale of Kfir jets (with U.S.-made engines) to Ecuador was vetoed. Coproduction agreements on F-16s and military communications items sought by Israel were not approved. A nuclear reactor sale was delayed and major Israeli arms requests were held up.

Beyond these specific instances of discord, there were other issues that emerged as the Carter administration asserted its positions concerning a settlement, positions that conflicted with Israeli perspectives.[26] The U.S. approach and the Israeli conception of peace were not congruent. The two governments saw the concept of peace similarly and believed that the end of war had to be accompanied by a normalization of relations between the parties. However, on the matter of secure boundaries the United States believed that minor adjustments in the pre-1967 war lines would be adequate; Israel sought broader changes and the establishment of defensible borders. The Palestinian element provoked the most direct clashes. Carter sought to involve the Palestinians and talked of the need for a Palestinian homeland or entity. Early in the administration there were a number of overtures to the PLO, suggesting there might be a modification of the U.S. policy on negotiations with them. These moves were of concern to Israel, which focused on the PLO commitment to the destruction of Israel and viewed the U.S. effort as an erosion in its position.

In the weeks following the Israeli election, both the United States and Israel staked out elements of their approaches to their bilateral relationship and to the Arab-Israeli conflict. Both Carter and Begin sought to play down the areas of controversy that emerged and to maintain a cordial and positive relationship. A crucial step took place in mid-July with the visit to the United States of Israel's new prime minister. Prior to that visit the Department of State, in a statement on June 27, 1977, reaffirmed the centrality of

Resolution 242, reiterated the basic elements of the Carter approach, and noted that withdrawal referred to withdrawal on all fronts, including the West Bank. The purposes of the visit were manifold, but the crucial agenda included the establishment of personal rapport between Begin and Carter and a discussion of the elements of a settlement. Their meetings occasioned no substantive changes in their respective policies but appeared to have laid a foundation for personal rapport and mutual confidence.

Begin was optimistic as a result of their meetings. At a press conference in Washington on July 20, he said, "I think I can say that we established a personal report . . . I can assure and reassure all the friends of Israel and of America there isn't any confrontation between our two countries. To the contrary, during the last few days, friendship between the United States and Israel has been deepened. And that personal rapport between the President and myself will be helpful in the future." Carter appeared optimistic, as did Begin, and stated, "I believe that we have laid the groundwork now, barring some unforeseen difficulty, that will lead to the Geneva conference in October . . . . We see [it] as being very likely."[27] During the visit Begin presented a plan for peace that was outlined at a press conference and dealt with the various aspects of a settlement. The "plan" was rejected by the Arabs.

Israel viewed the Carter-Begin meetings with a sense of relief because there had been concern about a possible hostile confrontation, but the mood was short-lived. After Begin's return to Israel the government (on July 26) recognized three previously illegal settlements on the West Bank (Kadum, Ofra, and Maale Adumim) as permanent, legal entities. The United States reacted sharply, Secretary of State Vance stating that the settlements were illegal and obstacles to peace: "We have consistently stated and reiterated during our discussions here in Washington that we are of the opinion that the placing of these settlements is contrary to international law and presents an obstacle toward peace."[28] Begin rejected Vance's criticism and defended his government's decision: "We left no doubt in our talks [in Washington] about our position. Jews have the right to live anywhere in Judea and Samaria [on the West Bank] and the Gaza Strip."[29] During an interview on July 29 Carter said, ". . . I think it's an obstacle to peace. . . . these settlements are illegal. . . . We think it's wrong to establish these settlements, it's wrong to insinuate that they are legal, it's certainly wrong to ever claim that they are permanent."[30]

Vance's visit to the Middle East in early August included stops in Egypt, Lebanon, Syria, Jordan, Saudi Arabia, and Israel. His basic purpose was to meet with regional leaders and to assess the situation as well as the prospects for convening a meeting in Geneva. He told reporters that he would take "proposals" and "suggestions" with him. Clearly, no major breakthrough occurred, for the positions of the parties, which were further clarified and elaborated, remained far apart. However, they agreed that their foreign ministers would meet with Vance and Carter in the United States during September, at the time of the U.N. General Assembly session, and the United States would utilize the opportunity to try to narrow the differences and lay the groundwork for a Geneva conference. Following a report by Vance to Carter, a White House statement said that President Carter "remains determined to do all that is possible to bring about a just and lasting peace in the Middle East" and, in that process, the United States "will use its influence, offer its advice, volunteer its suggestions, and work to bring the parties into fruitful negotiations."[31]

In the latter part of August, the United States tried to secure some movement with suggestions that if the PLO were to modify its stand on Resolution 242, it might open the way for a U.S. dialogue with the PLO and its possible participation in the Geneva peace conference. Carter suggested as much in comments made to reporters at Plains, Georgia, in early August, and the administration appeared to take the view that if the PLO endorsed Resolution 242 (in some fashion), recognition of Israel would be implied. This was a modification of the stand taken in 1975 during the Sinai II negotiations, and conjured up images of an earlier "trial balloon" contained in the 1975 "Saunders document." But the PLO did not respond to the overtures.

Israel's settlement activity generated further clashes with the United States. Soon after Vance left the Middle East, the Israeli government authorized additional civilian settlements, and Carter and Vance denounced them as illegal and obstacles to peace.

In September and October the United States concentrated its efforts on meetings and consultations, in Washington and New York, with the parties and with the Soviet Union. The basic question appeared to be that of Palestinian representation at Geneva, and the United States pressed its view that Palestinians must be involved in the peace process. On September 12 the State Department refocused attention on this issue:

> . . . the status of the Palestinians must be settled in a comprehensive Arab-Israeli agreement. This issue cannot be ignored if the others are to be solved. Moreover, to be lasting, a peace agreement must be positively supported by all of the parties to the conflict, including the Palestinians. This means that the Palestinians must be involved in the peacemaking process. Their representatives will have to be at Geneva for the Palestinian question to be solved.[32]

The United States sought to obtain agreement on a method for Palestinian involvement, and the concept of a unified Arab delegation, consisting of Egypt, Syria, Jordan, Lebanon, and the Palestinians, to participate at Geneva opposite an Israeli delegation emerged as a possible alternative. It remained unresolved which Palestinians would participate and what the nature of their relationship to the PLO would be.

Israeli Foreign Minister Moshe Dayan visited the United States, and subsequent to his visit and lengthy discussions with U.S. officials, on September 25, 1977, Israel's cabinet formally agreed to a U.S. proposal that Palestinian representatives constitute part of a unified Arab delegation at the opening session of a reconvened Geneva conference. Although this represented a shift in Israel's position, Dayan made it clear that it did not alter Israel's view of the PLO. It represented an Israeli responsiveness to U.S. efforts. Israel insisted that Palestinians could participate in the unified Arab delegation provided that they were not known members of the PLO, and they would have to be part of a Jordanian delegation. No negotiations would take place with this Arab delegation, and after the opening ceremonial session the Arab group would split up into delegations representing the various Arab states (such as Egypt, Syria, Jordan) for negotiations. There would also be no change in Resolution 242.

The process took a significant further step when, on October 1, 1977, the United States joined with the Soviet Union in a statement that brought the latter back to the forefront of the negotiating process and enhanced its role. The superpowers stressed the need for "achieving, as soon as possible, a just and lasting settlement of the Arab-Israeli conflict." In rehearsing the various elements of a settlement, they referred to the "legitimate rights of the Palestinian people," which seemed to imply a PLO role in the negotiating process and the establishment of a Palestinian state.

The administration believed that the Soviet Union should have a role in the process if it was constructive, and that such a step would help improve the prospects for a Geneva conference. Cyrus Vance said in 1983: "If they were prepared to play a constructive role, as I believe they were in 1977, then I feel it would be much better to include them, because they could become a spoiler if they are not included."[33] The matter of a cochairmen's statement prior to a Geneva conference was first raised in a meeting between Vance and Soviet Foreign Minister Andrei Gromyko in May 1977. Vance reports that "since then I had kept the Soviets generally informed of progress in the negotiations to head off attempts by them to interfere."[34] The communiqué itself was discussed by Vance and Soviet Ambassador to Washington Anatoly Dobrynin at the end of August, following Vance's Middle East trip and on a number of subsequent occasions in September. Vance reports that "the final text was developed in a lengthy session with Gromyko on September 30 and released the following day." The statement was designed to accelerate the efforts toward reconvening the Geneva conference in December by eliciting Soviet aid and to demonstrate that the Carter administration was prepared to work cooperatively with the Soviet Union on matters of crucial international importance.

The joint statement dismayed Egypt and Israel, and generated substantial furor and opposition that were particularly strong among supporters of Israel and among anti-Soviet elements in the United States. For example, Congressman John J. Rhodes, Republican minority leader of the House of Representatives, wrote in the *New York Times:* "The President succeeded in bringing our foremost adversary back into a position of influence in the Middle East and at the same time rousing deep unease about the stability of America's commitment to the only democracy in the Middle East."[35] It was viewed by some as a concession to the Soviet Union that secured no comparable Soviet concession in return.

Israel and its supporters focused their concern on the increased involvement of the Soviet Union, which had been effectively excluded by Kissinger from the peace process since the October War, and the reference to "the legitimate *rights* of the Palestinian people" (emphasis added), which the United States had not previously endorsed. Rabbi Alexander M. Schindler, chairman of the Conference of Presidents of Major American Jewish Organizations, noted that the statement "on its face, represents an abandonment of America's historic commitment to the security and survival of Israel."[36] Senator Henry Jackson and AFL-CIO President George Meany denounced it, and Meany warned that any attempt to undercut Israel would backfire politically for the president.[37] In Israel's view the United States appeared to be moving toward accepting the idea of a separate Palestinian state, it seemed to be leaning toward an imposed solution, and it fostered the impression that it might recognize the PLO—policies strongly opposed by Israel, but at the core of the Arab-Soviet position. Shlomo Avineri, formerly director general of Israel's Foreign Ministry, commented that the communiqué "made the Israelis lose whatever trust they still had in the sound judgement of the American administration. . . ."[38]

The Carter administration did not anticipate the extent and strength of the adverse reaction, both public and private, in part because of the exclusion of some of the president's political advisers from the decision-making process. Zbigniew Brzezinski notes in his memoirs:

. . . we clearly needed the input of the President's domestic advisers, because the foreign policy of a democracy is effective only as long as it is sustained by strong popular support. Insensitivity to domestic concerns could produce calamities, as was shown early in the Administration by the joint U.S.-Soviet statement on the Middle East which so outraged American friends of Israel.[39]

The administration soon set out to rectify the situation, reduce the strain, and restore domestic confidence in the president's handling of foreign policy through a multifaceted approach. Meetings with Israelis and other critics, including members of Congress, were arranged, and public statements to help reassure Israel and its supporters were crafted.[40] In a speech to the U.N. General Assembly on October 4, Carter reiterated the need for a "true peace" based on Resolutions 242 and 338, and noted that Israel must have "borders that are recognized and secure" and that "the commitment of the United States to Israel's security is unquestionable."[41] He also made it clear that "We do not intend to impose from the outside a settlement on the nations of the Middle East." These elements were stressed as a means of reassuring Israel. At the same time, however, Carter stated that "For the Arabs, the legitimate rights of the Palestinians must be recognized."

A "working paper" that dealt with reconvening the Geneva conference was devised by Carter, Vance, and Dayan during a meeting in New York on October 4. Dayan initially characterized the meeting as "brutal" but later seemed to recant, after a U.S. protest, and said it had been "difficult."[42] Although substantive areas of disagreement remained, the paper sought to reduce Israeli anxiety, to avoid a U.S.-Israel confrontation, and to clear the procedural obstacles on the path to Geneva. It was replete with compromises. The United States appeared to abandon its efforts to involve the Soviet Union and the PLO, and Israel agreed that it would deal with Palestinians at Geneva. Inter alia, it provided that "the Arab parties will be represented by a unified Arab delegation, which will include Palestinian Arabs. After the opening sessions, the conference will split into working groups," each to consist of Israel and an Arab state. "The West Bank and Gaza issues will be discussed in a working group to consist of Israel, Jordan, Egypt, and the Palestinian Arabs."[43]

In a U.S.-Israel statement issued on October 5, after the New York meeting, the October 1 statement was reduced in significance, for they noted that it was "not a prerequisite for the reconvening and conduct of the

Geneva Conference" and that Resolutions 242 and 338 "remain the agreed basis for the resumption of the Geneva Peace Conference."[44]

On October 11 the Israeli cabinet unanimously approved the "working" paper. In part this was to demonstrate Israeli flexibility in cooperating with the Carter administration on the procedural issues concerning a Geneva conference. But it also served to alter the rules of the game by removing the Soviet Union from the peace process and by demonstrating that the superpowers could not impose a solution or even take important actions without the involvement of the regional states. Nonetheless, Israel and the United States did not agree on the role of the Palestinians (especially the PLO) in the settlement process, the concept of a Palestinian homeland, the extent of Israeli withdrawal from the occupied territories, or the shape of Israel's final borders. Israel appeared to be "victorious" in the clash with the administration on the questions of the Palestinians and Soviet involvement.

The episode had a positive political benefit for the Begin coalition, in that Yigael Yadin and the Democratic Movement for Change (DMC) joined the government later in October. The decision reflected Yadin's concerns about U.S. policy and the nature of U.S.-Israel relations, and came after his visit to the United States, meetings with Vance and Brzezinski, and the U.S.-Soviet communiqué. He believed that the threat of American pressure was very real, and therefore the DMC was obliged to join the government to serve the interests of Israel. Yadin's 15 seats gave Begin a substantial majority (77 out of 120) in the Knesset.

The problem facing the United States was to secure Arab support, and on October 12 it sent the working paper to the Arab states for their consideration. The Arab governments sought changes to make it acceptable,[45] while the PLO rejected it outright. The basic obstacle seemed to be the form of Palestinian representation at Geneva. The PLO, generally supported by the Arab states, insisted that it was the only legitimate representative of the Palestinians, and Israel refused to deal with the PLO.

It was at this juncture that President Anwar Sadat of Egypt took the initiative that dramatically altered the situation, changed the nature of the peace process in the Middle East, and significantly affected the U.S.-Israel relationship.

Sadat's announcement on November 9, 1977, that he was prepared to go to the Israeli Knesset to discuss the Arab-Israeli situation was a surprise to the international community but was not a precipitous action. Contacts between Egypt and Israel had taken place through a variety of channels, particularly Romania and Morocco, and Israeli Foreign Minister Dayan had met secretly in Morocco with Egyptian Deputy Prime Minister Hassan al-Tuhami.

Sadat had some misgivings about the U.S. approach. He was not sanguine about the possibility of reconvening the Geneva conference and reconciling the diverse interests of the participants. Because of his distrust of the Soviet Union, the secret U.S.-Soviet talks that led to the joint communiqué, and the communiqué itself, increased his concern. By October, Sadat faced two alternatives: either risk being caught up in this "terrible vicious circle," or explore further the possibility of a settlement through direct contacts with Israel. Sadat also understood that Begin could be a legitimate partner to an agreement. Sadat's decision to visit Jerusalem, rather than pursue secret contacts, was prompted by his desire to create a psychological atmosphere in which he could secure important and rapid gains for Egypt. He also seemed to want to short-circuit U.S. efforts to reconvene the Geneva conference, and thus force the United States to focus its diplomatic energy on the possibilities created by his initiative.

In the years since Israel's establishment, no Arab state had recognized Israel or officially acknowledged negotiations with it. Now Egypt, the most powerful and populous Arab state, reversed this approach by the sudden visit of its president to Jerusalem and his address to the Knesset, in which he proclaimed: "we welcome you among us with full security and safety," and "we accept to live with you in permanent peace based on justice."

Sadat's gesture left Israel and the United States perplexed about Egyptian policy and Sadat's real intentions. The dominant U.S. reaction was that Sadat's move might isolate him and jeopardize his political future. The administration preferred Geneva and a process it could control. His initiative forced the United States to contend with the difficulty of supporting Sadat and helping him fend off his critics while keeping on friendly terms with Saudi Arabia and Jordan, both of which had significant objections to his policy. The United States responded with a hesitant approach, reflecting a reluctance to abandon its Geneva-oriented policy and an inability to adjust quickly to the new reality.[46] These considerations led it to counsel Sadat to refrain from making a separate peace, and to urge Israel to make a public offer of significant concessions that would help Sadat justify his initiative. Several days later it supported the initiative as a means to a settlement, and eventually downgraded its preference for Geneva.

On November 26, 1977, Sadat addressed Egypt's People's Assembly, calling for a Cairo conference "preparatory" to a Geneva conference and inviting all "parties" to participate. Israel accepted the invitation, while

Syria and the PLO denounced it. Jordan and Saudi Arabia remained "neutral." Several days later the United States agreed to participate, and Secretary of State Vance visited six Middle East nations between December 9 and 14, to persuade their leaders to lend their support and to participate. The Arab leaders refused, despite Vance's efforts and Sadat's assertion that he regarded the Geneva conference as a means for recovering the Arab territories and for obtaining recognition of the right of the Palestinians to a homeland. The Soviet Union refused to participate. The representatives of Egypt, Israel, the United States, and the United Nations met in Cairo on December 14 to discuss the procedures for reconvening the Geneva peace conference.

Israel's reaction to Sadat's initiative was designed to respond to U.S. expectations as much as to Egyptian demands. Begin prepared a detailed plan that included a framework for a peace treaty with Egypt and an approach to the Palestinian problem and the future of the West Bank and the Gaza Strip. It offered an Israeli withdrawal to the international border and Egyptian sovereignty over a demilitarized Sinai. It retained Israeli control of the West Bank and Gaza while suggesting that the inhabitants be accorded administrative autonomy. Security and public order would be "the responsibility of the Israeli authorities."

Begin's autonomy plan was a partial response to the fact that Egypt would not agree to a bilateral peace treaty unless the Palestinian issue was addressed. Begin sought to reconcile this factor with Israel's security requirements, with his government's ideological predispositions concerning the West Bank and Gaza, with other elements of Israel's national interest, and with domestic factors. Clearly, his main concern was the ultimate status of the West Bank and Gaza, for which a detailed plan was constructed in an effort to ensure that policy preferences would be maintained. For the Sinai Peninsula a less complex proposal was required because the issues were simpler. Even before formally submitting his detailed suggestions to the Israeli cabinet or to Sadat, Begin took them to Carter. Carter subsequently stated:

> I think Prime Minister Begin has taken a long step forward in offering to President Sadat, and indirectly to the Palestinians, self-rule. President Sadat so far is insisting that the so-called Palestinian entity be an independent nation. My own preference is that they not be an independent nation but be tied in some way with the surrounding countries . . . my own personal opinion is that permanent peace can best be maintained if there is not a fairly radical, new, independent nation in the heart of the Middle East area. . . . we are perfectly willing to accept any reasonable solution that the parties themselves might evolve.[47]

Encouraged by Carter's reaction that the approach was "constructive," Begin presented his proposals to Sadat in Ismailiya on December 25, 1977. Begin's plan for the West Bank (or Judea and Samaria, as the area was referred to by Israel) and Gaza proposed "administrative autonomy" for the inhabitants and called for the establishment of an administrative council that would control and regulate educational, social, religious, and economic activity in those areas while Israel would remain responsible for security. Thus it provided for self-rule but not sovereignty. Begin also reiterated Israel's claim of sovereignty over the area and preserved the right of Israelis to acquire land and settle there. Sadat found this formula unacceptable.

Egypt refused to enter into a discussion of the detailed Israeli proposal, and suggested instead that the two parties issue a general declaration of principles calling for the establishment of peace based on Israeli withdrawal from Sinai, the Golan Heights, the West Bank, and Gaza in accordance with Resolution 242, and a just settlement of the Palestinian problem on the basis of the Palestinians' right to self-determination. The Egyptian proposal was unacceptable to Israel, particularly because it conflicted with Begin's desire to keep the West Bank and Gaza under Israeli control.

Begin's autonomy plan and the Egyptian counterproposals became the centerpieces of the negotiations over the months leading to the Camp David summit. Begin's proposal was opposed by Egypt and the United States, both of which objected to indefinite Israeli control over the West Bank and Gaza.

On January 4, 1978, Carter met with Sadat at Aswan, and emphasized the importance of a "just and comprehensive" peace that included "resolution of the Palestinian problem in all its aspects. The problem must recognize the legitimate rights of the Palestinian people and enable the Palestinians to participate in the determination of their own future."[48] The "Aswan formula" reflected the extent of congruence of U.S. and Egyptian views, and the growing positive relationship between Carter and Sadat and between the United States and Egypt. A second issue concerned the linkage between an Egypt-Israel agreement and arrangements for the West Bank and Gaza. Israel sought to prevent a formal linkage, while Egypt and the United States insisted on such a connection.

Begin and Sadat agreed to set up two committees to pursue the talks. The Military Committee was to discuss the problems of Sinai, while the Political Committee was to seek agreement on a declaration of principles. The Military Committee began its work in Cairo on January 11, 1978, while the Political Committee convened in Jerusalem on January 17. Continued harsh criticism of Sadat's policy by other Arab states, Israel's construction of new settlements in Sinai (after it had agreed in principle to the restoration of Egyptian sovereignty there), and Israel's disregard of Egyptian sensitivities led Sadat to withdraw the Egyptian delegation and terminate the work of the Political Committee shortly after it convened. Egypt refused to reconstitute the Political Committee and sought to intensify pressure on Israel by increasing the U.S. involvement. Realizing that its views were closer to Egypt's than to Israel's, Sadat urged the United States to submit its own plan; Israel, for similar reasons, preferred a more limited U.S. role. Discussions between Egypt and Israel continued and the United States soon began to take an active role, with the approval and often at the request of the parties, to break the deadlock. The United States engaged in an intensive effort to mitigate Saudi and Jordanian criticism and to persuade Jordan to join in the talks.

As the negotiations after Sadat's visit began, the United States sought to ensure their progress and, as open disputes between Egypt and Israel developed, to persuade the parties to reduce public recriminations and continue private negotiations. As a part of this process, Sadat conferred with Carter at Camp David, Maryland, in early February 1978, and later announced that the United States was no longer a "go-between" but a "full partner in the establishment of peace," and that Israel's policy of building new settlements in the occupied terrotories was a barrier to negotiations. He clearly was suggesting a greater U.S. effort to influence Israel's position.

After Sadat's visit U.S. spokesmen criticized Israel's settlement policy as contrary to international law, and announced that the administration intended to sell military aircraft to Egypt and Saudi Arabia as well as to Israel, in part to encourage prospects for a settlement. Israel took a firm stand on the settlement question, and relations with the United States were strained further by Begin's assertion that Resolution 242 did not require Israeli withdrawal from either the West Bank or the Gaza Strip. The United States disagreed, and Vance reiterated:

> There now has been a question raised as to whether or not 242 does, in fact, apply to all fronts and, more specifically, to the West Bank and Gaza. In our judgment, it is clear from the past history—from the negotiating history—and from the conduct of the parties that 242 does, indeed, apply on all fronts.[49]

Throughout the spring of 1978, as the controversy over the proposed sale of the aircraft grew, efforts continued by Israel, Egypt, and the United States to work out a declaration of principles on which to base a peace treaty. Assistant Secretary of State Alfred Atherton traveled to the Middle East in February and April in an attempt to narrow the differences. Senior Israeli and Egyptian officials visited Washington to meet with Carter and their opposite numbers in the U.S. administration to work out a compromise, but the process seemed to generate more strain than accord in the U.S.-Israel relationship.

These diplomatic issues were soon overshadowed by events in the Middle East. On March 11, 1978, a busload of Israelis was attacked by Palestinian terrorists, and on March 14 Israel launched an invasion of southern Lebanon (Operation Litani) to drive the Palestinians from their positions close to the Israeli border. After initially securing a strip along the border between its territory and that of Lebanon, Israel's forces continued to move north, and eventually occupied all of Lebanon south of the Litani River. Israel began a phased withdrawal from southern Lebanon on April 11, after the U.N. Interim Force in Lebanon (UNIFIL) entered the sector to replace the departing Israeli troops and to help prevent infiltration into Israel. The last Israeli troops withdrew on June 13, 1978.

Although the United States was concerned that this violence would obstruct the peace process, Egypt and Israel continued to negotiate, albeit at a slower pace. At the end of March, Begin met with Carter in Washington, where he received new assurances of support for Israel, although his settlement policy was sharply criticized. The administration was concerned that the diplomatic process had been weakened by Begin's stand on the Palestinians, the settlements, and the interpretation of Resolution 242, and the U.S.-Israeli discord was particularly apparent because the parties did not agree on the central themes of the negotiations process.

The Israeli view of the meeting was negative, and reflected concern about Carter's approach and perspective.[50] Carter is quoted as saying: "The obstacle to peace is Israel's desire to perpetuate its political domination of the West Bank and Gaza. Let us hope that Israel will exchange political control for security arrangements . . . . At the same time, I want to give you credit for what you proposed in Sinai."[51] Carter states in his memoirs that "it was clear to everyone . . . that, unless he changed his positions, Begin was becoming an insurmountable obstacle to further progress."[52]

The visit was partly overshadowed by Israeli concern about the speed with which the United States sought aproval for its Security Council resolution concerning the Israeli invasion of southern Lebanon. The resolution, adopted on March 19, established UNIFIL and called upon Israel "immediately to cease its military action against Lebanese territorial integrity and withdraw forthwith its forces from all Lebanese territory." Israel's perception was that the United States "rammed" the resolution through the Security Council and that U.S. behavior was "hasty" and "brutal."

The Begin visit and the U.S. attempts to maintain the negotiations' momentum took place during a fierce U.S. debate over the administration's plans to sell jet fighter aircraft to Egypt, Saudi Arabia, and Israel as a "package deal." The proposed sale of planes quickly escalated into a major controversy between the United States and Israel, not so much over the sale of aircraft to Egypt as over the sale of F-15s to Saudi Arabia, which Israel described as a threat to its security. Begin had suggested that if the United States supplied Saudi Arabia with F-15 fighter bombers, it would make it a confrontation state against Israel. When Vance was asked about Begin's comment, he said:

> No. I respectfully disagree with that estimate of the Prime Minister's. Saudi Arabia is not a confrontation state. From all of our discussions with them at the highest level they have indicated that they do not and will not become a confrontation state.[53]

The Carter administration insisted that the planes would not be used against Israel, and that they were to protect Saudi Arabian and U.S. interests in the increasingly destabilized Persian Gulf. The American-Israel Public Affairs Committee and other opponents of the sale argued that it would build the Arabs' confidence that they could utilize military measures against Israel, and that it could only heighten Israel's insecurity and make it less willing to compromise. Despite Israeli opposition and the criticism of the U.S. Jewish community and many of Israel's supporters, both in and out of Congress, the Senate failed to disapprove the proposal by a vote of 54 to 44 on May 15, 1978. It was an important element in the administration's approach because the "package deal" was a symbol of U.S. support for the moderate Arab states, a tangible reward for Sadat's initiative, and a demonstration of Carter's evenhandedness. On May 12, in a letter to each member of the Senate, Carter wrote:

> It is my considered judgment that the aircraft sales to Egypt are essential to enable President Sadat to continue his efforts for peace. . . . To reject the proposed aircraft sale to Egypt would be . . . a devastating blow to President Sadat, to the military forces of Egypt, to the people of Egypt, and to the forces of moderation in the Middle East.[54]

The sale was also an indication of the importance of the U.S.-Saudi Arabian relationship. The decision to provide arms to the two Arab states and to "package" them with the sale to Israel signaled an important change in U.S. arms supply policy. Israel's virtual monopoly of sophisticated U.S. weapons systems in the Middle East was undone. The decision led to a further strain in the bilateral relationship because Israel perceived it as further indication of the Carter administration's "tilt" toward the Arabs and away from Israel, despite administration efforts to reassure Israel that the package was not meant to affect its security adversely. In a speech to the American Jewish Committee on May 18, Vice-President Walter Mondale said:

> We believe that our support for Egypt and Saudi Arabia will help promote that objective [a peaceful and stable Middle East] without threatening the security of Israel. And we believe that these actions are taken in the best interests of peace.[55]

The United States also continued to press Israel to clarify its position and sought Egyptian proposals that might facilitate the negotiation process. To this end Vice-President Mondale and a group of senior officials, accompanied by prominent U.S. Jewish leaders, visited Israel in connection with its thirtieth anniversary celebration. The trip demonstrated U.S. interest in persuading the parties to resume negotiations. Mondale hoped to ease U.S.-Israeli tensions but, although his reception was cordial, there was no significant effect on the strained relationship. Nonetheless, Mondale was able to persuade Israel and Egypt to convene a meeting of their representatives in London. Tensions continued, and at press conferences in late June and early July, prior to the meeting in England, Carter stated that Israeli government responses to U.S. requests for clarifications on the future status of the West Bank and Gaza were "very disappointing."

When the Israeli and Egyptian foreign ministers and the U.S. secretary of state met at Leeds Castle in July 1978, the sessions were long and the tone was informal. Despite some progress, the situation deteriorated. On July 23 Sadat asked Israel to return portions of Sinai (El-Arish) to Egypt as a symbolic gesture; Begin refused, adding, "Nobody can get anything for nothing." Sadat reacted angrily and ordered the Israeli military mission home, a symbolic gesture, since it had taken no substantive action since January. He termed the Israeli moves "negative and backward," and rebuffed an Israeli bid for new talks. Again Sadat asked the United States to act as a "full partner, not a mediator."

The parties had continued to maintain direct bilateral links, facilitated by the personal rapport between Israeli Defense Minister Ezer Weizman and Sadat, as well as through the Israeli military mission until its departure from Cairo at the end of July. Sadat also conferred with Shimon Peres, the head of Israel's opposition Labor Party, in July. The negotiations led to disagreements between the United States and both Egypt and Israel. With Egypt the discord focused on the nature of the U.S. role and on the Egyptian proposal for a settlement, which the Carter administration did not regard as a suitable basis for negotiations. The disagreements with Israel, which occasionally became particularly caustic, concerned Begin's interpretation of Resolution 242 as not necessarily applying to the West Bank and Israel's policy of establishing Jewish settlements there.

Within Israel there was debate as to whether the main negotiations should take place through the United States or bilaterally. Weizman's concern that the United States would tilt toward Egypt led him to prefer direct negotiations. Dayan preferred U.S. involvement because he saw the need to protect the bilateral relationship and to secure U.S. support for any agreement.

The deadlock threatened to halt the negotiations and alarmed the United States because it would be a setback for Sadat and the peace process, and might renew tensions between Egypt and Israel, thus increasing the danger of war. There was also concern because the term of the U.N. force in Sinai, to which Egypt had committed itself in Sinai II, was about to expire. These factors led Carter to try to break the deadlock through a new and dramatic initiative.

Although the United States expressed disappointment with Sadat's actions, Vance made a scheduled trip to the Middle East to persuade Egypt and Israel to resume the talks. He was warmly welcomed in Israel, where he met with Begin and his principal advisers and delivered a note from Carter. Vance subsequently met with Sadat in Alexandria and gave him a similar letter. On August 8 the White House announced that both leaders had accepted Carter's invitation to come to Camp David, Maryland, "for a meeting with the President to seek a framework for peace in the Middle East." Vance said, in a press conference with Sadat on the same day, that the United States would be a "full partner" in the negotiations. It is significant that only Egypt and the United States used this wording and that Israel did not, apparently withholding its acceptance of any change in the U.S. role. Begin's published reaction was as follows:

I don't know what it means to be a full partner. If it means that the American delegation takes interest in the talks and sometimes even brings a concrete proposal or formulation, that is one story. But I do not expect the United States to propose a so-called peace plan, because that would be unhelpful . . . . My personal advice would be for the United States to fulfill the very useful function of honest broker, and bring the two parties together for face-to-face negotiations.[56]

There were discordant voices in the administration who cautioned Carter against the decision and the risks involved, particularly to his prestige, if the summit should fail. Carter appeared to understand:

It is a very high risk thing for me politically, because now I think if we are unsuccessful at Camp David, I will certainly have to share part of the blame for that failure. But I don't see that I could do anything differently, because I'm afraid that if the leaders do not meet and do not permit their subordinates to meet in a continuing series of tough negotiations that the situation in the Middle East might be much more serious in the future even than it is now.[57]

CAMP DAVID

The meetings at Camp David were long (September 5-17, 1978), difficult, and complex. They were held in virtual secrecy, with no information available outside the compound, which led to extensive speculation in the media and by observers that often was incorrect. Carter clearly needed to emerge with an agreement, although clashes between the parties, and particularly between the United States and Israel, were common. Carter and Begin argued over Israel's continuing construction of settlements in the West Bank and Gaza. This proved to be a major point of controversy, given Begin's strongly held view that Israel had the right to do so and Carter's that the settlements were illegal and obstacles to peace. They also differed on the issue of Palestinian rights. Carter stressed the need for Israeli flexibility and concessions, arguing that Sadat could not modify his positions and yield. He was of the opinion that the summit might fail, to the disadvantage of all.

Various pressures were exerted by the United States on Israel. Among other devices, Carter suggested that he would report to Congress and the media on the results of the summit, and the Israelis believed that he would seek to blame them for the failure. Ultimately Israel conceded on a number of critical points, including the settlements in Sinai (the matter would be submitted to the Knesset for decision) and the Israeli military airfields there (Israel would relinquish control). Other issues that remained without agreement (such as Jerusalem) would be dealt with in letters accompanying the agreement but not included in it. Only after repeated crises was agreement finally reached.

The Camp David Accords did not constitute a peace treaty but instead consisted of two documents: "A Framework of Peace in the Middle East" and "Framework for the Conclusion of a Peace Treaty between Egypt and Israel." The Middle East framework set forth general principles and some specifics for a comprehensive peace settlement between Israel and its Arab neighbors. It dealt with the Palestinian problem and the future of the West Bank and Gaza, calling for a transitional period of not more than five years. In order to provide "full autonomy" to the inhabitants of those areas, the Israeli military government would be withdrawn upon the creation of a self-governing authority freely elected by the inhabitants of those areas, although the Israeli military would remain in specified areas of the West Bank and Gaza to protect Israel's security interests. "Egypt, Israel, Jordan and the representatives of the Palestinian people should participate in negotiations on the resolution of the Palestinian problem in all its aspects." It also called for negotiations to resolve the final status of the West Bank and Gaza, and Israel's relations with Jordan, based on Resolution 242 and Israel's right to live within secure and recognized borders.

The Israel-Egypt framework provided for a peace treaty in which Israel would withdraw from all of Sinai, including its settlements and airfields (a major concession, given previous Israeli positions), in phases according to a timetable to be determined, and for normal and peaceful relations to be established between the two states. The United States agreed to construct airfields for Israel in the Negev. Egypt agreed to normalization of relations, an exchange of ambassadors, and the opening of the Suez Canal to Israeli shipping.

The accords were signed ceremoniously at the White House on September 17, and became the basis for the negotiations that followed. The Egyptian cabinet unanimously approved the accords on September 19, and on September 28 the Israeli Knesset voted 84-19 (with 17 abstentions) to endorse them.

The general view was that the subsequent negotiations would not be difficult, since matters of principle had been settled at Camp David, and the process began with great optimism. The need was to convert the guidelines of the accords into operative details, in a treaty. This assessment soon proved faulty because the ambiguities of the accords and the differing perceptions and objectives of the parties were difficult to reconcile.

Negotiations began at Blair House in Washington on October 12, and were accompanied by reports of both progress and obstacles. By early November a peace treaty had been drafted, but difficulties developed when it failed to receive the approval of the Israeli cabinet and the Egyptian president. Both sides sought amendments and made new demands in an effort to improve the results they had obtained at Camp David. Camp David had avoided a number of crucial issues (such as the linkage between the two frameworks) by a calculated ambiguity—these issues now reappeared as sticking points in the negotiations. The strong and virtually unanimous Arab condemnation of Sadat and the Camp David accords suggested Sadat's isolation and the likelihood that no other Arab state would participate in the negotiations. Within Israel there was criticism from various quarters of the Palestinian component of the accords.

These obstacles to an agreement stemmed mainly from the differing pressures to which the Egyptian and Israeli leaders were subjected. Sadat was under great pressure to show the Arab world that his policy was yielding real gains, not only for Egypt but also for the Palestinians and the Arab cause in general. Begin came under attack primarily from the right, because of the concessions he had made. The decision to withdraw completely from Sinai raised questions concerning the significance and definition of secure borders in any peace settlement. Far more traumatic was the dismantling of the Sinai settlements, given the Israeli pioneering ethos. This was the first time in the modern era that Jews had voluntarily agreed to dismantle settlements. Strong opposition developed under the leadership of some of Begin's long-time disciples and colleagues.

The efforts to overcome the obstacles caused friction between Israel and the United States. The U.S. view was influenced by concern for Sadat's political standing and the need to prevent his isolation in the Arab world by ensuring that any agreement would go as far as possible to satisfy Arab demands. Consequently, U.S. efforts to secure concessions were directed much more frequently at Israel than at Egypt, and the United States sought to persuade Arab opinion that the Camp David accords were of value to other Arab states besides Egypt. Israel often saw the U.S. position as more rigid than Egypt's, especially on linkage, and its conduct fed Israeli suspicions and induced greater rigidity in the Israeli positions. For example, Israel announced on October 26, 1978, that it would "thicken" existing West Bank settlements. Apparently this was, in part, a response to assistant Secretary of State Harold Saunders' visit to the Middle East

(October 16-23) and his contacts with West Bank politicians, as well as a reaction to the U.S. responses to Jordanian queries about U.S. policy, which Israel regarded as detrimental to its interests and undermining its position. The U.S. reaction to the Israeli actions was negative.

In the efforts to implement Camp David, the conflicting goals and divergent interpretations of the accords soon became obvious, as did the differing central goals of the three states and leaders.

The United States sought to defend the accomplishment and to induce other Arab states (especially Jordan and the Palestinians) to participate in an effort to bolster Sadat and to enhance the prospects for successful negotiations. It emphasized the value of the accords to other Arabs if they joined in the peace process. The administration also sought to prevent Begin from concluding a bilateral Egypt-Israel treaty while extending control over the West Bank and Gaza. It opposed Israeli settlements in the West Bank as illegal and obstacles to peace. A significant dispute arose between Carter and Begin concerning Israel's commitment, made at Camp David, to refrain from construction of settlements. Begin and Israel saw the commitment as one for the three months that had been anticipated for the bilateral negotiation of a peace treaty with Egypt. Carter and Vance believed that Israel had agreed to refrain from establishing new settlements for the duration of the negotiations. In an interview in June 1983, Cyrus Vance stated:

> Both my notes and the president's notes indicate that during that session at Camp David, Begin agreed that no new settlements would be established during the negotiation for a self-governing authority on the West Bank, and that the question of any future settlements would be left up to the parties who would be involved in the negotiation leading up to the establishment of self-governing authority. What was being talked about at Camp David was the negotiation for the establishment of a self-governing authority—that period, however long that might take.[58]

The Carter administration sought Israeli efforts to create an atmosphere conducive to Arab acceptance of Camp David by refraining from construction of settlements, by accepting a linkage between the two Camp David frameworks, and by positive gestures in the West Bank and to the Arabs in general.

Israel's Camp David position was not unanimously supported within the government coalition. Opposition revolved around two issues: the concessions made in Sinai and the autonomy plan. Both were regarded as going too far in the direction of compromise with Egypt and the United States. Many saw the autonomy plan as leading to a Palestinian state—a result opposed by most members of the Knesset and by public opinion. Opposition also developed in the cabinet, and Begin apparently had some second thoughts about the contradition between his ideological preferences and his agreement at Camp David, especially concerning the West Bank. Israel's policy focused on "full autonomy" for the inhabitants of the West Bank and Gaza, the administrative nature of the self-governing authority, and its firm opposition to the creation of a Palestinian state. Israel also sought to limit the linkage between the Egypt-Israel agreement and the autonomy talks, and to consolidate its position in the West Bank by strengthening existing settlements and, after the three-month period of restraint, building new ones.

For the Begin government Camp David had the appeal of full peace and normalization with Egypt without the need for significant alterations in its perspective of and approach to the West Bank and Gaza. It did not have to modify its stand on Jerusalem or commit itself to Arab sovereignty (or give up its ultimate demand for sovereignty) in the West Bank and Gaza or even to a long-term stop of settlement construction. There was also concern that linkage between the two frameworks might provide the pretext for Sadat to undo Egypt's obligations under the peace treaty. Israel's decision makers (including the more "moderate" ones such as Weizman and Dayan) had reservations about Sadat's intentions, the reversibility of his commitment to peace, and his concessions in the peace process. Various demands by Egypt tended to reinforce Israeli doubts. For Begin there was a connection between the two Camp David frameworks, but they were not dependent on each other. There would be an effort to achieve a comprehensive settlement, but the Egypt-Israel peace could not be postponed because of a failure to reach agreement on the autonomy issue.

Egypt stressed the value of the Camp David accords to the Palestinians and the view that sovereignty over the West Bank and Gaza belonged to the Palestinian people. Egypt believed that autonomy would lead to the creation of a Palestinian state. It indicated its willingness to negotiate in place of Jordan should the latter fail to join the process, and sought a special status for Gaza. Egypt insisted on a linkage between the two Camp David documents. It opposed Israel's settlement policy in the West Bank and its position on autonomy, and sought Israeli confidence-building gestures to improve the prospects for other Arab participants to join the peace process. Sadat wanted more precise Israeli commitments to Palestinian self-determination (autonomy) and methods to institutionalize them through the linkage mechanism, in effect making normalization of relations hostage to progress on the Palestinian question.

Despite continuing efforts and some optimism in early December, Egypt and Israel failed to meet the December 17, 1978, deadline, although Vance made a last-minute effort at shuttle diplomacy. In a press conference on December 7, Carter sought to influence the process with the comment that "If the Egyptians and Israelis violate the three-month limit on negotiating this treaty, it will be a very serious matter to us, and I think to them." He also noted his differences with Begin on the matter of settlements. The administration believed that Begin, not Sadat, was the "chief problem" in the failure to reach agreement. Israel's cabinet rejected the terms Vance brought from Cairo in mid-December, blamed the failure to reach agreement on Egypt, and opposed the U.S. position on Egypt's proposals.

The Carter administration labeled this a "deliberate distortion," regarding the terms as fair and reasonable. The exchange of angry statements included Israeli accusations that the United States had a one-sided attitude favorable to Egypt and its protestation of unfair U.S. pressure. The United States was upset by Israel's rejection and its rhetoric and distortions. Israel suggested that the blame for the failure of the treaty to be signed had been "placed on the doorstep of Israel. This blame is not justified by the facts . . . ." It argued that Egypt had made new demands for concessions from Israel, and regretted that "the U.S. has apparently lent its support to these new Egyptian demands." It commented that "it is regrettable that the U.S. should have seen fit to approach the matter in an apparently one-sided manner."[59]

Israeli apprehensions were enhanced, and confidence in the United States further eroded, by the U.S. decision in December 1978 to establish diplomatic relations with China and sever links with Taiwan, which raised questions about the value and durability of U.S. commitments.

The failure to achieve agreement and the subsequent trading of charges provided the background for the continuing effort to reach accord. These efforts involved Carter in a direct and personal shuttle effort that culminated in success, although further disagreements emerged along the way. A meeting between Israeli Foreign Minister Moshe Dayan and Egyptian Prime Minister Mustafa Khalil took place at Camp David toward the end of February 1979, and later Carter announced the convening of a variation of the Camp David summit—Carter and Vance would represent the United States, Begin would participate, and Sadat would be represented by Khalil. Sadat had stated that he had made all the compromises he intended to make and the Israeli cabinet vetoed Begin's participation, ostensibly because Begin and Khalil were not of equal rank but actually because of the anticipation that the only purpose such a meeting could serve would be to pressure Israel to compromise its position in order to achieve agreement. Carter then invited Begin for private talks without Khalil, and this invitation was accepted. Ostensibly this change of position by Begin was a result of the altered format, but U.S. pressure proved decisive.

Disagreement over procedure was accompanied by differences in perspective concerning the issues in dispute. Carter stated, on February 27, that the differences requiring reconciliation were "absolutely insignificant" and "it's disgusting . . . that we're that close and we can't quite get it." Begin demurred, characterizing the differences between Israel and Egypt as "great issues relating first of all to our future and security." Begin and Carter met in Washington at the beginning of March. Despite an ostensibly friendly atmosphere, each party implied possible reconsideration of its approach to the peace process, and the Israelis also spoke of pressures exerted on them to accept the U.S. proposals.

Dayan told the Foreign and Security Affairs Committee of the Knesset that Carter had warned him that "the United States will conduct a reassessment of its entire Middle East policy if the deadlock in the negotiations is not resolved within the next ten days."[60] The *New York Times* said that "on most of the points still at issue, Administration officials acknowledge, the American position is closer to that of Egypt than to the Israeli view."[61] After considerable discussion Begin and Carter reached agreement on a number of crucial points that were subsequently accepted by the Israeli cabinet. Israel's press reported that Carter had pledged generous political, economic, and military aid, and noted that if Sadat rejected the agreed position, Israel would not be blamed.[62]

The final breakthrough occurred as a result of a dramatic intervention by Carter. His talks with Begin at Washington in March were followed by a visit to Cairo and Jerusalem, where he secured sufficient concessions from both sides to pave the way for agreement on the last details. Carter's trip made it clear that the treaty was of great importance to the United States, and to him personally, and that to refuse to reach an accord would humiliate and frustrate him, thereby probably incurring his wrath and a negative U.S. policy. The treaty was approved by the Knesset, after lengthy debate, and by the Egyptian cabinet on April 4. The formal signature of the peace treaty took place at an impressive ceremony at the White House on March 26, 1979. It was ratified and came into force on April 25, 1979.

Egypt and Israel ended the state of war, established peace, renounced the use of force to settle disputes, and pledged mutual recognition. Israel agreed to withdraw its armed forces and civilians from Sinai in stages—to a line running from El-Arish to Ras Muhammad—after nine months and to the international frontier (Rafah to the Gulf of Aquaba) after three years. Within a month of the completion of the first stage (the "interim withdrawal"), Israel and Egypt would exchange ambassadors, end economic boycotts, and open commerce between the two states. Sinai would be divided into zones with limitations on Egyptian personnel and equipment, and a U.N. force verifying compliance would be stationed in the zone adjacent to the Israeli border. U.N. observers would ensure Israeli compliance on its side of the border as well. The Suez Canal, Gulf of Aqaba, and Strait of Tiran would be regarded as international waterways. A joint commission would oversee the withdrawal, and a claims commission would settle any outstanding financial claims and arbitrate disputes. The United States agreed to continue surveillance flights over Sinai and to create an international force if the United Nations failed to do so.

The treaty also provided that one month after ratification, Israel, Egypt, the United States, Jordan, and representatives of the Palestinians living in the West Bank and Gaza would begin negotiations, to be completed in one year, for a self-governing authority in the West Bank and the Gaza Strip. The protocols, letters, annexes, and maps attached to the Egypt-Israel Peace Treaty dealt in detail with the phased Israeli withdrawal from the Sinai, the security arrangements, and the specific details for further negotiations on trade, economic, cultural, transportation, telecommunications, and other agreements between the two countries.

The United States and Israel also signed, on March 26, memoranda of agreement that provided specific American assurances to Israel, and reaffirmed and broadened the assurances provided in the 1975 Sinai agreements. One memorandum stated that:

> Should it be demonstrated to the satisfaction of the United States that there has been a violation or threat of violation of the Treaty of Peace, the United States will consult with the parties with regard to measures to halt or prevent the violation . . . and will take such remedial measures as it deems appropriate, which may include diplomatic, economic, and military measures as described below.

The memorandum brought a sharp protest from Egypt, and on March 28 President Sadat stated that it violated the peace treaty and that it "could be construed as an eventual alliance against Egypt." U.S. officials said that Egypt had been offered a similar security agreement but had refused it.

The Arab League, meeting in Baghdad between March 27 and 31, 1979, expelled Egypt from membership and rejected any cooperation with the peace treaty or the autonomy talks. The 18 Arab League countries that participated (Egypt, Sudan, and Oman did not attend) and the PLO severed diplomatic relations with Egypt and voted to impose an economic boycott. Saudi Arabia had joined the "radicals," and U.S. hopes that it would seek to minimize the anti-Sadat measures did not materialize, although a proposed oil embargo against the United States was forestalled. Sadat's first public criticism of Saudi Arabia came in his May Day speech: "The majority of the Arabs who severed their relations [with Egypt] did so out of courtesy to Saudi Arabia. Saudi Arabia paid a price to the minority to sever these relations. Some of those who acted out of courtesy and who got paid wrote to me." In response to Sadat's allegations, Saudi Defense Minister Prince Sultan announced, on May 14, that the consortium that operated Egyptian arms factories would go out of existence because "the signing of a peace treaty between Egypt and Israel clashes with the purpose of establishing the company."

Implementation of the treaty became the focal point of subsequent activity. The evacuation of Israeli forces from Sinai began on March 25, 1979, and the various committees were soon constituted. The first Israeli ship passed through the Suez Canal on April 29, 1979, and visits of senior officials and personalities soon began. The problem of oil supply by Egypt to Israel was resolved in November 1979.

The United States incurred various responsibilities under the treaty. On April 9 Carter asked Congress to authorize $4.8 billion in supplemental assistance for Egypt and Israel, to enable them to implement the treaty. Israel would get $2.2 billion in military credits and $800 million in military grants to help pay for the construction of two air bases in the Negev to replace bases relinquished in Sinai. Egypt would get $1.5 billion in military credits, $200 million in economic grants, and $100 million in economic loans. The United States agreed to provide arms to both states, the precise details becoming known only later, through various official and press reports.

An important element of the treaty concerned assurance of Israel's oil needs. In 1975 the United States undertook, as part of the Sinai II arrangements, to sell oil to Israel for up to five years if Israel could not secure it from other sources. A memorandum of agreement attached to the peace treaty reaffirmed the 1975 arrangement but extended the time limit to 15 years, and stated that the United States would seek the necessary statutory authorization for the oil transfer. On June 22, 1979, Israel and the United States signed a new agreement that provided, among other things, that if Israel was unable to secure oil from other sources, the United States would sell oil to Israel to meet its "normal domestic requirements" for 15 years, beginning November 25, 1979.

IMPLEMENTING CAMP DAVID: PEACE AND AUTONOMY

After the signing of the Egypt-Israel peace treaty, the peace process focused on Israeli withdrawal from Sinai, normalization of relations between Egypt and Israel, and negotiations on autonomy.

On May 25, 1979, in keeping with the previously agreed timetable, Egypt and Israel opened negotiations in Beersheba, Israel, to discuss implementation of the Camp David "Framework of Peace in the Middle East." The goal of the first stage of the negotiations was full autonomy for the inhabitants of the West Bank and Gaza under a freely elected, self-governing authority that would serve for a transitional period of not more than five years. The final status of the West Bank and Gaza was reserved for a second stage of negotiations—to begin as soon as possible but not later than three years after the self-governing authority was inaugurated. The "autonomy talks" involved only Egypt, Israel, and the United States—given the continued opposition of Jordan and the Palestinians. The United States appointed Ambassador Robert Strauss as its special negotiator. Minister of the Interior Yosef Burg was chosen to head Israel's team, and Prime Minister Mustafa Khalil led the Egyptian delegation.

In the summer of 1979 the Carter administration again tried to fashion a new approach to the Palestinians, a process that produced the curious Andrew Young affair. On July 26, Andrew Young, then U.S. ambassador to the United Nations, met with Zehdi Labib Terzi, the PLO observer at the United Nations, at the home of Kuwait's U.N. ambassador. The unauthorized meeting was in violation of the U.S. pledge to Israel made at the time of the Sinai II agreement, and maintained as U.S. policy since then, not to recognize or negotiate with the PLO. When the meeting became known, Young deceived the administration concerning the details and later admitted that he had not told the "entire truth" about the meeting.[63] The Israelis protested. Young resigned on August 15—an act that provoked an uproar and generated tensions between the black and Jewish communities in the

United States. The White House sought to heal the rift, but obviously was not successful, and Carter did not deny black charges that Israel and American Jews had forced Young's departure until over a month later.

Ambassador Strauss was sent to the Middle East to mollify Israel and to reassure it about U.S. policy. However, the mission was altered, and Strauss proposed to Israel and Egypt that they endorse a U.S.-sponsored U.N. resolution designed to attract Palestinians to the negotiating table by calling for Palestinian rights but stopping short of a Palestinian state envisioned in a proposed Kuwaiti draft. This initiative reflected the strategy of Carter, Brzezinski, Vance, and some foreign policy professionals. The administration seemed to believe that its version of the resolution would be seen by Israel and its supporters as consonant with Camp David, and therefore acceptable. They miscalculated. Strauss failed to gain Egyptian and Israeli support for the resolution. Israel's response was milder than Sadat's negative reaction. Strauss was frustrated by his failure and reportedly was critical of the new approach. Failing to achieve Israeli and Egyptian support, and faced with continuing Israeli concerns, the United States withdrew its resolution and pledged to veto any alternative proposal. The matter did not come to a vote in the Security Council.

Factors external to the autonomy negotiations also affected their course. In Israel there were divergent views in the Israeli body politic and in the cabinet—ultimately both Dayan and Weizman resigned—on the issue of settlements. Within Egypt there were also differences of perspective, but a significant goal was to ensure that the autonomy talks did not interfere with Israel's withdrawal from Sinai. For the United States the Arab-Israeli issues were soon overshadowed by the revolution in Iran, the holding of U.S. hostages, and the Soviet invasion of Afghanistan. Nevertheless, some progress was made, although the core issues did not prove susceptible to agreement.

The withdrawal of Israeli forces from Sinai proceeded with relatively minor difficulties. One of the issues was that of a force in Sinai to ensure compliance with the treaty limitations on forces and equipment. After some problems with the utilization of the U.N. Emergency Force the United States, Egypt, and Israel agreed, in May 1981, on a multilateral force to patrol the Sinai buffer zone after the final Israeli withdrawal. Toward the end of November 1981, Britain, France, Italy, and the Netherlands formally notified Egypt and Israel that they would participate in the Multinational Force and Observers (MFO). Israel said it would veto the participation of any state that did not support the Camp David agreements as the only basis for peace, thereby threatening the role of those that supported the

European Community's Venice Declaration.[64] In December, Israel and the United States reached an agreement that stated that the four members of the MFO disagreed with some Israeli and U.S. positions but would accept the Camp David process as the basis for their joining the MFO.

Each phase of the withdrawal was completed on or ahead of the original schedule, and on January 25, 1980, Israel moved its Sinai forces back to the El-Arish-Ras Muhammad line. Ambassadors were named, and they presented their credentials in Jerusalem and Cairo on February 26, 1980. Saad Mortada represented Egypt and Eliahu ben Elissar represented Israel. Egypt and Israel also agreed to open their border to tourists and to begin communications and commercial traffic across the frontier.

In the spring of 1980 another episode negatively affected the U.S.-Israel relationship. The United States was concerned about Israeli actions, especially with regard to West Bank settlements, that it saw as illegal or unhelpful, but vacillated on condemnation when it appeared one-sided, and sometimes further confused the situation with apparent policy shifts and inconsistencies. Among the more prominent of these was a unanimous U.N. Security Council vote on March 1, 1980, in which the United States joined, on Resolution 465, calling on Israel "to dismantle the existing settlements and in particular to cease, on an urgent basis, the establishment, construction and planning of settlements in the Arab territories occupied since 1967, including Jerusalem." This constituted an important shift in American policy.

Two days later the White House announced that the vote had been an error (it should have been an abstention) due to a failure in communication, and did not represent administration policy. The focus of Carter's concern was the resolution's references to Jerusalem, which the United States sought to have deleted. Yet the administration noted that the vote did not represent a change in existing U.S. policy on settlements, Jerusalem, the peace process, or support for Israel. The actions generated disdain by all parties. Israel was upset by the original vote and an apparent alteration in U.S. policy, and remained unsatisfied by subsequent explanations. The Arabs believed that Carter had been forced to retreat from his own policy and views under pressure from Israel and the Israel lobby. In the United States there was a general perception of ineptness.

In 1980 representatives of the parties met to continue the autonomy discussions. The issues were complex, there were constant breakdowns, and expressions of optimism, pessimism, and skepticism continued. There was not much chance of narrowing the gap between the parties despite substantial efforts by Sol Linowitz, who had replaced Robert Strauss as the senior U.S. negotiator.

In May 1980 Sadat suspended Egyptian participation in the autonomy talks, ostensibly because the Knesset discussed adopting a Basic Law affirming the status of Jerusalem as Israel's capital, although the proposed legislation did not meaningfully alter the existing situation. Egyptian spokesmen accused Israel of creating conditions that prevented "a suitable atmosphere for negotiations," and Sadat said he wanted time to evaluate past and future progress. Sadat seemed to be motivated by other factors, including the general lack of substantive progress, a desire to concentrate on the reorganization of his government, a need to protect his inter-Arab posture, and an effort to stimulate further U.S. pressure on Israel.

The suspension generated substantial concern and intensive diplomatic efforts. Letters were exchanged among Sadat, Carter, and Begin, and discussions were held to ameliorate the situation. The autonomy talks resumed in July but were suspended again by Sadat in early August. The stated rationale was that Israel's Knesset, on July 30, had adopted the "basic law" confirming Jerusalem's status as Israel's "eternal and undivided capital," by a vote of 69 to 15.

On August 20 the U.N. Security Council adopted Resolution 478, by a vote of 14 to 0, with 1 abstention (the United States), which censured Israel for the enactment of the "basic law." Secretary of State Edmund Muskie explained the United States position:

> . . . the question of Jerusalem must be addressed in the context of negotiations for a comprehensive, just, and lasting Middle East peace. That is the position of my government. But it is more. The status of Jerusalem cannot simply be declared; it must be agreed to by the parties. . . . But if we do not vote against the version before us today, neither can we find cause to support it. For the resolution is still fundamentally flawed. It fails even to reaffirm Resolution 242 as the basis for a comprehensive peace. . . . Further, the resolution before us calls upon those states that have established diplomatic missions in Jerusalem to withdraw them . . . . In our judgement this provision is not binding . . . . It does nothing to advance the cause of peace.[65]

Little progress on autonomy seemed likely, given the perspectives of the parties. Sadat talked of waiting for an Israeli election that might replace the Begin government. The United States continued to voice its concern about Israeli policies in the occupied territories, and Carter said that his concept of a "homeland" for the Palestinians did not mean that he supported the creation of a Palestinian state. A commitment by Egypt and Israel to resume the autonomy talks and their statement that they remained committed to the Camp David accords were secured by Linowitz in September.

The failure of the parties to reach agreement on autonomy by the self-imposed May 1980 deadline (and the May and August 1980 suspensions of negotiations) reflected the complex nature of the issues and the widely divergent positions of the two states. At the time of the May deadline, the negotiations had made some progress in translating "full autonomy" from concept to reality. On peripheral and essentially technical matters substantial agreement had been reached, but central problems remained unresolved. Linowitz summed up the progress in these terms:

> The gratifying fact is that considerable progress has been made in agreeing upon a substantial number of such powers and responsibilities that both Egypt and Israel believe should be transferred to the self-governing authority. These include such areas as agriculture, budget, finance, civil service, education, culture, health, housing, public works, judicial administration, transportation, communications, labor, social welfare, municipal affairs, local police, religious affairs, industry, commerce and tourism. In addition, significant progress has been made on some of the remaining most difficult substantive issues, including the questions of land and water in the West Bank and Gaza areas and the question of security arrangements. . . . In addition, substantial progress has been made in agreeing on the modalities—the mechanisms—for free elections in which the inhabitants of the West Bank and Gaza would choose the members of a representative authority to implement autonomy in the West Bank and Gaza areas.[66]

Much discussion focused on the problem of how to divide responsibility for internal and external security in the West Bank and Gaza. Israel's security and its protection from external attack had to be assured by the Israel Defense Forces, while the "strong local police force" of the self-governing authority had to have some role in internal security and public order. Egypt and Israel could not agree on the extent of the powers of the self-governing authority. Israel was clearly concerned that the Egyptian proposal would lead to the establishment of a Palestinian state.

Israel argued that autonomy should be limited to the inhabitants of the territories, while Egypt believed that it should extend to the actual territory. Israel saw the self-governing authority as an administrative council, while Egypt wanted this authority to have full legislative and executive authority as well as control of the administration of justice. Egypt sought a self-generating authority and the transfer to it of all powers from the military government. Israel sought to limit the powers of the authority through negotiation and believed that the military government should be the source of authority.

There was also discord on the sharing of the scarce water resources of the West Bank, the right of the Arabs of East Jerusalem to vote on questions relating to the self-governing authority, the status and use of private and public lands, and Jerusalem's final status.

Israel saw an autonomy agreement as a practical solution to the Palestinian question and as responsive to Israel's need for security, Egypt's wish to adhere to the Arab cause, and the Palestinian Arabs' desire to govern their own affairs. Israel's proposed autonomy plan would allow the Arab inhabitants fully to manage "areas of legitimate internal administration" while Israel "will retain those powers and functions which are essential to her defense and security." By contrast, Israel opposed Egypt's autonomy proposals partly because they "would set in motion an irreversible process which would lead to the establishment of an independent Arab-Palestinian state."[67]

Egypt sought total Israeli withdrawal from the occupied territories (including East Jerusalem), the dismantling of Israel's settlements, and the right of the Palestinians to self-determination. It sought to safeguard its Arab world position and to remain a part of the Arab community. It was important to Egypt to demonstrate that Sadat's approach was practical; thus Sadat had to avoid action that might undermine the Camp David process.

No negotiations were held between December 1980 and September 20, 1981, at which point they were resumed with the U.S. ambassador to Egypt, Alfred Atherton, and the U.S. ambassador to Israel, Samuel Lewis, acting as the U.S. representatives.

The extent, or lack, of progress on the autonomy negotiations can be attributed to a number of factors. Among the more significant was the failure to involve other participants, beyond Egypt, Israel, and the United States, in the process. The initial hope to include King Hussein of Jordan and representatives of the Palestinian people soon proved to be little more than wishful thinking. Hussein objected to the Camp David process for several reasons. His position was especially sensitive because of Jordan's sizable Palestinian population, the role envisaged for him by the Camp David accords in negotiations on Palestinian "autonomy," the decisions of the Rabat summit of 1974, and his susceptibility to various forms of pressure from Syria, Iraq, and Saudi Arabia. The overthrow of the Shah in Iran, the enhancement of the PLO's regional position, and the lack of any support for an alternative stand reinforced Hussein's "rejectionist" attitude.

By the time the Egypt-Israel peace treaty was signed, Hussein's initially cautious and noncommittal approach had been replaced by the view that Camp David was unacceptable. The PLO opposed the Camp David accords, the Egypt-Israel peace treaty, and the autonomy talks, partly because they were seen as legalizing the Israeli occupation and did not grant the right of self-determination to the Palestinians. Underlying the PLO view was its interest in establishing a Palestinian state in the West Bank and Gaza Strip under PLO leadership.

Despite the slow pace the United States continued to view the Camp David process as valid for the ultimate resolution of the conflict and preferable to any alternatives. This perspective flowed from the direct and extensive involvement of the administration in the peace process since its inauguration.

SHIFTING PRIORITIES

The U.S. priority for, and extensive focus on, the Arab-Israeli issue shifted as the Iranian revolution, the ouster of the Shah, and the taking of U.S. hostages in Iran affected the broader Middle East. The holding of the hostages for the last 14 months of the Carter administration led to preoccupation with this issue, to the virtual exclusion of other foreign policy questions. The Soviet invasion of Afghanistan in December 1979 generated concern not only about the future of that country but also about the potential threat to the Persian Gulf and U.S. friends in the Arabian Peninsula. The invasion shifted Carter's attention from the Arab-Israeli sector to a newly identified "Southwest Asia," the center of which was the Persian Gulf (with its oil and petrodollars) but which also included Afghanistan. The Soviet invasion led to the Carter Doctrine, which warned that the United States would respond to a Soviet threat to the vital Persian Gulf area with all means, including armed force if necessary, and reflected Carter's "reborn" anti-Communism. It extended a U.S. strategic umbrella over the Persian Gulf to contain Soviet expansionism.

Despite these developments the administration sought to ensure the continued implementation of the Camp David accords. It focused its efforts on the fulfillment of the provisions of the Egypt-Israel peace treaty and continued to participate in the autonomy talks. The area was not subject to substantial debate during the 1980 presidential campaign.

The Carter administration concluded its tenure with a mixed legacy for the Reagan team. In the Arab-Israeli sector Carter left the Camp David accords and the precedent of extensive presidential involvement in the Arab-Israeli peace process. But this involvement was overshadowed by the Carter Doctrine, which focused on the "vital" Persian Gulf and required the building of appropriate forces, such as the Rapid Deployment Force, and the securing of regional support and assistance.

SOME OBSERVATIONS

The relationship between the United States and Israel during the Carter years focused on the Arab-Israeli peace process and the desire to terminate the conflict, as both nations identified a danger and an opportunity. But they disagreed on the modalities and objectives of the peace process and developed significant personality clashes between Carter and Begin. There also was a reduced exclusivity in the relationship, especially after the Sadat visit to Jerusalem in November 1977.

The Carter tenure was replete with episodes of discord between the United States and Israel that generated numerous efforts by both powers to influence the policies of the other. The most noteworthy efforts revolved around the most prominent issues of the period. Israel's major success was in connection with the October 1, 1977, Soviet-U.S. joint communiqué. Although adopted with great fanfare by the administration, Israel was able to secure its abandonment within a matter of days. Israel mobilized its traditional supporters in the U.S. Jewish community and its non-Jewish supporters in Congress and elsewhere. It took advantage of strong public sympathy for Israel and against reinvolvement of the Soviet Union in the peace process, as well as the poor political preparation of the Carter administration.

The Carter administration had its most noteworthy success in effecting change in the Israeli position at Camp David and in the Egypt-Israel Peace Treaty. The main techniques involved high risk/high visibility presidential involvement and the suggestion that Israel could not allow the failure of the president, particularly if he would seek to place the blame for failure on Israel with Congress and public opinion. Israel was also influenced by articulated reassurances by the administration and by their tangible manifestation in the form of economic and military assistance. At the same time Israel gained important changes in its relationship with Egypt and in the nature of the Arab-Israeli conflict that were central to its position.

Israel was, therefore, influenced by the advantages of tangible accomplishment, the benefit of U.S. assistance, and the avoidance of presidential wrath through positive reaction to presidential entreaties.

NOTES

1. *New York Times,* Jan. 13, 1977.

2. Speech of Vice-President Walter F. Mondale to the World Affairs Council of Northern California, June 17, 1977.

3. Ibid.

4. Ibid.

5. Ibid.

6. Ibid.

7. *Department of State Bulletin,* May 30, 1977, p. 547.

8. Quoted in *Washington Post,* Oct. 3, 1977.

9. Zbigniew Brzezinski, Francois Duchene, and Kiichi Saeki, "Peace in an International Framework," *Foreign Policy* no. 19 (Summer 1975): 3-17.

10. *Toward Peace in the Middle East: Report of a Study Group* (Washington, D.C.: The Brookings Institution, 1975).

11. *Weekly Compilation of Presidential Documents,* Mar. 21, 1977, p. 361.

12. See Carter's press conference of Mar. 9, 1977.

13. See Carter's press conference of Mar. 9, 1977, and Mondale's speech of June 17, 1977.

14. In the joint U.S.-Soviet statement of Oct. 1, 1977, the United States agreed for the first time to the formulation that a solution had to include a means of ensuring "the legitimate *rights* of the Palestinian people." Emphasis added.

15. *Weekly Compilation of Presidential Documents.* Mar. 21, 1977, p. 361. Emphasis added.

16. In an interview on Sept. 16, 1977, Carter said: "I've never called for an independent Palestinian country. We have used the word 'entity.' And my own preference . . . is

that we think that if there is a Palestinian entity established on the West Bank, that it ought to be associated with Jordan, for instance." *Weekly Compilation of Presidential Documents,* Sept. 26, 1977, p. 1378.

17. See, for example, Carter's press conference on July 28, 1977. In a press conference on Sept. 29, 1977, Carter said: "We have no national position on exactly who would represent the Palestinians or exactly what form the Arab group [at Geneva] would take in which the Palestinians would be represented."

18. *Weekly Compilation of Presidential Documents,* Sept. 26, 1977, p. 137.

19. *Weekly Compilation of Presidential Documents,* Aug. 15, 1977, p. 1213.

20. *Department of State Bulletin,* Mar. 14, 1977, p. 226.

21. Quoted in *New York Times,* Jan. 26, 1977.

22. Quoted in *New York Times,* Apr. 5, 1977.

23. Quoted in *Christian Science Monitor,* May 11, 1977.

24. Quoted in *Washington Post,* May 25, 1977.

25. Quoted in *Washington Post,* May 22, 1977.

26. For details of the Carter administration's and Israeli views of the elements of a settlement, see Bernard Reich, "Israel's Policy and the Search for Peace in the Middle East," *Towson State Journal of International Affairs* 13 (Fall 1978): 1-15; and "Israel's Foreign Policy and the 1977 Parliamentary Elections," in Howard R. Penniman, ed., *Israel at the Polls: The Knesset Elections of 1977* (Washington, D.C.: American Enterprise Institute for Public Policy Research, 1979), pp. 255-82.

27. Quoted in *Washington Post,* July 21, 1977.

28. Quoted in *Washington Post,* July 27, 1977.

29. Ibid.

30. *Department of State Bulletin,* Sept. 5, 1977, pp. 305-06.

31. Quoted in *New York Times,* Aug. 15, 1977.

32. Text in *New York Times,* Sept. 13, 1977.

33. Vance interview, *Washington Times,* June 8, 1983.

34. Cyrus Vance, *Hard Choices: Critical Years in America's Foreign Policy* (New York: Simon and Schuster, 1983), p. 191.

35. *New York Times,* Oct. 14, 1977.

36. *New York Times,* Oct. 3, 1977.

37. Ibid.

38. Shlomo Avineri, "Peacemaking: The Arab-Israeli Conflict," *Foreign Affairs* 57 (Fall 1978): 51-69, p. 60.

39. Zbigniew Brzezinski, *Power and Principle: Memoirs of the National Security Adviser, 1977-1981* (New York: Farrar, Straus, Giroux, 1983), p. 73.

40. Carter sought to reassure a delegation of Jewish members of Congress and supporters of Israel of his commitment to that state during a session at the White House on October 6. He emphasized that he had no intention of imposing a settlement and rejected the view that the PLO had to be at Geneva. He also said, "I'd rather commit political suicide than hurt Israel." *New York Times,* Oct. 7, 1977.

41. *New York Times,* Oct. 5, 1977.

42. *New York Times,* Oct. 16, 1977.

43. Text as published in *New York Times,* Oct. 14, 1977.

44. *Weekly Compilation of Presidential Documents,* Oct. 10, 1977, p. 1482.

45. For example, Egypt sought an amendment that would name the PLO as one of the participants. See *Washington Post,* Oct. 20, 1977.

46. In an interview on "Face the Nation," on Nov. 20, 1977, Under Secretary of State Philip C. Habib said, in response to a question whether the United States might have to make a fundamental recalculation: "Recalculations don't occur on such immediate notice." He also stated that the president had indicated that "This visit would contribute to the process of negotiations and would contribute to the success—the ultimate success, we hope—of the Geneva conference." In a press conference on Nov. 30 Carter said that it would lead "ultimately, we believe, to a comprehensive consultation at Geneva." *Weekly Compilation of Presidential Documents,* Dec. 5, 1977, p. 1808.

47. "Interview with President Carter," Department of State news release, Dec. 28, 1977, p. 3.

48. "President Carter's Statement at Aswan," Department of State news release, Jan. 4, 1978, p. 1.

49. Press conference of March 24, in *Department of State Bulletin,* May 1978, p. 25.

50. Three Israeli journalists discuss the meeting in these terms: "At 10:30 a.m., March 28, 1978, the United States began dictating its ideas for achieving a Mideast solution." Eitan Haber, Zeev Schiff, and Ehud Yaari, *The Year of the Dove* (New York: Bantam Books, 1979), pp. 176-76; see also pp. 176-87.

51. Ibid., p. 181.

52. Jimmy Carter, *Keeping Faith: Memoirs of a President* (New York: Bantam Books, 1982), p. 312.

53. Vance press conference, Department of State press release, Mar. 24, 1978, p. 5.

54. *Weekly Compilation of Presidential Documents,* May, 1978, p. 896.

55. *New York Times,* May 19, 1978.

56. *Newsweek,* Aug. 28, 1978.

57. Carter press conference, Aug. 17, 1978, in *Department of State Bulletin,* Oct. 1978, p. 12.

58. *Washington Times,* June 8, 1983.

59. The Israeli perspective is outlined in Embassy of Israel, *Policy Background: There Is an Israeli-Egyptian Peace Treaty: Why Hasn't It Been Signed?* (Washington, D.C.: The Embassy, Dec. 19, 1978).

60. *Jerusalem Post,* Mar. 1, 1979.

61. *New York Times,* Mar. 1, 1979.

62. See *Jerusalem Post* and *Maariv,* Mar. 7, 1979, *Haaretz,* Mar. 11, 1979.

63. See *New York Times,* Oct. 29, 1979.

64. At its summit meeting in Venice in June 1980, the EC set forth its own initiative for a comprehensive Arab-Israel peace process to replace, without expressly saying so, the incremental approach of the United States. It was based on previous statements and on U.N. resolutions 242 and 338. The EC would seek to promote two principles: "the right to existence and to security of all the states in the region, including Israel, and justice for all the peoples, which implies the recognition of the legitimate rights of the Palestinian people." A number of other principles were stated. The Europeans argued that the Palestinian people and the PLO "will have to be associated with the negotiations." They opposed efforts to alter the status of Jerusalem and declared that Israeli settlements in the occupied territories were obstacles to peace, and that Israeli military occupation should be ended. To these ends they decided to make contacts with all the parties concerned and, in light of those consultations, to "determine the form which such an initiative on their part could take."

65. *Department of State Bulletin,* Oct., 1980, p. 78.

66. Sol M. Linowitz, "Prospects for Peace in the Middle East," *Middle East Insight* 2 (May 1982): 4-9, p. 6. See also interview with Sol M. Linowitz in *International Insight,* 1 (May/June 1981): 2-6; and Ruth Lapidoth, "The Autonomy Negotiations: A Stocktaking," *Middle East Review* 15 (Spring/Summer 1983): 35-43.

67. Embassy of Israel, "Policy Background: Autonomy—the Wisdom of Camp David" (Washington, D.C.: The Embassy, May 2, 1980), p. 2.

3

THE REAGAN ADMINISTRATION

In contrast with some of its predecessors, the administration of Ronald Reagan initially did not place the Arab-Israeli conflict, or its relationship with Israel, at the center of its foreign policy (or even its Middle East policy). When it came to office, it had no precise plan nor policy for that region. Israel and the Arab-Israeli problem were of marginal interest; domestic concerns had the highest priority. This changed, but slowly. By early 1983 the concept of strategic consensus, which focused on the Persian Gulf and Southwest Asia, had fallen into virtual disuse while the Arab-Israeli conflict, in its various and interrelated manifestations, had resumed its centrality in U.S. Middle East policy.

THE REAGAN FRAMEWORK

The president and his closest advisers believed that they had a mandate as a result of the Carter administration's domestic, especially economic, failures. They set out to implement their ideology and revamp the domestic system while relegating foreign policy to a lower priority. The initial foreign policy hallmark was a strong anti-Soviet posture, particularly in rhetorical terms, which included an antiterrorist and antiradical component.

The administration was committed to the restoration of U.S. power and prestige in the international system, and to regaining the confidence of its allies and the respect of its adversaries through a clear, consistent, coherent, and realistic foreign policy. The humiliation resulting from the taking of U.S. hostages in Iran in November 1979 could not be repeated. The failures associated with the Iranian revolution, which raised questions about the quality of U.S. intelligence, the credibility of the United States as an ally, and its capability to respond to threats distant from its shores, needed to be undone. The administration would, as Reagan had suggested during the campaign, eliminate perceptions of indecisiveness, ineptitude, and vacillation, and speak with a single and powerful voice in foreign policy. This intention was accompanied by a dramatic increase in military spending and a search for bases or facilities.

Reagan's campaign rhetoric, and the Republican platform on which he ran, went beyond the customary pledges of friendship, suggesting strong and consistent support for Israel and its perspective of the Arab-Israeli conflict. He was opposed to dealing with the PLO until that organization dramatically changed its policies by renouncing terrorism, accepting Resolution 242, and acknowledging Israel's right to exist. He perceived Israel to be strategically significant, and an important ally and asset to the United States in the struggle against the Soviet Union:

> Israel is the only stable democracy we can rely on in a spot where Armageddon could come. The greatest responsibility the United States has is to preserve peace—and we need an ally in that area. We must prevent the Soviet Union from penetrating the Mideast. . . . If Israel were not there, the United States would have to be there.[1]

Reagan supported some Israeli actions that had been criticized by previous administrations, such as its settlement policy and its actions with regard to Jerusalem: "An undivided city of Jerusalem means sovereignty for Israel over the city. . . . The West Bank should be a decision worked out by Jordan and Israel. I would never have supported dismantling [of Israeli settlements on the West Bank]."[2] Reagan saw the Palestinian issue as less than the political problem identified by the Carter administration and more as a question of refugees:

> Palestine was never a country. It was a territory, an area, and it was a British mandate. And it was the British Government that created the Kingdom of Jordan, which is 80 percent of what used to be Palestine. The Israelis have less than 20 percent of what was Palestine. The Palestinian refugee problem, it seems to me then, is an 80 percent-20 percent problem of Jordan and Israel.[3]

During the campaign vice-presidential candidate George Bush expressed views similar to those of Reagan—and had done so earlier, while campaigning against him for the Republican presidential nomination. In a position paper on the Middle East, Bush wrote: "It is in the strategic interest of the United States to maintain Israel's strength and security. The security and freedom of that small democracy are fundamental to American strength and Middle East stability."[4] He also argued for the maintenance of the U.S. position concerning the PLO, and suggested the need to encourage Jordan to support the Camp David process and to negotiate with Israel concerning the West Bank.

Secretary of State Alexander Haig advocated a more assertive foreign policy and saw himself as its "vicar," with responsibility for the "formulation, conduct and articulation" of U.S. foreign policy.[5] The downgrading of the national security adviser's role, with Richard V. Allen reporting not to the president but to presidential counselor Edwin Meese, contributed to Haig's assertiveness. Haig's foreign policy background was mixed but clearly oriented toward Soviet-focused global issues and the centrality of Europe. Haig described the Soviet threat as relentless, and was suspicious of détente and of Soviet intentions. His Middle East background was limited—he had had little experience with the region and had said little in public about it. However, while seeking the Republican presidential nomination, he spoke of Israel as a strategic asset whose "very existence serves to deter Soviet aggression."[6] His views of the Soviet Union and of Israel comported well with those expressed by Reagan.

The tone for the Reagan administration's foreign policy was set during the presidential campaign and reiterated at Reagan's first White House press conference. He attributed many of the world's problems to the policies of the Soviet Union. Reagan's ideological framework included an active, aggressive Soviet Union bent on "expansionism," which required the United States to think in terms of containment and, perhaps, confrontation. It was believed that the Soviet Union's methods might well involve it in many of the world's conflict areas, given the assumption that it thrives on exploitation of instability and encourages turmoil through subversion. The logical and appropriate response should, therefore, include the enhancement of U.S. military capability, the restoration of U.S. decisiveness, and the mobilization of other states against the Soviet danger. The administration believed it could capitalize on regional anxiety about the Soviet Union to establish strategic alliances under U.S. guidance. In the Middle East the administration spoke in terms of a "strategic consensus."

EARLY INDICATORS OF MIDDLE EAST POLICY

The Reagan administration was slow to develop a comprehensive approach to the Middle East. The primary initial emphasis was on the Soviet strategic threat in the Persian Gulf sector and not on the Arab-Israeli conflict.

Although Reagan had taken a pro-Israel stand during the election campaign, it was not immediately clear what policy the new administration would pursue in the Middle East, especially since the existing process—which included Camp David, the Egypt-Israel peace treaty, and the autonomy talks—had lost its momentum. Unlike their Carter administration counterparts, the secretary of state and the president's national security adviser had not been identified with Middle Eastern issues. The new administration had no ready-made blueprint like the Brookings Report, which had appeared to figure prominently in the Carter administration's initial approach to the Middle East. Unlike Carter, who saw "a fine opportunity for dramatic improvements," Reagan did not identify "propitious circumstances." While both Carter and Vance lost little time in assuming an activist policy stance, the Reagan administration moved more slowly.

By early February 1977 the Carter administration's interest in the Middle East had become fairly precise. In contrast, by mid-February 1981 the assistant secretary of state for Near Eastern affairs had not been named officially, and the National Security Council did not have its senior staff member for the area. The assessment was that no major Arab-Israeli eruption was likely and the prospects, at that moment, for success in further negotiations were low because of the transition between American administrations, the preparations for the Israeli elections at the end of June 1981, and the prospects that a Labor government would return to power. The initial euphoria following the Egypt-Israel peace treaty of March 1979 had been replaced, after more than 18 months of negotiations, by a more tedious and deliberate process. The momentum had slowed, and the urgency that had characterized earlier periods of the conflict and of the peace process was gone.

The administration was uncertain about the process by which negotiations might continue, although the goal of a settlement within the broad confines of the "Camp David process" was retained. In contrast with the focus of the Carter administration on Palestinian participation, and even overtures to the PLO, Reagan seemed to approach the issue with some variant of the Jordanian option in mind: "I've always believed that Jordan could be very helpful, and others have tried to get Jordan into the peace talks. We should continue trying that."[7] The administration's perspective of the Palestinians was colored by Reagan's view of the PLO as a terrorist organization. Shortly after his election Reagan said, "Yes, I think the PLO has proven that it is a terrorist organization. And I have said repeatedly I separate the PLO from the Palestinian refugees. No one ever elected the PLO."[8] During his confirmation hearings, Haig sought to differentiate between the PLO and components of that organization—refusing to label the overall group as terrorist while suggesting that elements were.

In a number of specific instances the views of the Reagan administration seemed closer to those of Israel than the Carter administration's positions had been, but these perspectives were not tested in the negotiations process. Precise areas of concord and discord remained to be identified, but the impression derived from the campaign and the initial actions of the new administration appeared to "tilt" in favor of Israel. An example of the assertive nature of the administration's support for Israel was provided in mid-February, when the State Department condemned as "absurd" the possibility that the nonaligned nations might seek to expel Israel from the United Nations. During the campaign Reagan had said that U.S. support for the United Nations would be jeopardized by such an effort. The State Department spoke of U.S. opposition to Israel's expulsion and of the "gravest consequences" for the United Nations should it proceed in such a manner.

The approach emerged in a series of indicators. It appeared that the Middle East would gain attention and priority as a function of the worldwide superpower rivalry and its regional manifestations. In August 1979 Reagan wrote: "Stripped of rhetoric, the paramount American interest in the Middle East is to prevent the region from falling under the domination of the Soviet Union."[9]

In an early interview Reagan spoke of the need for a ground military presence of the United States in the Middle East for it to be able to respond to the Soviet threat.[10] Haig stated that the administration did not feel a particular sense of urgency with respect to the autonomy negotiations. There seemed to be greater interest in the Persian Gulf and in the Arabian Peninsula, particularly Saudi Arabia, and one newly appointed ambassador suggested that Saudi Arabia was "the nexus" of U.S. policy in the Middle East.

STRATEGIC CONSENSUS:
THE FIRST MIDDLE EAST INITIATIVE

The slow trend toward increased awareness of the Persian Gulf sector started at the beginning of the 1970s with the British withdrawal from the Gulf, and was given impetus by the October War of 1973, the accompanying oil price increase, and related factors that ensured the politicization of oil. This trend was accelerated by the Iranian revolution, the dramatic increase in oil prices (especially in 1979), the Iraq-Iran war, the Egypt-Israel peace treaty, and the Soviet invasion of Afghanistan.

Iran, which had been seen as an "oasis of stability" and a pillar of U.S. policy in the Gulf sector, shifted to a new role that contributed to regional instability while it faced internal turmoil. This was accompanied by a strongly anti-U.S. policy.

The Egypt-Israel peace treaty of March 1979 reduced the dangers of conflict in the Arab-Israeli sector of the Middle East. At the same time enhanced awareness of the Persian Gulf and the heightened sense of danger there suggested an increased focus on that sector with particular emphasis on the need to strengthen military capabilities. The combination of influence and counterinfluence in the Gulf was a major element in the strategic assessment of the area. It included concern for oil, the stability of the smaller Gulf states, the relationship with Saudi Arabia, and, ultimately, the future direction and alignment of Iran.

In an effort to link the various elements of its world view, including its conception of the Middle East, the administration gave first priority in the region to the Persian Gulf and Arabian Peninsula, and the Soviet threat there. The general view was that the U.S. position in the vital Gulf sector had to be restored and U.S. power enhanced to counter the threat.

Thus, the new administration focused early on an anti-Soviet strategy that sought to link moderate, anti-Communist Middle Eastern states that would subscribe to the notion of an anti-Soviet strategic consensus. The belief was that Egypt, Israel, and Saudi Arabia could, and would, form the basis of such a strategic consensus. Israel's strategic utility was identified.

In testimony in March 1981, Haig told the Senate Foreign Relations Committee there was a need to establish a "consensus, in the strategic-regional sense, among the states of the area, stretching from Pakistan in the east to Egypt in the west, including Turkey, Israel, and the other threatened states."[11] The goal appeared to be the construction of a geopolitical grouping, not a formal alliance, to contain the Soviet Union and its threat to the region. The United States would seek to strengthen, through military, economic, and political cooperation and assistance, a number of regional states, including Israel, Egypt, Turkey, Pakistan, Jordan, and Saudi Arabia. The approach bore some of the hallmarks of earlier U.S. efforts in the region, most notably the Dulles "northern tier" notion of the mid-1950s. Haig also attributed Saudi reluctance concerning the Arab-Israeli peace process in part to concern about the Soviet threat. The connection between strategic consensus and the Arab-Israeli conflict was tenuous:

> It is our strong belief that improving the security of the region is intimately related to progress in the peace process between Israel and the Arab states. In fact, only when local states feel confident of United States reliability and secure against Soviet threats will they be willing to take the necessary risks for peace. It is thus important to handle the Arab-Israeli question and other regional disputes in a strategic framework that recognizes and is responsive to the larger threat of Soviet expansionism.[12]

It was believed that if the United States was perceived as a reliable ally and the regional states were more secure, consensus would be more probable. To a significant degree this was a continuation of the Carter Doctrine.

The administration believed it was necessary to convince the Persian Gulf states that the United States was a reliable partner—the proposed sale of AWACs to Saudi Arabia was a partial test of this. There was the need to establish a credible deterrent to the potential Soviet incursion in the Persian Gulf area, with the expectation that basing facilities and locations to preposition equipment would become available through cooperation with regional states that might similarly identify a potential Soviet threat and might be prepared to cooperate with other regional states and the United States to deal with such a threat.

In April 1981 Haig visited Israel, Egypt, Jordan, and Saudi Arabia in an effort to secure support for strategic consensus. He sought to convince them that the Soviet Union was the main threat to the area, and that joining in a strategic consensus with the United States was an appropriate countermeasure. The idea faced a number of obstacles as the regional states made it clear that they held a different perception of the nature and priority of the Soviet threat and of the most appropriate means to deal with it. These states were more concerned with regional problems and threats, and for the Arab states this meant the Arab-Israeli conflict and Israel.

Saudi Arabia and Jordan identified Israel as their main concern, and suggested that Israeli policies were partly responsible for the increased Soviet presence in the region and its ability to make inroads in the Middle East. This led to frustration within the administration, which saw Saudi Arabia as playing a pivotal role because of its geopolitical position, its oil and petrodollar reserves, its dependence on Western military equipment and training and nonmilitary technology, and its fervent anti-Communism. The Saudis, however, were unwilling to commit themselves to the United States and its perspective. They sought to keep their distance despite their concern about a Soviet threat. Saudi Arabia and Jordan also reiterated the areas of discord between themselves and the United States on the Palestinian issue and the terms on which it should be resolved, reminding Haig of the Arab world's opposition to the Camp David process and the Egypt-Israel peace treaty.

Israel approached the subject of strategic consensus from a different perspective. It saw the idea as having merit and suggested a willingness to cooperate with the United States, although it had strong reservations about increasing Arab military capability, in particular through the supply of AWACs to Saudi Arabia. It was pleased that the United States did not necessarily link the Arab-Israeli conflict with the threat to Persian Gulf security. In addition, Israel was eager to cooperate in the strategic realm, thereby proving itself to be a reliable ally and strategic asset. It would also reduce the Arab-Israeli priority and, therefore, the probably inevitable U.S.-Israeli clashes on that subject.

It soon became clear that while the traditional U.S. interest in thwarting Soviet regional ambitions was newly invigorated by the Iranian revolution and by the Soviet invasion of Afghanistan, the regional states were not similarly concerned. Furthermore, there was a failure by the administration to realize fully the nature and extent of local sensibilities on such questions as the establishment of closer cooperation between regional states, and between the states of the region and the United States, especially in areas of military cooperation and the establishment of military facilities for use (permanent or temporary) by U.S. forces. Haig found a reluctance on the part of the Arab states, including Egypt, to formalize their links to the United States. Sadat, for example, refused to conclude a formal treaty arrangement with the United States concerning access and rights at Ras Banas, although the United States was granted use of the facilities if it would upgrade and improve them.

THE ARAB-ISRAELI CONFLICT: A LOWERED PRIORITY

The decision makers of the Reagan administration seemed to be in agreement on an approach to the Persian Gulf, but the Arab-Israeli situation did not elicit the same consensus. Secretary of State Haig and Secretary of Defense Weinberger seemed to have divergent perspectives. Haig was not as concerned about Arab demands relating to the Arab-Israeli issue as was Weinberger, who seemed more willing to placate the Arabs (especially Saudi Arabia) as a means of securing support for strategic consensus and for a response to the perceived Soviet threat.

The centrality of the Arab-Israeli conflict, which had dominated previous periods, was diminished by the focus on the Persian Gulf, the preoccupation of the major policy makers with that sector, and their differences concerning Israel and the appropriate means for dealing with the Arab-Israeli conflict. The autonomy talks and the Egypt-Israel peace process were relegated to a lower priority, in part because there was no urgency and no perceived opportunity for a renewed effort. In addition, the upcoming Israeli elections (and the likelihood that the Labor Alignment under Shimon Peres might gain control of Israel's Knesset and government) suggested there was little utility in taking action prior to the summer, when, if early predictions proved correct, the new Israeli government might be prepared for a renewed approach to the peace process. Such a policy would be facilitated by the accession to power of Peres and the Labor Alignment, which campaigned on a slogan of territorial compromise in the West Bank.

Or so Washington reasoned. No special U.S. negotiator was appointed to replace Ambassador Sol Linowitz, and the process was left to the parties and the professionals who had long been engaged in its resolution. Camp David was supported: U.S. efforts focused on implementation of the Egypt-Israel peace treaty (including the withdrawal of Israeli forces from Sinai, the dismantling of the settlements there, and the normalization of relations between Egypt and Israel) and on the autonomy negotiations. These efforts were handled through ordinary diplomacy, without resort to a superambassador or special negotiator, although there were occasional special efforts. The Arab-Israeli situation had not yet achieved centrality in the Reagan approach to the region. Israel did not object to this approach, and the links were cordial during the first months of the Reagan tenure.

EPISODIC DIPLOMACY: INCREASED ARAB-ISRAELI ACTIVITY

Despite the inclination to pay less attention to the Arab-Israeli conflict, a series of episodes (or "crises") turned attention to it, although the major change in U.S. policy occurred only with the commencement of the war in Lebanon in June 1982. Prior to that time the U.S. effort in the Arab-Israeli sector of the Middle East was characterized by "episodic diplomacy"—the administration responded to developments as they occurred, but otherwise seemed content with a generalized view that the existing process should be maintained.

The shift from episodic to comprehensive diplomacy developed in response to the chain of events that occurred between the spring of 1981 and the September 1982 Reagan initiative. These included PLO attacks across the border from Lebanon into Israel, the Israeli raid on the Iraqi nuclear reactor in June 1981, the July 1981 Israeli bombing of PLO headquarters in Beirut, the suspension of F-16 deliveries to Israel, the Habib-arranged Israel-PLO cease-fire, the Fahd plan and reactions to it, the AWACS debate, the Israel-U.S. memorandum of understanding on strategic cooperation, the Israeli "annexation" of the Golan Heights, continued terrorist actions, and the war in Lebanon.

THE SYRIAN MISSILE MOVEMENT IN LEBANON

The first significant event in the shift of U.S. priorities, and the one that brought Philip Habib back into diplomatic service, was the emplacement of missiles in Lebanon by Syria in April 1981, in apparent violation of tacit agreements worked out in the mid-1970s, when Syrian forces had been sent into Lebanon in connection with the civil war.

The movement of missiles into Lebanon was a result of clashes between Syrian forces and the Phalangists in and near the city of Zahlah. An artillery battle in early April 1981 was followed by Syrian air strikes against Phalangist positions. Israel came to the aid of the Phalangists by attacking Syrian positions and shooting down two Syrian helicopters on April 28. The next day Syria moved SAM-3 and SAM-6 missiles into Lebanon, ostensibly to defend Syrian aircraft against further Israeli attacks.

Israel soon made it clear that such missile emplacements were unacceptable—they were seen as a threat to Israel's security—and it was suggested that they would be destroyed if they were not removed. At an election rally in mid-June, Begin indicated that Habib would be given time to accomplish his task, but that if he failed, "there will be no war, but I promise you there will be no missiles either . . . . If you [Habib] don't move them, then we will."[13] It was subsequently clarified that this was not meant as an ultimatum with a deadline, and Begin told Habib that Israel was prepared to allow him additional time to deal with the issue.

The United States sought to end the confrontation, and Habib was sent to the region to defuse the crisis and prevent conflict. The immediate concern was to avert an Israeli strike at the missiles. On April 29 State Department spokesman Dean Fischer said that the United States had not given Israel a "green light"—an apparent effort to clarify an impression given earlier by National Security Adviser Richard Allen that "hot pursuit" reaching the source of terrorism is "justified." On May 3 Reagan wrote to Begin, requesting a delay in military actions against the missiles to allow time for diplomacy.

The administration understood Israel's concern and realized that direct military action was a possibility. The continued efforts by Habib reflected this perspective, as did Reagan's comment on June 16, 1981, that the Syrian missiles in Lebanon were "offensive" and aimed at Israel.

Despite sustained efforts, often in the shadow of new crises that diverted his attention, Habib made no apparent progress in securing the removal of the missiles or fully defusing the situation. Israel occasionally noted the lack of progress and limits to its patience, but no deadlines were set and no action was taken until June 1982, during the war in Lebanon.

THE IRAQI NUCLEAR REACTOR RAID—JUNE 1981

Concord between the United States and Israel concerning the missiles in Lebanon was soon overshadowed by discord on a series of other matters, beginning in June 1981.

On June 7, 1981, Israeli Air Force jet aircraft (U.S.-supplied F-16 jets, escorted by F-15s) bombed and destroyed the French-built Iraqi nuclear research facility (Osirak) near Baghdad as it was nearing completion. The mission was undertaken without prior consultation with the United States, which was not notified until several hours after the completion of the raid. Although the Israeli aircraft flew over Jordanian and Saudi air space, and U.S. AWACS aircraft were patrolling in northeast Saudi Arabia, the Israeli planes apparently flew beyond the range of those aircraft and thus went undetected. The attack raised questions about potential Iraqi retaliation and expansion of the resultant conflict between Iraq and Israel.

Israel's government argued that the action was in self-defense and necessary because, it believed, the Iraqi reactor had the potential to produce weapons-grade material for the development of nuclear weapons that might endanger Israel's security, and because Iraq had made clear its intention to use such a weapon against Israel, since the two countries were technically in a state of war. Israel also argued that once the reactor had become operational ("hot"), an attack could not be undertaken without exposing the inhabitants of the Baghdad area to a massive and potentially lethal radioactive fallout. Begin said that the decision was made "many months" prior to its being carried out and the date had been postponed repeatedly. He rejected the wave of international criticism touched off by the raid and warned that "Israel will not tolerate any country—Arab or otherwise—developing weapons of mass destruction" that might be used against Israel. He also stated that "Israel's attack was carried out for 'supreme' legitimate self-defense" and that "there will never be another Holocaust."[14]

The United States disagreed with Israel's assessment. The initial U.S. response came in the form of a statement issued by Department of State spokesman Dean Fischer on June 8:

> The United States government condemns the reported Israeli air strike on the Iraqi nuclear facility, the unprecedented character of which cannot but seriously add to the already tense situation in the area. Available evidence suggests U.S.-provided equipment was employed in possible violation of the applicable agreement under which it was sold to Israel and a report to this effect is being prepared for submission to the United States Congress in accordance with the relevant U.S. statute.[15]

Fischer also called attention to the fact that Iraq was a signatory to the nuclear nonproliferation treaty and had agreed to accept the safeguards of the International Atomic Energy Agency (IAEA) for work on nuclear weapons. The United States had no evidence that work on nuclear weapons was being carried out by Iraq. Pentagon spokesman Henry E. Catto, Jr., noted that while "you cannot but admire their [the Israelis'] technical proficiency, which is what they displayed, we [still] strongly condemn the act," and stressed that the United States "had absolutely no foreknowledge of this."[16]

Members of Congress were cautious about issuing statements that were more critical of Israel than those of the administration, but there was concern that the action would further complicate the Habib effort as well as the broader attempts to achieve an Arab-Israeli peace settlement and to encourage strategic consensus. Some members of Congress shared Israel's concerns.

Walter Stoessel, Jr., under secretary of state for political affairs, testified before the House that the "Israeli air force units were equipped with defense articles furnished to Israel by the United States under the foreign military sales program. The United States was not consulted in any way about any phase of this action, nor were we informed of it in advance."[17] Stoessel also noted that Iraq denied that its nuclear program was designed for anything but the "peaceful use of nuclear energy," and that Iraq had signed the nonproliferation treaty, whereas Israel had not. The IAEA checked the reactor periodically, and no violations had been found earlier that year.

In a letter to Congress, Haig reported that a substantial violation of the military sales act might have occurred, and therefore a review would be conducted to consider the Israeli claim of self-defense. The point of law under consideration was section 3(c)(2) of the Mutual Defense Assistance Agreement of July 23, 1952 (TIAS 2675), which states in part:

> The Government of Israel assures the United States Government that such equipment, materials, or services as may be acquired from the United States . . . are required for and will be used solely to maintain its internal security, its legitimate self-defense, or to permit it to participate in the defense of the area of which it is a part, or in United Nations collective security arrangements and measures, and that it will not undertake any act of aggression against any other state.

Furthermore, for the duration of the review period, and while discussions with Israel continued, Reagan suspended the shipment of four F-16 aircraft that had been scheduled for delivery to Israel that week.[18] While still endorsing some of Israel's justifications, Reagan went further than any previous president in suggesting that Israel had abused the agreement. He was hopeful that interested governments would continue to cooperate with the Habib mission, and he pointed to the raid in support of his view that the only answer to Middle East tensions is true peace.[19]

On July 13, after meetings between Begin and State Department Counselor Robert McFarlane, McFarlane read a statement to reporters with Begin standing by:

> The governments of the United States and Israel have had extensive discussions concerning the Israeli operation against the atomic reactor near Baghdad. The discussions have been conducted with the candor and friendship that is customary between friends and allies. The governments of the two countries declare that any misunderstanding which might have arisen in the wake of the aforementioned operation have been clarified to the satisfaction of both sides.[20]

It was expected that this would lead to the lifting of the suspension of the delivery of the F-16s.

Iraq accused Israel of collusion with Iran, and Arab governments condemned the Israeli raid as an act of terrorism. France termed the Israeli attack "unacceptable," and its foreign minister, Claude Cheysson, protested that it was a "breach of international law."

The matter was brought to the United Nations, where a draft resolution sponsored by Third World states and endorsed by Iraq "strongly condemned and censured Israel" and provided for severe sanctions, including compensation. The United States was prepared for some form of censure but indicated that it would veto a resolution of the type and severity offered by Iraq. U.S. Ambassador Jeane Kirkpatrick met with the Iraqi representative and worked out a compromise resolution that "strongly condemned" Israel's action, but did not call for sanctions, and was unanimously approved by the Security Council on June 19. Ambassador Kirkpatrick supported the resolution because Israel "failed to exhaust all diplomatic recourses available in dealing with her concern" over Iraq's nuclear reactor. However, she also noted that "nothing in the resolution will affect my Government's commitment to Israel's security" and that the Security Council resolution had not "harmed Israel's basic interests."[21]

THE RAID ON BEIRUT AND THE CEASE-FIRE

Exchanges of fire between PLO terrorists operating from Lebanon and Israeli forces continued across the Israel-Lebanon border. On July 17 Israel bombed PLO targets in West Beirut, resulting in significant casualties and loss of life. In a television interview Foreign Minister Shamir stated:

> We did not bomb Beirut. Of course, there are occasionally adverse reactions to actions that we take . . . by people who are not in the same situation that we are in. For the U.S. and other nations this is but one

detail of the general international landscape. For us it is a war for survival.

Israel regretted all civilian casualties but, he noted, every war has casualties:

> We warned this time that we would not refrain from attacking terrorist bases and headquarters, even if they seek sanctuary amidst civilian populations. And you must also realize that the same people who live in the buildings that house their headquarters are people connected in one way or another with the Palestinian organization's activities.[22]

Lebanese authorities said that Israel used U.S.-made F-4 Phantom jets.

Because of the continued fighting, and to assist Habib's efforts to achieve a cease-fire, Reagan postponed the anticipated announcement that the United States would resume the shipment of F-16s to Israel that had been suspended following the raid on Baghdad. A second shipment was also withheld. Haig said that no decision on the planes was issued not because of "any specific action of the Government of Israel" but because the "situation has escalated to such a degree the President felt it would have been highly inappropriate to send additional armaments into the area."[23] Haig elaborated on the rationale in a number of interviews in which he focused on the inappropriateness of shipping arms to an area of tension and stated that the review was being conducted only because of the Iraqi raid, and not the Lebanese attack.[24] He suggested that the attack on Beirut was in partial response to the attacks on Israel from Lebanese territory in which innocent Israeli lives were lost.[25]

The United States sought a cease-fire, and the Israeli cabinet met extensively to consider the suggestion. State Department spokesman Dean Fischer deplored the "intensified violence" and remarked that "these recent tragic events underscore the fact that only peace can provide for the long-term security and well-being of all in the area." He attributed the loss of "innocent life" on both sides to the "progressive escalation of violence."[26]

Israel was reluctant to agree to a cease-fire, which would give the terrorists the opportunity to recuperate from their losses and continue the massive buildup of weapons that the Israelis believed they had been receiving from several sources, including Syria and the Soviet bloc. Israel also was concerned about negotiating with the PLO, either directly or indirectly, and it publicly reiterated its refusal to participate in such negotiations.

Following a cabinet meeting on July 21, Begin read a government statement in which Israel agreed that Habib could begin contacts with the president and government of Lebanon, "with the aim of establishing peaceful relations between Israel and Lebanon from where the terrorist organizations incessantly attack the territory of Israel and murder and maim its citizens." The statement reiterated Israel's refusal to negotiate "directly or indirectly, with the Arab terrorist organizations whose declared aim is the destruction of Israel and its people . . . . Likewise, the government of Israel does not authorize anybody to conduct negotiations with the aforementioned organizations."[27] The effect of the decision was that Habib could negotiate a cease-fire, but not with the PLO, although it was apparent that the PLO would have to be a party.

Habib arranged a cease-fire on the Israel-Lebanon border. The hope, voiced in Washington and Jerusalem, was that this would ease regional tensions and the strain between Israel and the United States resulting from the miniwar between the PLO and Israel and from the Israeli strikes at the Iraqi nuclear reactor and PLO positions in Beirut. Reagan and Haig believed that this would be a first stage in promoting regional peace and stability, and that it could be followed by further efforts on the part of Habib, including an attempt to defuse the Israel-Syria missile crisis. Whatever the means and procedure, the PLO was clearly the second party to the cease-fire, although Israel insisted that Habib was not authorized to deal with the PLO. Within Israel the government was criticized for the bombing of the PLO offices in Beirut, on the grounds that it was militarily ineffective and damaging to Israel's image abroad, especially in the United States. There was also criticism of the cease-fire because it was arranged with the PLO (albeit indirectly), thereby giving the latter a substantial political victory.

The cease-fire went into effect at 1:30 P.M. local time on July 24, 1981. Habib announced in Jerusalem that "all hostile military actions between Lebanese and Israeli territory in either direction will cease." Begin confirmed the statement after the cabinet had endorsed it. The Israeli government was anxious to avoid any impression that there was a deal with the PLO. It stressed that the term "cease-fire" was not used because that would imply an agreement between two parties to a conflict, and it insisted that Israel had made no deal with the PLO, which it continued to regard as a terrorist organization with which negotiations could not be conducted.

Government officials noted that they had responded to a call from the United States and that Habib negotiated with the government of Lebanon, which had been "in contact with other parties." The chief of staff of the Israel Defense Force, Rafael Eitan, argued that the PLO had accepted the arrangement because it had been broken, or was on the verge of it, as a result of Israel's massive blows. But, he also believed, the PLO would take advantage of the cease-fire to regroup and resupply its forces. Virtually from the outset Israel reported PLO violations of the cease-fire, involving shooting and Katusha rocket attacks, and the PLO reported Israeli violations.

On August 17 Haig announced that "following discussion with the government of Israel, consultation with Congress and completion of the Administration's review, the President has lifted the suspension of military aircraft deliveries to Israel."[28] By the time the suspension was lifted, the delay included 10 F-16s and 2 F-15s (the latter were part of a package of 15 that had been scheduled for delivery in mid-August). The ban ended without a formal determination as to whether Israel had violated its agreement with the United States by using U.S.-supplied equipment in the raid on the Iraqi reactor. Haig said that the United States had completed its "intensive" review of Israel's use of U.S.-supplied aircraft in its attacks on Iraq's reactor and on PLO headquarters in Beirut, but had not reached a conclusion on whether the raids violated the agreement, which required the use of the planes for defensive purposes only.

Begin was pleased with the resumption of the shipments and stated that "a wrong was done to Israel. But now President Reagan has decided to right that wrong. I hope it will not be repeated."[29] He argued that the embargo was "absolutely unjust and unjustifiable." Earlier Israel had expressed dismay and anger at the suspension of the delivery of F-15s and F-16s. A spokesman for the Israeli Foreign Ministry had described it as an "unjust and damaging action, bordering on breach of contract."[30] Spokesmen stressed that this was the first time there had been a halt in the delivery of items for which contracts had been signed. The deliveries of planes began in late August.

THE FAHD PLAN

Attention was refocused on the Arab-Israeli sector with the articulation, by Crown Prince Fahd of Saudi Arabia, of a "peace plan" in August 1981. At the time the U.S. reaction was cool, but the plan later reemerged as a matter of interest to the United States and, consequently, of concern to Israel.

In an interview on August 7, 1981, Fahd proposed an eight-point plan for resolution of the Arab-Israeli conflict. Among the principles were: Israeli withdrawal from all Arab territory occupied in 1967, including Arab

Jerusalem; dismantling of Israeli settlements built on Arab land after 1967; guaranteed freedom of worship for all religions in the holy places; the right of the Palestinian people either to return to their homes or to receive compensation; a several-month transitional period for the West Bank and Gaza under U.N. auspices; establishment of an independent Palestinian state, with Jerusalem as its capital; all states in the region living in peace; and the guarantee of these principles by United Nations (or members of the United Nations). He noted that these points were taken from U.N. resolutions.

The proposed plan was the first relatively clear pronouncement by a senior Saudi official on the conflict and on a method for its resolution. It offered an alternative to both the rejectionist Arabs who called for war and the Sadat-Camp David peace approach. Some saw it as a turning point in the conflict and in Saudi policy, while others viewed it more skeptically, as an effort to influence the AWACS debate. Because of its vagueness it was unclear to what extent, if any, the Saudis were prepared to accept Israel and to deal with it.

Israel rejected the plan outright on August 9, 1981, with the statement that it was "a phased program for the destruction of Israel," although some Israelis saw merit in its implied recognition of Israel.

The initial U.S. reaction came in the form of a State Department statement:

> On initial examination it appears to be largely a restatement of previously known Saudi government decisions of principles outlined in United Nations Security Council Resolutions 242, 338 and other United Nations resolutions relating to the Arab-Israeli conflict. . . . we of course welcome any expressions from states in the area of a desire to seek a peaceful resolution of the problems confronting the Middle East.[31]

It occasioned no controversy in the U.S.-Israel relationship.

THE AWACS SALE

The decision of the Reagan administration to sell, among other military systems, five AWACS aircraft to Saudi Arabia became a test of the importance of Saudi Arabia to the United States and a major factor in the U.S.-Israel relationship. Saudi Arabia sought additional equipment for the F-15s it had purchased earlier, along with five AWACS aircraft to improve its defense intelligence, and viewed this request as a test of the U.S.-Saudi relationship and of Israel's ability to veto such an arrangement. The Reagan administration received this arms request soon after its inauguration and decided to endorse it. Israel saw the sale as a direct threat. The lines were drawn between the United States and Israel. Opponents of the sale secured a majority in the House and early had identified a majority in the Senate who opposed the sale for a variety of reasons.

The administration concentrated its efforts on preventing a Senate veto and mounted several arguments for the sale: It would help Saudi Arabia to defend its oil facilities; it would rebuild confidence in the United States as a reliable partner and credible ally in the region; and it would further increase U.S. military capabilities. The administration claimed that the United States would benefit from shared intelligence derived from the planes' presence in the region. It also sought to downplay the quality and effectiveness of the Saudi military (and especially its air force) as a potential threat to Israel. It was argued that future U.S.-Saudi relations would be adversely affected if the sale were rejected.

Israel opposed the sale but apparently concluded that it could not block it without a direct challenge to the president. Israel's decisions were influenced by its view that it faced a "no win" situation in which the president would win and Saudi Arabia would get the planes or Reagan would be defeated by Israel and its lobby, thus raising the ire of the administration and leading to possible negative repercussions for the U.S.-Israel relationship. The last-minute decision of Senator William S. Cohen, a vocal opponent of the sale, to vote with the administration reflected some of Israel's concerns. He switched "to support the sale largely to avoid a Presidential defeat that he said would result in Israel's being made 'a scapegoat' if the Middle East peace process was harmed."[32] Israel sought compensatory actions rather than confrontation with the administration, but the matter could not be readily controlled, and the initial recompense (the U.S.-Israel memorandum of understanding on strategic cooperation) did not appear to Israel to be commensurate with the provision of AWACS to Saudi Arabia.

The Senate vote was an important victory for the administration and particularly for Reagan, who spent much time and effort to achieve it. The final vote (52-48) reflected the intensive and extensive efforts of the administration, especially the president, to change the votes of individual senators, primarily with the argument that Senate failure to allow the sale would harm the president's prestige and hinder his ability to conduct foreign policy. The decision pleased the Saudis (although there were reservations about the difficulty of achieving it and a sense of having been insulted by questions about their military competence and political stability), as did the favorable comments about the Fahd plan that soon followed. Then, in a press conference on October 1, 1981, Reagan commented: "Saudi Arabia we will not permit to be an Iran."

For Israel this comment was a further indicator of a U.S. tilt away from its close association with Israel. There was concern about the willingness to provide sophisticated equipment to the Arabs that might erode Israel's military position. Concern within the Israel lobby, the U.S. Jewish community, and in Israel was also generated by comments made during the debate by the president and others that raised questions about the motivations of those who sought to thwart the proposal. Reagan's press conference comment that "it is not the business of other nations to make American foreign policy"[33] reflected tension in U.S.-Israeli relations. There were also allegations of anti-Semitism and talk of a choice between Reagan and Begin, implying a conflict of loyalty. The potential of an anti-Semitic backlash played a role in the Senate's decision, although its precise effects are difficult to determine. One observer wrote:

> Senator S. David Durenberger said he had "never experienced anything like this in my life, in terms of basic prejudice." Senator Mark Hatfield found a "resurgence of anti-Semitism. I think there's a latent anti-Semitism in this country, and my mail has shown a definite increase." Richard Nixon lamented and suggestively linked "intense opposition by [Menachem] Begin and parts of the American Jewish community." From many respectable quarters came the counsel—usually offered as well-meaning, but taken as potentially threatening and intimidating by many who heard it—that Jewish Americans should stop lobbying against the sale lest they provoke sentiment against Israel or sentiment against Jews.[34]

These and similar comments generated anxiety and concern in the American Jewish community and among other supporters of Israel.

The administration embarked on an effort to reduce the tensions and improve relations with Israel and with the American Jewish community. Reagan reassured Israel that the United States remained committed to help Israel retain its military and technological advantage.[35] Informal meetings were held with prominent Jewish figures to explore various aspects of the relationship and to "explain" various actions and statements of the administration during the AWACS debate. Secretary of Defense Weinberger described the injection of criticism of the Jewish lobby into the AWACS debate as an "ugly tone" and reaffirmed Reagan's commitment to Israel and to the Camp David process.

REEMERGENCE OF THE FAHD PLAN

When originally suggested, the Fahd plan elicited no strong positive reaction beyond the Arab world and had been dismissed by the Reagan administration. On October 29 Haig and Reagan said they regarded it as a basis for negotiation, and State Department spokesman Alan Romberg said that the United States "welcomed certain elements" of the plan, such as the suggestion that all nations should live in peace, but viewed others as problematic. Why the administration suddenly reversed itself on the merits of the Fahd plan was unclear, but some suggested that it was a way to indicate that the Saudis were being helpful in the peace process, as had been argued by the administration and its supporters during the AWACS debate. These comments, when added to the AWACS approval by the Senate, further concerned Israel and its supporters, who saw it as additional evidence of a U.S. tilt toward Saudi Arabia and away from Israel.

Israel continued to see the Fahd plan in negative terms. In an interview on ABC-TV's "Issues and Answers" on November 1, Begin stated that it was an obstacle to peace and "a plan how to liquidate Israel in stages," particularly since it called for a Palestinian state under PLO control with Jerusalem as its capital. Begin expressed concern over the fact there were those in the United States and Europe who expressed support for parts of the plan and suggested that it was a "complete deviation from the Camp David Agreement." In a statement to the Knesset on November 2, Begin elaborated on several of his objections: Fahd's call for Israeli withdrawal meant that Israel would be asked to sacrifice its security; the dismantling of Israeli settlements would erase Israel's "inalienable right" to the West Bank; if a Palestinian state were established, Israel would be involved in an unending war with it. Begin called attention to Fahd's seventh point, which called for peace among nations of the area but did not mention Israel by name and could not be interpreted as recognition of Israel, either explicitly or implicitly. He requested that the Knesset send a nonpartisan delegation to the United States to present Israel's opposition to the Fahd plan to Congress and to the American people.

The Arab states and the PLO were to hold a summit meeting at Fez, Morocco, in late November to consider the proposal, but that meeting ended on November 25 without decision. Saudi Arabia was embarrassed and the United States was disappointed. King Hassan announced that the summit would be resumed at a later date. Arab endorsement awaited the reconvened Fez summit.

STRATEGIC COOPERATION

Reagan and Begin met at Washington in September 1981 and discussed a number of issues in the bilateral relationship, including a closer strategic connection between the two states. In a letter to Begin in late October, Reagan reaffirmed his commitment to arrangements for strategic cooperation between the two countries. In the wake of the AWACS debate, and given the administration's efforts to reduce the tensions in the bilateral relationship and to reassure Israel concerning the military balance, strategic cooperation was an appropriate course of action. It would also serve to demonstrate administration success in implementing its concept of strategic consensus. In early November, Begin announced in the Knesset that a high-level Israeli military delegation would visit the United States for preliminary talks to prepare a "memorandum of understanding" for subsequent signature by Weinberger and Israeli Defense Minister Ariel Sharon when the latter would visit Washington at the end of November. Begin said that the proposed visit, at the invitation of Weinberger, would help to realize the strategic cooperation announced during his meeting with Reagan in September.

The memorandum of understanding on strategic cooperation was negotiated and signed during the visits to Washington by the Israeli team and the minister of defense. Sharon met with Weinberger on November 30, 1981, and it was subsequently announced that they had reached agreement on a strategic cooperation accord.[36] The preamble noted that the memorandum "reaffirms the common bonds between the United States and Israel and builds on the mutual security relationship that exists between the two nations." The focus was on the Soviet Union: "The parties recognize the need to enhance strategic cooperation to deter all threats from the Soviet Union to the region." Article I provided, inter alia, that "United States-Israeli strategic cooperation, as set forth in this memorandum, is designed against the threat to peace and security of the region caused by the Soviet Union or Soviet-controlled forces from outside the region introduced into the region." Strategic cooperation between the parties would be carried out in various fields, and a coordinating council and joint working groups would seek to further the purposes of the agreement by addressing various issues of military cooperation.

The memorandum was praised by the Likud leadership and denounced by the Labor Alignment's leadership, both primarily for political reasons. Begin's office said it was "an important achievement, as it would strengthen Israel's ties with the United States and improve her international status." The Labor Alignment saw its focus on a Soviet threat to be of little value to Israel, and noted that no previous international document signed by the United States was specifically directed against the Soviet Union. Thus, it argued, Israel became the first country in modern diplomacy to tie itself in a formal agreement with the United States specifically directed against the Soviet Union.

The agreement did not commit the United States to come to Israel's aid or to provide protection, but only to cooperate with Israel against Soviet and Soviet-controlled forces posing threats to the region. Sharon argued that the agreement was a means of meeting the threat to Israel and the "free world" from the Soviet Union and "forces controlled by the Soviet Union." Begin was particularly anxious to have the agreement concluded because he regarded it as a major political achievement as well as a personal one. A motion of no confidence in the Knesset, objecting to the agreement, was defeated by a vote of 57-53 on December 2, 1981.

The agreement was short-lived. The Reagan administration suspended the memorandum following a decision by the Knesset, by a vote of 63-21, to extend Israel's law and jurisdiction (in effect to annex) to the Golan Heights on December 14. The United States reacted quickly. It argued that this act violated Resolution 242 and the spirit of the memorandum of understanding because the United States was not consulted prior to the action. On December 17 the United States supported Security Council Resolution 497, which declared the Israeli action "null and void and without international legal effect." On December 18 the State Department announced that, because of Israel's action, "the President has instructed Secretary Weinberger and Secretary Haig not to proceed at this time with discussions intended to implement the Memorandum of Understanding. . . ." The coordinating council meeting scheduled for January would not be held, and the planned U.S. purchase of Israeli military components would be delayed.

Subsequently Begin attacked U.S. policy and charged that the United States had "abrogated" the memorandum and, therefore, that it was "null and void." On December 20, he told U.S. Ambassador Samuel Lewis that Israel regarded "your announcement of the suspension of the discussion of the memorandum of understanding as its cancellation. . . . We take note of the fact that you have canceled the memorandum of understanding." The text of Begin's statement was read over Israeli radio by the cabinet secretary. It was caustic. Begin queried whether Israel was a "vassal," a "banana republic," or a "fourteen-year-old boy" who was being punished for misbehaving. He said that the United States was not "morally" entitled to "preach" to Israel about bombing the Iraqi reactor or Beirut, and the resultant loss of civilian lives, because of similar U.S. actions in World War II and Vietnam. "You have broken the President's word" by canceling the agreement to purchase Israeli military equipment. He also stated that the effort to secure Senate approval of the AWACS sale was accompanied by an "ugly anti-Semitic campaign."[37] Israel argued that the Golan action had nothing to do with the cooperation agreement.

In January 1982 Weinberger said that it was Israel, and not the United States, that canceled the agreement, and the State Department issued a statement noting its unwillingness to reopen the agreement:

> The President decided that we would not be able to go forward with the memorandum of understanding for the time being as the spirit in which the memo of understanding had been signed had not been upheld. We hope for a restoration of a spirit of partnership which would include consideration by each of the broader policy interests of the other.[38]

The memorandum of understanding remained suspended, and U.S.-Israel relations were characterized by tension and controversy.

EPISODIC DIPLOMACY CONTINUES

Despite these developments, and others in the fall of 1981 and the spring of 1982, which helped to introduce the administration to the realities of the Arab-Israeli conflict, a comprehensive approach to that problem did not develop. There were occasional flurries of activity, often in response to specific regional events, but a comprehensive approach did not replace "episodic diplomacy" until the summer of 1982, in the aftermath of the war in Lebanon.

During this period of episodic diplomacy, some attention was also paid to maintaining the peace process that derived from the Camp David accords and the Egypt-Israel peace treaty. Implementation of the peace treaty and continuation of the autonomy talks remained goals of U.S. policy, although they were not given the priority they had had in the Carter administration prior to the Iran revolution and the Afghanistan invasion. Two milestones proved significant: Sadat's assassination followed by the accession of Hosni Mubarak to the presidency of Egypt, and the completion of Israel's withdrawal from Sinai, as required by the peace treaty.

The assassination of Egyptian President Anwar Sadat on October 6, 1981, raised questions in Israel and in the United States about Sadat's successor, Hosni Mubarak, and the continuity of Egyptian policy, especially with respect to the implementation of the Egypt-Israeli peace treaty, the autonomy negotiations, and the anti-Soviet strategic consensus of the Reagan administration. Mubarak and members of his government offered assurances to Israel and to the United States that Egypt would meet all of its responsibilities under the peace treaty. Sadat's funeral was attended by Begin and Haig, who met with Mubarak to discuss the implementation of the peace treaty and the continuation of the autonomy talks. Former presidents Carter, Ford, and Nixon also attended. Carter and Ford suggested that the United States should begin a dialogue with Palestinian leaders. Israel was perturbed by this suggestion, and the following day (October 13) Reagan reiterated the U.S. policy of not recognizing the PLO and not negotiating with it.

Mubarak pursued Sadat's basic approach to the peace process, and the implementation of the Egypt-Israel peace treaty took place as scheduled, although with somewhat dampened enthusiasm, at least on the Egyptian side.

The autonomy talks did not alter their slow pace, nor were the central issues resolved. There were occasional efforts to achieve a "breakthrough," but these proved unsuccessful. In mid-November 1981 senior Israeli and Egyptian officials met to discuss the key issues in the autonomy talks. These discussions took place in an atmosphere of Israeli concern about the perceived "drift" in U.S. policy toward the Fahd plan, which, Israel believed, helped to block movement toward an autonomy agreement. Israel was also concerned because the Reagan administration had failed to name a replacement for Ambassador Linowitz as special representative for the peace process. After two days of talks in Cairo the effort was abandoned and the "working team" resumed its deliberations. In January 1982 Haig made two visits to the region to explore the means best suited to proceeding toward an autonomy agreement. The visits were labeled as "fact-finding," in that he was to learn firsthand about the issues. The trips served the purpose of orientation for Haig but did not advance movement toward a settlement.

THE WAR IN LEBANON

The war in Lebanon was a major watershed in U.S.-Israel relations and had a significant effect on many elements of the bilateral relationship. It was also the catalyst in altering the Reagan administration's approach to peacemaking in the Arab-Israeli conflict, from its episodic character to a more comprehensive framework.

Activity in the spring of 1982 reflected the administration's continued focus on the potential Soviet threat and on efforts to ensure implementation of the Egypt-Israel peace treaty, especially Israel's withdrawal from Sinai, scheduled for April 1982, and additional elements of normalization between Egypt and Israel. Ambassador Habib continued trying to reduce regional tensions and ensure compliance with the cease-fire that he had arranged the previous summer. Israeli complaints of violations of the cease-fire, and about the Syrian missiles that were still in Lebanon, raised concerns about possible Israeli military responses. In early May the tension escalated with the shelling of northern Israeli villages and limited Israeli aerial action in southern Lebanon. Israel subsequently increased its military strength in the north. In a newspaper interview on May 14, IDF Chief of Staff Eitan said: "It is a fact that there is no cease-fire." Escalation of PLO shelling across the border between Israel and Lebanon and the attempted assassination of Shlomo Argov, Israeli ambassador to the United Kingdom, in London were the proximate causes of Israel's decision to launch "Operation Peace for Galilee."

On June 6, 1982, Israel began a major military action against the PLO in Lebanon. It sought to remove the PLO military and terrorist threat to Israel and to reduce the PLO's political capability. Israel's concerns were articulated by David Kimche, director general of Israel's Foreign Ministry, in these terms:

> The situation on the eve of our attack on the PLO was that it had not only effectively destroyed the unitary Lebanese state, but had imposed a form of gangster rule on the country. . . . A state-within-a-state was created, replete with its own army and police, tax system, budget and source of manpower in the refugee camps. . . . The fortifications, the arsenals, the sheer quantities of arms and ammunition that we uncovered in southern Lebanon amply justified all our fears.[39]

The action was in "response to 14 years of PLO terrorist warfare launched from Lebanese soil against Israel and the Jewish people." Israel noted that between 1968 and 1982 over 1,000 civilians were murdered and 4,250 were wounded by PLO terror attacks. The targets were Israeli towns, Israeli diplomats, hostages, and tourists, both Jews and non-Jews, and all were civilians. Further, since the Habib-arranged cease-fire of July 24, 1981, there had been 290 attacks or attempted attacks in Israel and abroad, resulting in 29 deaths and 271 injuries. In a speech at Israel's National Defense College on August 8, 1982, Begin said: "The terrorists did not threaten the existence of the State of Israel; they 'only' threatened the lives of Israel's citizens and members of the Jewish people." He noted that they had violated the cease-fire, resulting in civilian casualties in the north, explosions in Jerusalem and Jewish blood spilled in the Diaspora. There had been constant problems since the cease-fire went into effect, and while they did not threaten the existence of the state, they did threaten the lives of civilians.

At the launching of the operation, the cabinet of Israel made public its decisions:

1. To instruct the Israel Defense Forces to place all the civilian population of the Galilee beyond the range of the terrorists' fire from Lebanon, where they, their bases and their headquarters are concentrated. 2. The name of the operation is "Peace for Galilee." 3. During the operation the Syrian army will not be attacked unless it attacks our forces. 4. Israel continues to aspire to the signing of a peace treaty with independent Lebanon, its territorial integrity preserved.

The immediate goal was to put the Galilee out of the range of PLO shelling—a distance of about 40 kilometers (25 miles)—but Israel also sought to destroy the PLO infrastructure. Begin told Reagan on June 6 that Israel "does not covet one inch of Lebanese territory" and "we wish to sign a peace treaty with a free, independent Lebanon." Ultimately Israel went beyond the self-imposed 40-kilometer limit. The PLO's military infrastructure was far more extensive than had been thought, and Israeli intelligence had underestimated the extent of the PLO presence and capability. Thus the decision to pursue the PLO and destroy depots, headquarters, and other elements of its infrastructure. At the same time Israel had the opportunity to reduce the military and political stature of the PLO and thereby to affect the political dimension of the conflict.

The Israeli incursion into Lebanon came suddenly, and Israeli ground forces moved swiftly north from the border, destroying and capturing numerous PLO strongholds and positions. Within a week Israel was in control of much of the southern portion of the country—some 40 percent of Lebanon. Thousands of PLO fighters were killed and others captured. Clashes with Syrian military forces, primarily in the Bekaa Valley, resulted in substantial Syrian losses of aircraft, missile batteries, and tanks, as well as numerous casualties. By the middle of June, Israel had virtually laid siege to Beirut, which housed PLO headquarters in its western portion, and PLO and Syrian troops were trapped there. Israel maintained steady military pressure to secure the PLO's withdrawal.

Within Israel there were differences over the war and its conduct, but in general the reaction was one of support for a war that was deplored but considered necessary. A "no confidence" motion brought in the Knesset against the government by the Democratic Front for Peace and Equality failed to poll more votes than the seats that party held, and no significant opposition to Operation Peace for Galilee was heard in the Knesset. Public opinion seemed to be similarly supportive. In a poll conducted between August 10 and 19, 1982, in response to a question concerning their voting preferences if the elections were held then, Israelis gave an overwhelming vote of confidence to Prime Minister Begin's Likud: That would have been an absolute majority for Likud, the first in Israel's history. Even more significant was the wide margin over the opposition Labor Party, especially when compared with their virtual equality in the 1981 elections. At the same time the public was queried about the war itself: "If you had known before June 6 all that you know now, would you have supported the government's decision to launch the opration?" Over 80 percent responded in the affirmative (among Likud supporters it was more than 90 percent, and among Labor supporters it was 73 percent). When asked if Israel should have gone beyond the 40-kilometer limit, 64 percent answered "yes." When asked if Israel should have entered Beirut, 46 percent answered in the affirmative.[40]

The war generated substantial controversy in the U.S.-Israel relationship. Among the questions was the extent of direct or indirect U.S. encouragement. A persuasive case can be made that the United States, aware of Israel's concerns about the situation, made no significant effort to discourage Israeli action. Zeev Schiff, one of Israel's foremost military commentators, has summed up the situation in these terms:

Although the Americans sounded circumlocutory warnings for public consumption, the American nay was so feeble that the Israelis regarded it merely as a diplomatic maneuver designed to exonerate the United States should the military operation go sour. Based on trustworthy intelligence, Israel was confident that the United States would welcome a military operation in Lebanon if it struck at the base of Moscow's allies—the Palestine Liberation Organization (PLO) and Syria—without resorting to dangerous extremes.[41]

In summary, Schiff said, "Whether wittingly or unwittingly, Washington gave Jerusalem the green light to invade Lebanon, and Israel interpreted the lack of a strong American position as support for all its objectives."[42]

Ambivalence seemed to characterize the administration's initial response to the war. The official position was that the United States did not collude with Israel and did not welcome the invasion, but neither did it condemn it. At the same time Ambassador Habib was instrumental in securing the termination of hostilities between Israel and the PLO, the lifting of the siege of Beirut, arranging cease-fires, and negotiating for and arranging the withdrawal of the PLO from Beirut. Yasir Arafat agreed, as early as July 3, to the evacuation of his fighting personnel from Beirut, but the problem was complex and it was not until August that all of the necessary elements were in place. Contingents of the multinational force, composed of U.S., French, and Italian troops, began to arrive on August 21. The PLO began to leave for Tunisia, Syria, Sudan, Algeria, North Yemen, South Yemen, Jordan, and Iraq on the same day, and the evacuation was completed by September 1. Subsequently U.S. troops withdrew from Lebanon (on September 11), as did the Italians and French soon thereafter.

With the termination of hostilities the administration adopted the view that there was a new opportunity to move toward resolution of the broader Arab-Israeli conflict. This resulted from an assessment of the strategic accomplishments of the war in a number of specific areas.

Inter-Arab Relations

The invasion of Lebanon came at a time of substantial disarray within the Arab world. The Arab states were unable to unite their military resources or to mobilize their political will to act against Israel. The Arab world watched and lamented, but did not act, as Israel's forces destroyed the PLO's military capability, significantly damaged Syria's might and prestige, forced the acceptance of a cease-fire, and laid siege to Beirut with the PLO trapped therein. Toward the end of June 1982, a meeting of Arab League foreign ministers convened at Tunis, but the few who appeared were unable to reach any important consensus, let alone a plan for effective action. Subsequent efforts were equally unimpressive. Despite substantial discussion of the oil weapon since 1973, its relative impotence was demonstrated in 1982. If in fact the weapon existed, it had eroded in power and was not employed in any meaningful way to affect the policy decisions of either the regional states or the external powers. The worldwide oil glut and the softness of the market, which led to disarray in the ranks of OPEC, was a factor.

The more radical Arab states lost prestige and influence in the wake of the conflict, given the poor showing of Syria and the PLO and the lack of participation by others. They did not demonstrate that their approach to the "problem of Israel" was more effective than that of the more moderate states, such as Egypt. Syria, which had long sought leadership of the eastern front and of the bloc of more radical Arab states, lost significantly as a result of the conflict, and its position in Lebanon deteriorated. Its military situation was also weakened, although it was subsequently upgraded with substantial Soviet resupply. Syrian forces remained inferior to their Israeli counterparts and could expect no meaningful help from the other Arab states. The Israeli presence in Lebanon further threatened Syrian security. Syrian relations with the PLO were also strained, and became a matter of open conflict in the spring and summer of 1983. There were no effective Arab actions in support of the PLO during its darkest hours, although some rhetorical support was provided.

The Role of the United States

The regional reaction to the United States improved after the initial days of the conflict, when it was seen as closely associated with the Israeli invasion. The U.S. role as Israel's patron, and the administration's apparent acquiescence in the Israeli action, generated Arab hostility. However, as the war continued, and particularly with Haig's resignation and his replacement by George Shultz, the atmosphere improved. When Habib became extensively involved in the efforts to secure the evacuation of PLO and Syrian forces from West Beirut, the United States extended its contacts with the Arabs and often clashed with the Israelis, thus improving its overall posture in the Arab world. Habib's success in securing the evacuation of the PLO and Syrian forces from Beirut added to the improved U.S. position, and the administration sought to capitalize on this momentum.

The Role of the Soviet Union

The Arabs again experienced the failure of Soviet military equipment, training, and doctrine, as utilized by Syria, and to a limited extent by the PLO, in dealing with Israel and its U.S. equipment, doctrine, and training (although modified by the Israel Defense Forces). Some of the best equipment in the Soviet inventory was found lacking in comparison with the U.S. and Israeli equipment that it confronted. This was particularly obvious in the substantial losses of the Syrian Air Force in encounters with the Israeli Air Force, and in the substantial damage inflicted by Israel on Syrian missile sites in Lebanon. Mutual recriminations between Moscow and Damascus regarding the blame for the losses did little to improve the role and influence of the Soviet Union. The Soviet failure to provide any tangible aid (military, economic, diplomatic, or political) to its allies during the hostilities raised, once again, doubts about the utility of the Soviet connection for the Arab states.

This provides a partial explanation of the subsequent Soviet decision to replace Syrian losses with later models of similar equipment and more sophisticated equipment (such as the SA-5 missile) and to dispatch large numbers of Soviet advisers. The SA-5s have a greater range than the previous air defense capability provided to Syria—they can reach a large segment of Israel's airspace, as well as portions of Lebanon and Jordan, and much of the eastern Mediterranean, where the U.S. Sixth Fleet had been sailing since the war began. The SA-5s, not previously deployed outside the Soviet Union, reporesented a major escalation in Soviet support for Syria, as did the increased number of Soviet personnel assigned.

The Danger of Warfare: Conventional or Unconventional

The PLO's capability for military or terrorist activity against Israel was significantly reduced with the destruction and capture of equipment and bases of operations, and with the dispersal of PLO forces. An IDF spokesman reported that Israel uncovered 540 weapons depots in Lebanon and that it took 4,330 truckloads to transport the captured supplies to Israel. The equipment included ammunition, armored combat vehicles (including tanks), antitank weapons, small arms, mortars, Katyusha rocket launchers, field artillery pieces, and antiaircraft weapons. At the same time Syria's losses, Egypt's peace with Israel, Iraq's war with Iran, and the general unwillingness of the Arab states to join in a war against Israel made a full-scale Arab-Israeli war unlikely.

For Lebanon the war had a mixed outcome. Although there was widespread destruction and a substantial number of casualties, there also arose the prospect of removing foreign forces from the country, thereby providing an opportunity for the central government to extend its authority and to reestablish its sovereignty throughout its territory.

For Israel the general accomplishments of the war could be identified in more specific terms. Northern Israel was removed from the range of PLO guns, and relative peace was restored. The threats of terrorism and of war were reduced, at least in the short term. The prospects for war with the Arabs were reduced by the demonstration of clear Israeli military superiority and the obvious disarray in Arab ranks, as well as by the unwillingness (and probable inability) of the Arab states to confront Israel. The prospects of PLO terrorist activity against Israel were also reduced wtih the loss of PLO positions and equipment, the dispersal of the PLO forces, and disagreements within its ranks. The prospects for peace were enhanced in that the futility of war and terrorism should have been increasingly realized by the Arab states and the PLO, as it was by the United States in advocating the September initiative. At the same time Israel's relations with Egypt, while formally reduced with the recall of the Egyptian ambassador from Tel Aviv and remaining relatively "cool," nevertheless survived the war and its immediate aftermath.

Despite the positive results of the war for both Washington and Jerusalem, there were increased tensions between the United States and Israel. The United States seemed to respond positively to the initial Israeli incursion, but when Israel moved beyond the 40-kilometer line there was increasing U.S. concern.

Alexander Haig's resignation, which occurred during the war but was primarily a result of other factors, was seen as a blow to Israel because he had been an advocate of its cause and its strongest supporter in the senior ranks of the administration, providing a counterweight to the views of Secretary of Defense Weinberger. In addition, George Shultz, who was chosen to replace Haig, had extensive Saudi business ties by virtue of his prior association with the Bechtel Corporation, and was linked to Weinberger. He also had disagreed with Reagan's views on the Middle East during the presidential election campaign. The initial Israeli concern about Shultz soon gave way to an assessment that he pursued a policy in keeping with the president's views and, at times, at variance with Weinberger's.

Haig's resignation suggested that Weinberger, who was seen by Israel as a negative factor, could secure a greater role in the formulation of Middle East policy. Weinberger was a strong advocate of Saudi centrality in U.S. policy, and he now could pursue that perspective with little opposition. When the Israeli attack on West Beirut began in mid-August, Reagan warned Israeli Foreign Minister Shamir that the special relationship between Washington and Tel Aviv could be threatened by such a move. Following the Israeli bombing of the Lebanese capital, Reagan told reporters,

"I lost patience a long time ago." Relations between the two countries became particularly strained in this period, as was evidenced by U.S. abstention on a U.N. Security Council resolution calling on Israel to return some of the areas captured during the fighting. Reagan was upset by what he saw as Israeli intransigence, but believed that the United States should refrain from taking actions that were too harsh and could result in increased tensions. Instead, he sent a letter to Begin expressing his "outrage" over the bombing of West Beirut and demanding adherence to the cease-fire.[43]

It is in this context of significant strategic changes and uncertainty in the U.S.-Israel relationship that the administration began to think in terms of a new approach. The appointment of George Shultz provided an opportunity, and he was charged with devising an appropriate "plan" to deal with the altered situation.

Reagan's decision to take a major step and to be assertive resulted from a number of factors. The invasion of Lebanon, Haig's departure, Shultz's accession, and the regional alterations were important, but Reagan's personal perspectives (his personality and his concept of "right and wrong") were crucial. Reagan himself said, "I was determined to seize that moment." Shultz reviewed U.S. policy and sought wide consultation within and outside the administration. The discussions were conducted in secrecy, primarily to prevent Israel from learning about the effort and, in the view of many officials, possibly subverting it. The secret was well kept, a factor that later generated Israeli suspicions of the president's initiative.

THE "FRESH START" INITIATIVE

The initiative for peace in the Middle East outlined by Reagan in a television address on September 1, 1982,[44] was an important watershed in U.S. Middle East policy and in U.S.-Israel relations.

Reagan set forth the position of his administration on some of the central elements of the Arab-Israeli conflict. This was not a "plan" for resolution of the conflict—the administration was careful to distinguish it from a specific and detailed blueprint for action that would include methods and timetables. It was argued that Resolution 242 and the Camp David accords provided an appropriate "plan." Reagan sought to take advantage of the strategic alterations in the region. "It seemed to me that with the agreement in Lebanon [to evacuate the PLO fighters from Beirut] we had an opportunity for a far-reaching peace effort in the region, and I was determined to seize that moment." He believed that the United States bore special responsibility for dealing with the problem.

This view reflected a peculiarly American trait—"a neat package syndrome"—that suggests the need to try to resolve disputes and prevent their deleterious international effects. Reagan articulated this general conception when he said: "Our involvement in the search for Mideast peace is not a matter of preference, it's a moral imperative." In calling upon the parties to recognize each other's needs and aspirations, he said that "in making these calls upon others, I recognize that the United States has a special responsibility. No other nation is in a position to deal with the key parties to the conflict on the basis of trust and reliability." Reagan also modified his approach to the peace process when he stated that the United States would "put forward our own detailed proposals" and would support positions that it saw as "fair and reasonable compromises."

A sense of need and of responsibility was thus combined with a perception of a special opportunity. The president spoke of a "fresh start" as well as of continuity with the Camp David process, which the initiative was intended to reinvigorate, and he noted that the proposals were in keeping with Resolution 242. He reiterated a long-held U.S. position that negotiation between the parties was the only method to resolve the conflict. Reagan called for Israel to withdraw from occupied territory but not fully to the 1967 lines. The right of Israel to exist within secure and defensible borders was reasserted, and it was stated that "America's commitment to the security of Israel is ironclad." Reagan altered his perspective of the Palestinians by saying that they had strong feelings that their cause was "more than a question of refugees" and, further, that he agreed with that perspective. The Palestinian people had to exercise their legitimate rights. Jordan and representatives of the Palestinians were invited to join the negotiations on the future of the West Bank and Gaza Strip.

Reagan did not identify exactly what role the Palestinians might play in the negotiation process nor who, other than Hussein, might represent them, but the PLO was not included. It was not mentioned (except in the context of withdrawal from Beirut) in the initiative and, in an interview on September 2, Shultz reiterated the long-standing U.S. policy with regard to the PLO. Reagan envisaged a five-year transition period during which the future of the West Bank and the Gaza Strip would be worked out, as had been discussed in the Camp David accords. He spelled out his view that these territories should constitute neither an independent Palestinian state nor fall under Israeli sovereignty; rather, they should become a self-governing entity in association with Jordan. The city of Jerusalem should remain undivided, but its precise final status must be negotiated. A moratorium on the creation (a "freeze") of Israeli settlements was suggested. Reagan's view of Israel's settlements in the West Bank and Gaza was modified when he called for a freeze; he added that they were "in no way necessary for the security of Israel."

Many of the points were not new, although the articulation of specific positions was a departure from previous U.S. policy statements. In particular the envisaged preferred future for the West Bank and Gaza was more precise than previously discussed:

> The final status of these lands must, of course, be reached through the give and take of negotations. But it is the firm view of the United States that self-government by the Palestinians of the West Bank and Gaza in association with Jordan offers the best chance for a durable, just and lasting peace.[45]

Implicit in the distinctive features of the Reagan initiative were three assumptions that are key to understanding the approach and its fate.

The initiative envisaged Palestinian self-government in association with Jordan, thus making King Hussein central to the process on the Arab side. He was invited to join the peace talks, with the view that such a decision would constitute a significant breakthrough. In a sense Reagan was trying to identify a role for Hussein similar to the one played by Sadat. This comported well with a conception articulated the previous July, when Reagan said that the United States had "been trying to establish a bond with them [the Jordanians] so that we can bring them into the peace-making process with Israel, and we've called it 'create more Egypts.' "[46]

Prior to identifying the role for King Hussein, there were consultations with him in late August that generated the administration's view that he was willing to participate in the process, provided the appropriate mandates (approval and/or acquiescence) could be secured from the Arab states and the PLO. Toward the end of August, Hussein revealed his thinking when he stated that the Camp David process remained unacceptable and that a new initiative was called for. He also said that "we will be moving in the very near future to hold serious discussions with the PLO, who have indicated a desire to do so, to formulate the concept of future Palestinian-Jordanian relations" and that "this may be a step along the way to enable us to co-operate jointly to establish a just and durable peace." The Reagan administration clearly believed that Jordan could be drawn into the process with appropriate U.S. incentives and backing from the moderate Arab regimes. Without this assumption there could be no Arab interlocutor.

Thus, the administration seemed to believe that despite his constant refusal to participate in the Camp David process, Hussein would join in this initiative after securing a mandate from the Arab summit scheduled to meet at Fez (the timing of the initiative sought to take advantage of the projected summit), and that the PLO and the Saudis, not necessarily in concert, would facilitate this effort. The Saudi factor was never articulated very precisely but had to undergird the initiative. It was believed that Saudi Arabia sought stability and a resolution to the Palestinian problem in part because its continuation helped to promote regional instability and provided a pretext for Israeli actions. The administration, and particularly Secretary of Defense Weinberger, had focused on the importance of Saudi Arabia, and this was one of the areas where the Saudis were envisaged as being of potential assistance.

A second key assumption pertained to Israel. Although it was obvious that the Reagan view of the West Bank was incompatible with Begin's, it was believed that there might be a mechanism to alter this situation. The initiative seemed to assume (although the administration was careful not to articulate, and often to deny, any effort to achieve it) that there could be an alteration in the policies of the Begin government or in the government itself, under appropriate circumstances. A willingness of Hussein to negotiate with Israel, as had Sadat, might provide the necessary catalyst. Despite repeated denials that the United States sought to bring about a change of government in Israel, the rumors were rife and the logic of the initiative seemed to include such an assumption.[47] In early September, in an interview published in *Bamahaneh,* Begin accused U.S. officials and journalists of interfering in the internal affairs of Israel through leaks to the press, statements by various officials, and aid to rival political parties.[48]

A third implicit assumption was that of a connection between the initiative and the situation in Lebanon. The basic goals were to secure the withdrawal of all foreign forces, to extend and secure the sovereignty of the government throughout the territory of Lebanon (in part by equipping and training its armed forces), and to achieve the economic and social reconstruction of the country. This was seen as a relatively straightforward process whose earliest elements could be achieved readily, and there were some in the administration who spoke of the withdrawal of foreign forces within a matter of weeks. The connection between the two issues was made by Reagan when he said that "the evacuation of the PLO from Beirut is now complete and we can now help the Lebanese to rebuild their war-torn country."

U.S. efforts to ameliorate the situation were made public in early September. After consulting with Habib, Reagan announced the formation of an interagency steering group to coordinate the political, economic, and security assistance planned to help the Lebanese government restore its authority throughout the country, and reiterated his objective of securing the removal of all foreign forces. Because of the relative stability of the situation, Reagan said that U.S. and other contingents of the multinational force would begin withdrawing from Beirut ahead of schedule, on September 10. Thus, the sequence of events envisaged was the withdrawal of all foreign forces from Lebanon, the building up of the Lebanese army and the reconstruction of the country, the promotion of stability and the extension of effective sovereignty to the entire territory of Lebanon, and negotiations to implement the elements of the Reagan initiative.

INITIAL REACTIONS

On September 2 the Israeli cabinet rejected the Reagan proposal as presented on U.S. television and as conveyed (with some modifications) to Prime Minister Begin. There were specific objections and a general perception that it sought to deny Israel many of the benefits it could reap from the war. A major argument was that it departed from the conceptual framework agreed to at Camp David. The proposal seemed prematurely to determine the outcome of negotiations on several points, including the status of Jerusalem as the capital of Israel and the future of the West Bank and Gaza. The Camp David accords deliberately left open the final status of these areas and contained no provision concerning Jerusalem. There were, instead, letters attached to the accords stating the positions of the parties. There were other points of concern, since the proposal represented a shift in the U.S. role from that of honest broker to that of advocate affecting the outcome of the negotiations. Commenting on the initiative, former U.S. negotiator Ambassador Sol Linowitz said:

> President Reagan's peace proposal sharply changes the role of the United States in the Middle East negotiations. Until now the United States has acted as a mediator seeking to find common ground between the parties. The plan advanced by the President, however, sets forth American positions on some of the most controversial aspects of the negotiations.[49]

The very fact that the United States articulated its position prior to an agreement by the Arabs to negotiate seemed to Israel to reduce the chances for negotiations. Reagan also called for a unilateral freeze of settlements by Israel without any quid pro quo from Jordan. This was not included in the

Camp David accords but addressed in a separate letter, and was a matter of significant controversy, given the divergent U.S. and Israeli interpretations of the length of time Israel had agreed to forego settlement construction. Israel was concerned that the United States had defined autonomy to include "the land and its resources," which had been left for negotiation because the Camp David accords specified that the inhabitants of the areas would enjoy full autonomy.

There were other aspects of the initiative that concerned Israel. Begin preferred the Camp David process within the new context created by the war in Lebanon, particularly the decreased capabilities of the PLO. Israel was also concerned that Hussein (and perhaps other Arab leaders, most likely King Fahd of Saudi Arabia) had been consulted in advance but that the initiative was presented as a fait accompli to Israel. In a speech to the Knesset on September 8, 1982, Foreign Minister Yitzhak Shamir said: "The United States Government did not see fit to consult with us on this new program, which concerns our borders, our security and our positions. This is something that is simply not done." Israel viewed this as a violation of the spirit and letter of the Sinai II pledges, made in 1975, to consult concerning the peace process and of the general spirit of the U.S.-Israel relationship.[50]

There was concern because the proposals seemed to deviate from the Camp David process, despite Reagan's assertions to the contrary, and to focus on points deliberately avoided at Camp David (and since). The initiative seemed to generate a new procedure with a Palestinian focus and an approach to the West Bank that the Begin government had sought to avoid. The proposal seemed to embrace the views of Shimon Peres, Begin's major opponent and leader of the opposition Labor Alignment, who had advocated a "Jordanian option" both in the 1981 election campaign and subsequently.[51]

The Israeli cabinet unanimously rejected the initiative, but Peres suggested that it had "positive points" and was "a basis for dialogue," and endorsed it, albeit with some reservations. The Reagan administration indicated that it was not surprised by the rejection but did not consider it Israel's final and irrevocable word. The timing of the president's speech, just days prior to the scheduled Arab summit meeting at Fez, raised questions about U.S. motives. Some observers felt that it would help to prevent a strongly anti-U.S. tone at Fez and might help to secure the needed backing for Hussein to participate in the process. Israel saw it as a further attempt to curry favor with the Arab states at its expense.

The Arab reaction was, on the whole, more positive, partly as a result of the fact that their expectations of the Reagan administration were low. While some elements in the Arab world rejected the proposal, others identified "new" and "positive" elements, and were pleased with Israeli discomfort and the changes that could be identified in U.S. policy, even if they were denounced as insufficient. For the Arab world a major objection centered on the U.S. refusal to support the establishment of an independent Palestinian state in the West Bank and Gaza. However, it had its own difficulties in formulating an appropriate response. The main and initial Arab response came at the Fez summit, where the Arab leaders restated the designation of the PLO as the sole legitimate representative of the Palestinians and refused to grant Hussein the required mandate to negotiate on their behalf.

IMPLEMENTING THE INITIATIVE

Ambassador Philip Habib was appointed the president's special representative for the Middle East (a "superambassador"), with overall responsibility for implementing the initiative as well as for coordinating the negotiations concerning Lebanon. He was to be assisted in the first task by Ambassador Richard Fairbanks and in the second by Ambassador Morris Draper.

The administration's resolve to continue with the initiative became increasingly obvious over time. When asked by reporters on December 23, 1982, what he considered his greatest foreign policy accomplishment, Reagan responded: "I think that the initiative that we've taken in the Middle East is probably the greatest accomplishment, and I have great hopes for that. If we can bring peace to that very troubled area, I think we will have made a very great accomplishment."[52] In his 1983 State of the Union Address Reagan said: "All the people of the Middle East should know that, in the year ahead, we will not flag in our efforts to build on that [Camp David] foundation to bring them the blessings of peace."[53] Shultz similarly suggested continued and increased efforts.

Developments in, and with respect to, the Middle East were to capture the limelight and affect the peace efforts of the Reagan administration in the following months. These included the assassination of President-elect Beshir Gemayel of Lebanon; the election of Amin Gemayel as president of Lebanon; the massacres at the Shatila and Sabra refugee camps; the appointment in Israel of the Kahan Commission, its investigation, and its subsequent report; and various acts of violence perpetrated against the multinational force, against the foreign forces, and against the American Embassy in Beirut.

With the evacuation of the PLO from Beirut, and the withdrawal of the U.S., French, and Italian troops of the multinational force, tension and violence escalated quickly in Lebanon. Following the assassination of President-elect Beshir Gemayel, Israeli forces moved into West Beirut in an effort to preserve order and stability. Subsequently several hundred Palestinians were massacred in the Shatila and Sabra camps near Beirut, and Israel was accused of being involved. The massacres and the initial refusal of the government to order an official investigation strained Israel's relations with the United States and further damaged its image in the international community.

The United States reacted quickly to the reports of the massacre. Reagan met with his advisers, condemned Israel for its indirect responsibility, called for its immediate withdrawal from West Beirut, and supported a U.N. Security Council resolution to that effect. On September 20 Reagan announced that U.S. marines would return to Lebanon as part of a broader multinational force. He also stated that the new spiral of violence was potentially a great setback for his peace initiative. The initial decision by the Begin government not to establish a commission of inquiry generated strong negative views in the United States, both in Congress and in public opinion. Even staunch supporters of Israel were concerned. More than 30 members of the House signed a personal letter to Begin calling for the establishment of a commission of inquiry, and members of the Senate were similarly critical of Israel's actions.

Israel's government ultimately decided to establish a commission of inquiry to investigate the events and to report its findings and recommendations. That decision, strongly influenced by the U.S. reaction, helped to defuse the crisis and to prevent a further erosion of U.S. support and sympathy. When the Kahan Commission reported its findings in the spring of 1983, it generated strongly positive reactions in the United States and was a major factor in a dramatic improvement in Israel's image in U.S. public opinion.

Implementation of U.S. policy took two forms: the administration waited for Hussein to agree to join the process, and it concentrated on the immediate problems of Lebanon. In both areas it clashed with Israel. The U.S. "peace team" worked to secure the withdrawal of foreign forces from Lebanon and to provide for the reconstruction of the country and the improvement of the capability of the Lebanese armed forces. Both Reagan and Shultz reiterated the view that a satisfactory conclusion to the negotiations for withdrawal of foreign forces was a necessary first step and, while they expressed optimism on this point on numerous occasions, they recognized that the process was going more slowly than they would have preferred. The talks between Israel and Lebanon continued into the spring of 1983, and while they appeared to be going very slowly, there were occasional reports of progress.

At the same time the United States continued its efforts to improve the situation in Lebanon. U.S. economic and military aid, as well as the presence of U.S. marines as part of a multinational force and of U.S. advisers to help train the Lebanese military to assume greater responsibility for internal security, became visible parts of a comprehensive effort to respond to the situation created by the 1982 war and to try to restore Lebanon to a sovereign and prosperous position in the region.

The central issues in U.S.-Israel relations included both the substance of the issues and the lack of basic trust betrween the two states in the wake of the war. Begin felt betrayed by the Reagan initiative and saw the United States as "selling out" to the Arabs. Reagan reportedly felt deceived by Israel's actions. The United States also had to defend itself against Arab accusations that it had shirked its responsibility in Lebanon because Habib had guaranteed the safety of the Palestinians and the massacre had occurred despite these assurances. Relations were strained further when the administration opposed increased aid authorizations to Israel, and argued that the action should not be interpreted as a direct affront to Israel but should be seen in the context of efforts to reduce U.S. aid programs. Israel saw it as a significant shift in U.S. policy.

The administration seemed especially frustrated by the lack of progress in the Lebanon-Israel negotiations concerning Israel's withdrawal. Israel sought to secure important political gains, particularly the establishment of "good neighborly relations," from the war. Lebanon objected to any mention of normalization, an action that might endanger its relations with the other Arab states. This issue, and others of an ancillary nature, slowed the talks. Although the Reagan administration professed that it had no illusions that foreign troop withdrawals could occur "overnight," there was hope that the pace would be quicker than it was. In some quarters Israel was accused of a deliberate effort to undermine the Reagan initiative by stalling on the withdrawal issue. The negotiations between Israel and Lebanon, with U.S. participation, continued into the spring of 1983, and aspects of the frustration appeared in early 1983. A scheduled visit by Begin to Washington was delayed, and there was modification of the U.S. view of

Camp David's requirement of a five-year transition period for the West Bank and Gaza.

Other events generated tension and seemed to separate U.S. and Israeli perspectives, and to give added incentive to Hussein and the Arabs to support the peace process. Criticism of Israeli actions came often. On January 11, 1983, the State Department faulted Israel for authorizing an advertising campaign to promote West Bank settlement, called the action "unfortunate and counterproductive," and reiterated "the U.S. position . . . [that] settlements are an obstacle to peace in the Middle East." Incidents involving Israeli forces and U.S. marines in Lebanon in early February contributed to the tensions.

At about the same time it was reported that Secretary Weinberger had rejected a proposed agreement with Israel under which Israel would have shared military information with the United States about the performance of U.S. military equipment used by Israel and about Soviet equipment in the hands of the Syrians and the PLO gained as a result of the war in Lebanon. Weinberger apparently believed that the Israeli price was too high for the intelligence the United States would receive, and that Israel would gain access to sensitive military information he believed should not be shared wtih any other country. This further intensified the tensions between the two states.

"WAITING FOR HUSSEIN"

The publication of the Kahan Commission's report, and the resulting relaxation of tension between the United States and Israel, shifted the focus back to Hussein. Washington had been "waiting for Hussein," as it had on previous occasions. The administration held the view, often expressed publicly, that Hussein was ready to bargain if given the appropriate mandate by the other Arabs, especially the PLO. The Israelis were never confident of this and often expressed their skepticism. The effort to secure Hussein's participation was almost continuously confronted by setbacks, although the Reagan administration sought, and often found, the positive aspect of each roadblock and pronounced itself "hopeful" of continued progress.

The administration sought Jordanian participation not only because Jordan was seen as indispensable if the West Bank was to be on the agenda for discussion, but also because a positive response from Hussein would help to elicit change in the Israeli position, thus improving the prospects for peace. This perspective was articulated clearly by Shultz in an interview published in *U.S. News and World Report* on November 8, 1982:

> The next step in the process is for King Hussein of Jordan, with support from the Arab world and participation of some form of Palestinian representation, to express a willingness to sit down and negotiate with Israel on the future of the occupied West Bank and Gaza Strip areas. This is something that has to take place. If he does so, it will be very difficult for any Government of Israel to say no. And I'm quite certain it wouldn't say that.

Reassurances were important in the effort to secure Hussein's participation, and various U.S. statements were made to produce the desired effect, despite (or perhaps because of) their negative effect on the U.S.-Israel bilateral relationship. On August 30, 1982, in apparent response to the continued comments of Israeli Defense Minister Sharon, Larry Speakes said that "the U.S.—this administration, as its predecessors—is committed to the territorial integrity and sovereignty of Jordan and our support for its enduring character. We do not agree that Jordan is a Palestinian state."[54]

The Fez summit did not provide the desired mandate, but the Reagan administration sought to interpret the summit in a positive way by suggesting that the endorsed plan represented an agreed stance by both moderate and radical Arab states replacing the existing discord. Also, the reference to the Security Council guaranteeing "peace among all states of the region" could be taken to include Israel, thereby facilitating implementation of the initiative. But, as Shultz said, "the key thing is, will somebody show up at the negotiating table? The fact that people have positions is not so important as will they come to talk about it."[55] In an address on September 12, 1982, Shultz stated that "the absence of Jordan and representatives of the Palestinian inhabitants of the occupied territories from the negotiations has been the crucial missing link in the Camp David process." Therefore, he believed, "success in the peace process depends on Arab support for these vital missing partners to join the negotiations and become partners for peace."[56] The administration remained optimistic partly because of the statements of moderate Arab leaders, such as Hussein, who periodically suggested that peace was essential and that they wanted to help achieve it. For example, King Hussein, in an interview broadcast by the BBC on September 14, 1982, said:

> I am going to play a very, very active part in helping, pushing forth every possible attempt for the establishment of a just and durable

peace. But, beyond that, there are limitations which I recognize, and which I hope the world recognizes.[57]

Similar perspectives were suggested to Reagan during a visit in October by an Arab League delegation.

At the same time discussions between Hussein and Yasir Arafat began in Amman, ostensibly with a view to reaching an agreed position in response to the initiative, and thereby providing for Jordanian participation. Positive interpretations of these meetings continued to buoy the administration's perspectives.

Hussein visited the United States in December. In an interview prior to the visit, Reagan again displayed his optimism and said that "Hussein [is] sincerely desirous of peace in the Middle East. I think he will be cooperative. And I think we can count on him for that." At the same time Reagan noted the priority of Lebanon and its linkage to the initiative: "But the main thing right now . . . is to get what now constitute armies of occupation—the PLO, the Syrians, and the Israelis—out of Lebanon. . . . That is the first step. And then we move to the peace process. . . ."[58] This optimism remained the public face of the administration even though nothing productive emerged publicly as a result of Hussein's visit. Nevertheless, Reagan said that they had concluded "productive talks and . . . we've made significant progress toward peace."[59] It was during the December visit that Reagan reportedly promised Hussein that if he offered to enter the talks, the United States would try to halt the building of Israeli settlements in the West Bank and Gaza, a pledge acknowledged by the Department of State in mid-April. If the United States failed, it would not press Hussein to join in the talks.[60]

Hussein had made his participation contingent on receipt of a mandate from the Arab states and/or the PLO. Consequently the negotiations between Hussein and Arafat were significant, as were the decisions of the Palestine National Council, which met at Algiers in February 1983. The council confirmed its rejection of the Camp David accords and rejected consideration of the Reagan plan as a suitable basis for a just and lasting solution of the Arab-Israeli conflict. It restated the role of the PLO as the sole representative of the Palestinian people and rejected any effort to assign that right to someone else—thereby excluding a representative role for Jordan.

The administration remained sensitive to Hussein's difficulties, and in remarks on February 22, 1983, Reagan said that "King Hussein should be supported in his effort to bring together a joint Jordanian-Palestinian team to negotiate the future of West Bank, Gaza, and Jerusalem."[61]

Reagan also pledged his "personal commitment" to the peace talks and to Resolution 242. Additional efforts to induce Hussein's participation included the possibility of arms sales and other assistance—the former consisting of the option to purchase F-16 aircraft. At the same time the United States took an increasingly tough stance with Israel, including a statement by Reagan on March 31, 1983, that 75 U.S. F-16 fighter jets would be withheld until Israel withdrew from Lebanon. Reagan cited legal reasons for the delay, noting that "under the law . . . those weapons must be for defensive purposes . . . . While those [Israeli] forces are in the position of occupying another country . . . we are forbidden by law to release those planes."[62]

A last U.S. effort to influence these negotiations occurred on April 8, 1983, when State Department spokesman John Hughes suggested that the United States would seek to stop Israeli construction of new settlements in the West Bank if Hussein would join the negotiations.

> If Jordan publicly announces its willingness to enter such negotiations we are determined to do our best to assure that the results of those negotiations are not prejudiced from the outset by activities of any party which reduce the prospects of a negotiated peace.

At the same time, in response to a question, he noted that establishing new settlements could be considered that form of activity, but he also added that his comments should not be interpreted as "a threat to cut off aid or take any other action against Israel."[63]

On April 10, 1983, Jordan's cabinet announced that Jordan would not participate in the peace process, and could not and would not negotiate on behalf of the Palestinians because Hussein was unable to reach agreement with Arafat, apparently because of the veto by the radical elements of the PLO of a tentative Hussein-Arafat agreement. Arafat told Hussein that he would not sign the joint communiqué that would have allowed Hussein to lead a Jordanian-Palestinian delegation to negotiate under the terms of the Reagan initiative. Jordan noted, with some exasperation and frustration, "we leave it to the PLO and the Palestinian people to choose the ways and means for the salvation of themselves and their land, and for the realization of their declared aims in the manner they see fit."

The cabinet statement reviewed Jordan's role in the peace process and focused on the fact that it had considered the "political option" and Resolution 242 as prime factors in the process to recover Arab territories occupied through military aggression by Israel. It noted that Jordan found that the

Reagan plan "contained a number of positive elements" and that it "presented the vehicle that could propel the Fez peace plan forward, and Jordan proceeded to explore this possibility." As a result of the PLO's decision, "We in Jordan, having refused from the beginning to negotiate on behalf of the Palestinians, will neither act separately nor in lieu of anybody in Middle East peace negotiations."[64]

Israel reacted to Hussein's statement with satisfaction and relief. The satisfaction was a result of its view that Hussein would reject the offer to negotiate. Israel had disagreed with the United States concerning the possibility of Hussein's accepting the offer to participate; the sanguine U.S. approach was viewed with skepticism in Israel, and Hussein's announcement vindicated the Israeli assessment. There was also a degree of relief that the difficult issues involved in West Bank negotiations would not have to be confronted at that time. Israel had been "let off the hook," in that it would not have to respond to the pressures, from both the United States and the Israeli body politic, that would have followed a positive decision by Hussein. U.S. pressures to be "forthcoming" in response to Hussein probably would have included an effort to have Israel refrain from settlement activity in the West Bank. Hussein's decision removed the prospect of pressure and allowed Israel to pursue its own course with regard to the area, at least for the time being. It meant that the United States would have to identify a potential negotiating partner if it wished to make progress toward an Arab-Israeli settlement.

At the same time Issam Sartawi, a noted Palestinian who had met with Israelis and was seen as a leader of the more "moderate" elements within the PLO, was shot and killed in Portugal, apparently by a member of a more radical Palestinian faction. This was seen as a warning to Hussein and Arafat. Despite the Hussein announcement, and its emphasis by the killing of Sartawi, the Reagan administration stated that it was "hopeful" that the process might be continued. The basis for this somewhat optimistic statement was difficult to identify; it reflected the fact that the administration could not admit defeat of a proposal that it saw as a significant foreign policy achievement and for which there was no viable alternative.

MAINTAINING THE INITIATIVE

By the latter part of April 1983, the Reagan administration was faced with a significant dilemma. Hussein refused to participate, and progress on discussions for the withdrawal of foreign forces from Lebanon was slow.

The direct U.S. involvement in the region was growing and becoming more dangerous. The terrorist attack on the American Embassy in Beirut in April, with a substantial loss of life, raised questions about the U.S. involvement. It prompted some members of Congress to call for the withdrawal of the marines from their peacekeeping activities but strengthened Reagan's resolve to continue the effort; he noted that it would not deter the United States from carrying out its search for peace. The administration was also subjected to substantial criticism of its handling of the initiative. One particularly caustic commentary said: ". . . President Reagan's Middle East initiative was a model of disaster in its execution. Before it got the *coup de Grace* from the P.L.O., it had been fatally weakened by the inept, uninformed, half-hearted diplomacy of the President and Secretary of State Schultz. They were not serious."[65]

In an effort to resuscitate the initiative, the president blamed the impasse on the radical elements in the PLO and decided to send Shultz to the region. He would focus on the withdrawal of foreign forces from Lebanon, but also would consult on the status of the broader initiative. Shultz began by holding exploratory meetings with Begin and Gemayel, in an effort to achieve better understanding of their positions. His shuttle diplomacy sought to reconcile their perspectives and led to an agreement after some 35 sessions of Israeli-Lebanese negotiations, conducted over several months by U.S. ambassadors Habib and Draper.

The Israel-Lebanon agreement did not constitute a "peace treaty" but the countries agreed "to respect the sovereignty, political independence and territorial integrity of each other," and to "confirm that the state of war between Israel and Lebanon has been terminated and no longer exists." The "existing international boundary between Israel and Lebanon" was to be the border between the two states. Israel undertook "to withdraw all its armed forces from Lebanon." Both agreed to refrain from various hostile actions, including hostile propaganda, against each other.

A Joint Liaison Committee, in which the United States would participate, was to be established and "entrusted with the supervision of the implementation of all areas covered by the present agreement." To carry out its functions under the agreement, each party, if it desired, "may maintain a liaison office on the territory of the other party." An annex concerning security arrangements, which provided for the establishment of a "security region," was specifically delineated in the agreement. "The Lebanese authorities will enforce special security measures aimed at detecting and preventing hostile activities as well as the introduction into or movement through the Security Region of unauthorized armed men or military equipment."

The forces permitted were specifically defined. A Security Arrangements Committee, operating within the framework of the Joint Liaison Committee, would be established to supervise the implementation of the security arrangements contained in the agreement and its annex. Joint supervisory teams (Israel-Lebanon) "will conduct regular verification of the implementation of the provisions of the security arrangements in the agreement and this annex." The annex provided that "within 8 to 12 weeks of the entry into force of the present agreement, all Israeli forces will have been withdrawn from Lebanon. This is consistent with the objective of Lebanon that all external forces withdraw from Lebanon." The United States assured Israel that it was not obliged to begin a pullout until Syria and the PLO did.[66]

On May 17 Israel and Lebanon signed the U.S.-mediated agreement, in the Israeli town of Kiryat Shmona and at Khalda in Lebanon, in four languages: English and French (the binding versions), Hebrew, and Arabic. U.S. Ambassador Morris Draper noted:

> The goal of the United States in the future will be to assure that this agreement is carried out efficiently in the spirit of full cooperation as attested by the recent visit to the area by Secretary of State Shultz, as well as by the consistent view of President Reagan. The United States will not take its responsibility lightly.[67]

The Lebanese representative, Antoine Fattal, said: "If we today are signing this agreement . . . it is because Lebanon is in need of urgent tranquility and order. Lebanon wants to survive."[68] The Israeli negotiator, David Kimche, said that the accord marked "a beginning of a new chapter in our histories" and called on Syrian President Assad to withdraw his forces from Lebanon. Reagan hailed the agreement as "a significant step forward" and said "we have crossed an important threshold in the path to peace. . . . It can lead to the restoration of Lebanon's sovereignty throughout its territory while also insuring that southern Lebanon will not again become a base for hostile actions against Israel."[69]

Subsequently, Shultz met with Syrian president Assad and Saudi Arabian officials. He told reporters that Syria had "a legitimate point" in questioning whether the establishment of an Israeli security zone in southern Lebanon threatened Syrian security, but he remained optimistic and pledged that, despite "difficulties ahead," the United States would continue to do "everything we can" to settle the crisis. Israeli Foreign Minister Shamir said that Shultz's shuttle diplomacy had "succeeded in bridging some of the differences which prevail between Lebanon and Israel. I believe that the agreement we reached with your aid, if it will be scrupulously kept by all parties, has achieved that goal" of peace and sovereignty for Lebanon and security for Israel's northern border. He also noted that "Israel for its part will implement this agreement as soon as possible" and that implementation "will depend on the positions of the other camps, the PLO and the Syrian army."[70]

Syria rejected the agreement, and Palestinian leaders, meeting in Damascus, also opposed it. Syria objected to the Israeli security presence in southern Lebanon, claiming that it infringed on Lebanese sovereignty and Syrian security. Despite the professed concern for the future of Lebanon, Assad's motives seemed more Syria-oriented. Syria sought to regain the Golan Heights, and if this was not possible through a process such as that proposed by the Reagan initiative, then it would play the "spoiler" by preventing negotiations. Assad wanted to ensure that any negotiations would take Syria's concerns into account and that Syria's leadership of the negotiating team and control of its positions would be assured. Syria also sought to maintain (and enhance) its role and influence in Lebanon, a historical aspect of the Syria-Lebanon relationship that harks back to the period when Lebanon was a part of greater Syria. There was concern that Israeli or pro-Israeli control of the Bekaa Valley and the contiguous areas would provide relatively easy military access to Damascus in the event of conflict. Despite his opposition to the agreement, Assad sought to avoid a direct conflict with Israel, if Syria could not be assured of additional Arab support, thereby avoiding a repeat of the losses suffered during the 1982 war.

The Soviet Union's negative reaction was multifaceted. On May 9 Tass issued a statement in which it charged that the United States and Israel were "grossly violating" Lebanese territory, and it demanded the "unconditional withdrawal" of Israeli troops from Lebanon as the "first and foremost" condition for bringing peace to that country. It insisted that U.S. and other foreign troops should be withdrawn so that Lebanon would be free of all foreign troops, and could be united and independent. The Soviets also charged that Israel was preparing another Middle Eastern war. Soviet support for the Syrian position took the form of statements as well as continued military supply (and military advisers) and economic assistance.

The agreement, accompanied by Syria's rejection of it with strong Soviet support, had a positive effect on U.S.-Israel relations.

Subsequently Reagan said he would lift the ban on the sale to Israel of 75 F-16 aircraft, which he had held up in the wake of Israel's invasion of Lebanon and the subsequent retention of its troops there. Reagan had hailed the agreement as a "positive step," and Shultz said there was no longer any reason to hold up the planes. During Shultz's shuttle effort there had been indications that the aircraft had been an indirect inducement for Israel's acceptance of the accord, although it was denied that he had made any direct offers of aid to secure Israel's assent.

Reagan's decision appeared to be influenced by the increased Soviet support for Syria and the substantial Soviet military resupply and troop presence there. Defense Secretary Weinberger earlier had told the House Foreign Affairs Committee that the "additional threat" posed by a Soviet-backed military buildup in Syria heightened the need for Israel to have advanced warplanes. Weinberger seemed to modify his views of Israel, and noted the strong bonds between the two states and Israel's strategic value. He also said that "the revival or restitution of that memorandum [the memorandum of understanding on strategic cooperation of 1981] could take place at virtually any time, depending on the wishes of the Israeli Government."[71]

Improved relations between the United States and Israel reflected their congruent positions on the regional situation and the fact that there were no outstanding major issues of controversy between them, although it did not mean that they agreed on all elements of the relationship, or on all aspects of the situation in the Middle East.

Shultz returned to the Middle East in early July, following a long-planned visit to Asia, and met with a number of regional leaders, including King Fahd, President Gemayel, King Hussein, President Mubarak, President Assad, and with the Israelis, but failed to achieve any agreement concerning the withdrawal of Syrian troops from Lebanon or Arab acceptance of the Israel-Lebanon agreement. The Arab leaders proved unable or unwilling to exert any influence on Assad to accept the withdrawal agreement, and thus the simultaneous withdrawal of Israeli, Syrian, and PLO forces from Lebanon. Shultz summarized his discussions thus: "I wish I could report that somehow we see progress in the direction of simultaneous [Syrian and Israeli] withdrawal as we wish to see, but I can't give any such report."[72]

Subsequently Israel decided "to begin its part of the general withdrawal by redeploying its own forces further south, along a line following the Awali River." This decision reflected political, military, and economic factors, and would reduce Israel's casualties and costs while awaiting Syria's (and the PLO's) willingness to withdraw. The United States had to agree to the plan despite its (and Lebanese) preference that Israel's troops continue to serve as a buffer, and peacemaker, between warring Lebanese factions. The issue was complicated by the continuing power struggle within the PLO and within the Arab world concerning that organization's future.

The projected visit of Menachem Begin to Washington at the end of July 1983 was canceled by Begin, for "personal reasons." Reagan then invited Israel's minister of defense and former ambassador to Washington, Moshe Arens, and Israel's minister of foreign affairs, Yitzhak Shamir, to Washington for discussions concerning Lebanon, especially the Israeli redeployment, and the overall peace process. They reassured the administration that the redeployment would not lead to a de facto partition of Lebanon, and that it was the first phase in a total withdrawal of Israeli forces that would occur with the withdrawal of Syrian and PLO forces from Lebanon.

The first anniversary of the "fresh start" initiative was not particularly auspicious. No negotiations had begun under its auspices. Hussein, after months of deliberation, had refused to participate, and no other Arab interlocutor was prepared to come forward. The problems of Lebanon, which had become a surrogate for the initiative, showed some amelioration but no dramatic breakthrough. The Israel-Lebanon agreement was an important accomplishment, but it was virtually stillborn as a result of Syrian, PLO, and Soviet opposition. Progress was made on extending the authority of the Gemayel government beyond small sectors of Beirut, on rebuilding the Lebanese army to establish broader central government authority, and on the reconstuction of Lebanon, but this was limited and slow.

U.S.-Israel relations, which had been seriously impaired by the war, the massacre, and the Israeli rejection of the Reagan initiative, and by a host of lesser events, returned to their former level. There were no major issues of controversy, given the absence of a substantive peace effort where the differing views of the two parties might clash. Despite increasing concern with other issues, such as Central America and Chad, Reagan remained committed to resolution of the problems of Lebanon and to the broader peace process. A restructured American "team," which included new special negotiators, a new assistant secretary of state (Richard Murphy), and a number of ambassadorial shifts and new appointments (including Nicholas Veliotes in Cairo), was put in place. Robert C. McFarlane, deputy national security adviser, was named to replace Philip Habib as special negotiator, and he made an initial visit to the Middle East at the beginning of August 1983 to assess the situation, but no substantial results were achieved. Later, when he became Reagan's National Security adviser, Donald Rumsfeld became the special negotiator.

Menachem Begin's decision to resign as prime minister of Israel, announced in late August 1983, suggested the prospect of some alteration in the style of U.S.-Israel relations but no substantial alteration in their content. The effort to resolve the Arab-Israeli conflict remained the focus of the Reagan administration's Middle East policy as well as of Israel's government. The continuing peace process, and the regional and international content in which it would be pursued, suggested that U.S.-Israel relations would not deviate substantially from the course established by the summer of 1983.

SOME OBSERVATIONS

The relationship during the Reagan years was complex. Israel and the United States clashed over divergent interpretations of the regional situation, of the peace process, and of Israel's security needs. Israel struck at the Iraqi reactor and at PLO positions in Beirut, and took action on other issues where it believed its national interest was at stake, even when it understood this would lead to clashes with the United States. The United States could react, but could not alter the Israeli decisions. On less central issues, such as Israel's withdrawal to more secure lines in Lebanon in 1983, Israel deferred to U.S. entreaties. Similarly, Israel was able to respond to Shultz's shuttle to achieve an agreement between Israel and Lebanon because it believed that such an agreement was in its interest, because it wanted to be responsive to Shultz's effort, and because it would refurbish its peace-oriented image. U.S. reassurances played a significant role; after the agreement was signed, Reagan lifted the ban on the sale to Israel of F-16 aircraft that had been held in abeyance.

The AWACS clash demonstrated another element of influence. Israel was restrained in responding to the AWACS sale because of a desire not to confront the president directly, once he had made it a matter of personal and presidential prestige, and to avoid striking at the core of the relationship. Its supporters were careful to avoid the possible anti-Semitic repercussions of a presidential defeat. At the same time, reassurances once again proved important.

The Reagan administration's relations with Israel went through a series of alterations, but the main watershed was the war in Lebanon. The war and associated developments called into question various aspects of the links between the two states. However, following the failure of Hussein to join the peace process and with the increased Soviet involvement in Syria, the Lebanon-Israel accord, and the Syrian-Soviet opposition to it, the U.S.-Israel relationship reverted to its previous positive levels. Israel was able to influence the tenor of the ties by taking advantage of public sympathy following the Kahan report and the increased involvement of the Soviet Union, which generated further support for Israel. The relationship appeared to come full circle by the summer of 1983, when the two states seemed linked by a congruence of policy that included recognition of Israel's strategic anti-Soviet value and its desire for peaceful resolution of the Arab-Israeli conflict. This comported with Reagan's initial perceptions of Israel and its position in the Middle East, and suggested a period of positive relations between the United States and Israel.

NOTES

1. Quoted in Hedrick Smith, "Reagan: What Kind of World Leader?" *New York Times Magazine,* Nov. 16, 1980, pp. 174-75.

2. Ibid., p. 175.

3. Ibid.

4. Quoted in *Near East Report,* Jan. 9, 1980, p. 7. See also *Near East Report,* Mar. 19, 1980, pp. 51-52.

5. *New York Times,* Jan. 29, 1981.

6. Quoted in *Washington Post,* Dec. 23, 1980.

7. Reagan interview, *U.S. News and World Report,* Jan. 19, 1981, p. 26.

8. Reagan press conference, Nov. 6, 1980, in *New York Times,* Nov. 7, 1980.

9. Ronald Reagan, "Recognizing the Israeli Asset," *Washington Post,* Aug. 15, 1979.

10. *New York Times,* Feb. 3, 1981.

11. *New York Times,* March 20, 1981.

12. "Middle East Regional Security" (Washington, D.C.: Bureau of Public Affairs, Department of State, Mar. 23, 1981).

13. Jewish Telegraphic Agency (JTA), *Daily News Bulletin,* June 16, 1981, p. 2.

14. *Washington Post,* June 10, 1981.

15. "Department Statement," *Department of State Bulletin,* Aug. 1981, p. 79.

16. *New York Times,* June 10, 1981.

17. U.S. Congress, House Committee on Foreign Affairs, *Hearings, Israeli Attack on Iraqi Nuclear Facilities,* 97th Cong., 1st Sess., 1981, p. 3. Washington: U.S. Government Printing Office, 1981.

18. "Secretary's Letter to the Congress," *Department of State Bulletin,* Aug. 1981, p. 79.

19. Larry M. Speakes, "Situation in the Middle East: Statement by Deputy Press Secretary," *Weekly Compilation of Presidential Documents (WCPD),* June 15, 1981, p. 614.

20. JTA, *Daily News Bulletin,* July 15, 1981, p. 3.

21. *New York Times,* June 20, 1981.

22. Quoted in JTA, *Daily News Bulletin,* July 27, 1981, p. 1.

23. *New York Times,* July 21, 1981.

24. Interview on "Nightline," July 20, 1981, in *Department of State Bulletin,* Sept. 1981, p. 29.

25. Interview with Haig on CBS "Morning News," July 24, 1981, in *Department of State Bulletin,* Sept. 1981, p. 59.

26. *New York Times,* July 18, 1981.

27. Quoted in JTA, *Daily News Bulletin,* July 22, 1981, p. 3.

28. "U.S. Lifts Suspension of Aircraft to Israel: Secretary's Announcement," Aug. 17, 1981, *Department of State Bulletin,* Oct. 1981, p. 61.

29. *New York Times,* Aug. 17, 1981.

30. JTA, *Daily News Bulletin,* Aug. 12, 1981, p. 1.

31. Ibid., p. 2.

32. *New York Times,* Oct. 29, 1981.

33. *New York Times*, Oct. 20, 1981.

34. Stephen S. Rosenfeld, "Dateline Washington: Anti-Semitism and U.S. Foreign Policy," *Foreign Policy* no. 47 (Summer 1982): 172-83, pp. 174-75.

35. *New York Times*, Oct. 30, 1981.

36. The text of the agreement is in *New York Times*, Dec. 1, 1981.

37. The full text of the statement is in *New York Times*, Dec. 21, 1981.

38. JTA, *Daily News Bulletin*, Jan. 11, 1982, p. 1.

39. "Israel in the Middle East," address by Dr. David Kimche at the Royal Institute of International Affairs, Chatam House, London, Nov. 2, 1982, pp. 2, 4.

40. *Jerusalem Post* (int. ed.), Aug. 29-Sept. 4, 1982, p. 3.

41. Zeev Schiff, "The Green Light," *Foreign Policy* no. 50 (Spring 1983): 73-85, p. 73.

42. Ibid., p. 85. He has accurately described the situation in these terms: "Washington knew what was about to happen. It possessed information in abundance about Israel's intentions and operational plans for Lebanon. Israel's incursion into Lebanon did not come as a surprise. Then Israeli Defense Minister Ariel Sharon did not hand the Pentagon his specific war plans, but there is no doubt that Washington, through its contacts, was well apprised of the plans before they were implemented. Washington knew about the highly visible concentration of forces on the borders of Lebanon and that Israel intended to invade Lebanon with a large army. Thus Washington's vague murmurings and apparent indifference were interpreted by the Israeli government as a green light for Operation Peace for Galilee." Ibid., p. 74.

43. *Department of State Bulletin*, Sept. 1982, p. 22.

44. For the text of the Reagan initiative, see "A New Opportunity for Peace in the Middle East," Department of State, *Current Policy* no.417 (Sept. 1, 1982) and *New York Times*, Sept. 2, 1982. For a "semiofficial" argument in support of the proposal, see Alan J. Kreczko, "Support Reagan's Initiative," *Foreign Policy* no. 49 (Winter 1982-83): 140-53.

45. "A New Opportunity for Peace in the Middle East."

46. Reagan question-and-answer session, July 1, 1982, *Weekly Compilation of Presidential Documents*, July 5, 1982, p. 862.

47. See, for example, the Shultz interview on "Today," Sept. 21, 1982; *New York Times* report on official comments and the Bush address, Sept. 23, 1982; Nicholas

Veliotes, on "Meet the Press," Sept. 26, 1982, where he evades the question; and Reagan's news conference of Sept. 27, 1982.

48. See *New York Times* and *Washington Post,* Sept. 10, 1982.

49. Sol Linowitz, "An Old Pro's View," *Newsweek,* Sept. 13, 1982, p. 31.

50. The matter was particularly significant. Henry Kissinger spelled out this factor: "Having taken the unprecedented step of introducing a plan without consultation with Israel, we have to be careful not to turn an emergency measure into a regular procedure. Opposition to Israel must not become a congenital feature of our foreign policy lest we break Israel's back psychologically. This is not the case now; I am simply warning against turning what was a probably unavoidable first step into a permanent feature of our diplomacy." Interview with Henry Kissinger, *The Economist,* Nov. 13, 1982, p. 28.

51. See Shimon Peres, "A Strategy for Peace in the Middle East," *Foreign Affairs,* 58 (Spring 1980): 887-901.

52. *Weekly Compilation of Presidential Documents,* Dec. 27, 1982, p. 1658.

53. *New York Times,* Jan. 26, 1983.

54. *Weekly Compilation of Presidential Documents,* Sept. 6, 1982.

55. Quoted in *New York Times,* Sept. 11, 1982.

56. Secretary of State George Shultz, "The Quest for Peace," Department of State, *Current Policy* no. 419 (Sept. 1982): p. 3.

57. *New York Times,* Sept. 15, 1982.

58. *Weekly Compilation of Presidential Documents,* Dec. 27, 1982, p. 1646.

59. Ibid., p. 1661.

60. See Karen Elliott House, "Hussein's Decision," *Wall Street Journal,* April 14 and 15, 1983.

61. *Weekly Compilation of Presidential Documents,* Feb. 28, 1983, p. 275.

62. *New York Times,* Apr. 1, 1983.

63. *New York Times,* Apr. 9, 1983.

64. The full text of the Jordanian cabinet statement of Apr. 10, 1983, on King Hussein's refusal to join the Reagan initiative is in *New York Times,* Apr. 11, 1983.

65. Anthony Lewis, "The Bungled Initiative," *New York Times,* Apr. 24, 1983.

66. *New York Times,* May 17, 1983, and May 18, 1983.

67. *New York Times,* May 18, 1983.

68. Ibid.

69. Ibid.

70. *New York Times* and *Washington Post,* May 10, 1983.

71. *New York Times,* June 15, 1983.

72. Quoted in *Washington Post,* July 8, 1983.

4

ECONOMIC AND MILITARY ASSISTANCE

U.S. economic and military assistance to Israel has become a salient aspect of the relationship, particularly since the October War. From 1949 to 1983 U.S. aid totaled more than $25 billion, including more than $16.5 billion in military loans and grants; more than $6.5 billion in economic loans and grants under the Security Assistance Program; and more than $2 billion in other programs, including Food for Peace, housing guarantees, Export-Import Bank loans, and aid for resettling Soviet Jews (see Tables 4.1 and 4.2).

Aid for Israel has evolved from a rather modest, primarily economic effort to a substantial and multifaceted program. Between 1946 and 1971 the overwhelming portion of aid was economic, and most of that was loans. The military portion also was in the form of loans. U.S. aid was not the major source of assistance—German reparations, United Jewish Appeal funds, sales of Israel bonds, and direct foreign investments were the major sources of capital imports for Israel. Military aid was provided primarily by other countries, especially France. The program shifted in the 1970s. The total amount of U.S. aid climbed dramatically, and much of it was military assistance. The turning point was the October War, although other factors, including the long-time high levels of defense expenditures and substantial external debt incurred by Israel, were elements in the equation even prior to the conflict.

Since the 1973 war Israel's need for both economic and military assistance has grown considerably, in spite of the economic progress it has made. Its increased needs primarily are a result of the growth of military expenditure, the rise in the price of oil and other essential imports, and the

TABLE 4.1 U.S. Loans and Grants to Israel: 1946-82 (U.S. Fiscal Years; millions of dollars)

Program	Postwar Relief (1946-48)	Marshall Plan (1949-52)	Mutual Security Act (1953-61)	Foreign 1962-78	1979
I. Econ. assist.—total	—	86.5	507.1	3,393.6	790.1
Loans	—	—	248.3	1,330.6	265.1
Grants	—	86.5	258.8	2,063.0	525.0
A. Aid and predecessor	—	63.7	311.5	2,935.4	785.0
Loans	—	—	96.0	900.5	260.0
Grants	—	63.7	215.5	2,034.9	525.0
(Sec. supp. asst.)	(—)	(—)	(—)	(2,769.5)	(785.0)
B. Food for Peace	—	22.7	195.6	458.2	5.1
Loans	—	—	152.3	430.1	5.1
Grants	—	22.7	43.3	28.1	—
Title I—Total	—	—	165.1	448.6	5.1
Repay. in $—loans	—	—	—	335.1	5.1
Pay. in. for. curr.	—	—	165.1	113.5	—
Title II—Total	—	22.7	30.5	9.6	—
E. Rel, ec. deu. & WFP	—	—	—	2.2	—
Vol. Relief Agency	—	22.7	30.5	7.4	—
C. Other econ. assist.	—	0.1	—	—	—
Loans	—	—	—	—	—
Grants	—	0.1	—	—	—
Peace Corps	—	—	—	—	—
Narcotics	—	—	—	—	—
Other	—	0.1	—	—	—
II. Mil. assist.—total	—	—	0.9	7,911.6	4,000.0
Loans	—	—	0.9	4,461.6	2,700.0
Grants	—	—	—	3,450.0	1,300.0
A. Map grants	—	—	—	—	—
B. Credit financing	—	—	0.9	4,461.6	2,700.0
C. Intl. mil. ed. trng.	—	—	—	—	—
D. Tran.—excess stock	—	—	—	—	—
E. Other grants	—	—	—	3,450.0	1,300.0
III. Total econ. & mil.	—	86.5	508.0	11,305.2	4,790.1
Loans	—	—	249.2	5,792.2	2,965.1
Grants	—	86.5	258.8	5,513.0	1,825.0
Other U.S. Loans	—	135.0	57.5	412.5	68.7
Ex.-Im. Bank loans	—	135.0	57.5	412.5	68.7
All other	—	—	—	—	—

*Details may not add to totals due to rounding.

**Values in these columns are net of deobligations.

Assistance Act (FAA)			Total FAA	Total Loans and Grants	Repayments and Interest	Total Less Repayments and Interest
1980	1981	1982	(1962-82)	(1946-82)	(1946-82)	(1946-82)
				**		**
786.0	764.0	806.0	6,539.7	7,156.0	850.2	6,305.8
261.0	—	—	1,856.7	2,079.6	850.2	1,229.4
525.0	764.0	806.0	4,683.0	5,076.4	—	5,076.4
785.0	764.0	806.0	6,075.4	6,491.8	367.8	6,124.0
260.0	—	—	1,420.5	1,509.3	367.8	1,141.5
525.0	764.0	806.0	4,654.9	4,982.5	—	4,982.5
(785.0)	(764.0)	(806.0)	(5,909.5)	(5,909.5)		
1.0	—	—	464.3	664.1	482.4	181.7
1.0	—	—	436.2	570.3	482.4	87.9
—	—	—	28.1	93.8	—	93.8
1.0	—	—	454.7	601.7	482.4	119.3
1.0	—	—	341.2	323.1	216.5	106.6
—	—	—	113.5	278.6	265.9	12.7
—	—	—	9.6	62.4	—	62.4
—	—	—	2.2	2.2	—	2.2
—	—	—	7.4	60.2	—	60.2
—	—	—	—	0.1	—	0.1
—	—	—	—	—	—	—
—	—	—	—	0.1	—	0.1
—	—	—	—	—	—	—
—	—	—	—	—	—	—
—	—	—	—	0.1	—	0.1
1,000.0	1,400.0	1,400.0	15,711.6	15,704.2	3,306.6	12,397.6
500.0	900.0	850.0	9,411.6	9,404.2	3,306.6	6,097.6
500.0	500.0	550.0	6,300.0	6,300.0	—	6,300.0
—	—	—	—	—	—	—
500.0	900.0	850.0	9,411.6	9,404.2	3,306.6	6,097.6
—	—	—	—	—	—	—
500.0	500.0	550.0	6,300.0	6,300.0	—	6,300.0
1,786.0	2,164.0	2,206.0	22,251.3	22,860.2	4,156.8	18,703.4
761.0	900.0	850.0	11.268.3	11,483.8	4,156.8	7,327.0
1,025.0	1,264.0	1,356.0	10,983.0	11,376.4	—	11,376.4
305.9	217.4	24.0	1,028.5	1,139.4	673.0	466.4
305.9	217.4	6.5	1,011.0	1,121.9	671.1	450.8
—	—	17.5	17.5	17.5	1.9	15.6

Source: Agency for International Development, "U.S. Overseas Loans and Grants and Assistance," in *International Organizations, Obligations and Loan Authorizations, July 1, 1945-September 30, 1982* (1983), p. 18. (Washington: Agency for International Development, 1983).

TABLE 4.2 U.S. Assistance to Israel, 1948-83 (millions of dollars)

Year	Total U.S. Aid[1]	Total U.S. Aid to Israel	Economic Loans to Israel
1948	3,017	—	—
1949	8,267	—	—
1950	4,850	—	—
1951	4,380	0.1	—
1952	3,839	86.4	—
1953	6,496	73.6	—
1954	5,793	74.7	—
1955	4,864	52.7	30.8
1956	5,402	50.8	35.2
1957	4,976	40.9	21.8
1958	4,832	61.2	49.9
1959	4,954	50.3	39.0
1960	4,804	55.7	41.8
1961	4,737	48.1	29.8
1962	7,034	83.9	63.5
1963	7,314	76.7	57.4
1964	5,215	37.0	32.2
1965	5,310	61.7	43.9
1966	6,989	126.8	35.9
1967	6,440	13.1	5.5
1968	6,894	76.8	51.3
1969	6,791	121.7	36.1
1970	6,787	71.1	40.7
1971	8,078	600.8	55.5
1972	9,243	404.2	53.8
1973	9,875	467.3	59.4
1974	8,978	2,570.7	—
1975	7,239	693.1	8.6
1976	6,413	2,229.4	239.4
TQ	2,603	278.6	28.6
1977	7,784	1,757.0	252.0
1978	9,014	1,811.8	266.8
1979	13,845	4,815.1	265.1
1980	9,694	1,811.0	261.0
1981	10,549	2,189.0	0
1982	12,076	2,219.0	0
1983	12,744	2,497.5	0
Total	258,120	25,607.8	2,105.0

[1]Does not include Export-Import Bank loans.
[2]Less than $50,000.
[3]This figure includes $21 million in economic assistance reprogrammed from the Israeli account in FY81.

TQ = Transitional Quarter.

Source: Agency for International Development, *U.S. Overseas Loans and Grants from International Organizations* (annual). (Washington: Agency for International Development)

Economic Grants to Israel	Military Loans to Israel	Military Grants to Israel	Soviet Jewry Resettlement Funds
—	—	—	—
—	—	—	—
—	—	—	—
0.1	—	—	—
86.4	—	—	—
73.6	—	—	—
74.7	—	—	—
21.9	—	—	—
15.6	—	—	—
19.1	—	—	—
11.3	—	—	—
10.9	0.4	—	—
13.4	0.5	—	—
18.3	**[2]	—	—
7.2	13.2	—	—
6.0	13.3	—	—
4.8	—	—	—
4.9	12.9	—	—
0.9	90.0	—	—
0.6	7.0	—	—
0.5	25.0	—	—
0.6	85.0	—	—
0.4	30.0	—	—
0.3	545.0	—	—
50.4	300.0	—	—
50.4	307.5	—	50.0
51.5	982.7	1,500.0	36.5
344.5	200.0	100.0	40.0
475.0	750.0	750.0	15.0
50.0	100.0	100.0	0
490.0	500.0	500.0	15.0
525.0	500.0	500.0	20.0
525.0	2,700.0	1,300.0	25.0
525.0	500.0	500.0	25.0
764.0	900.0	500.0	25.0
806.0[3]	850.0	550.0	13.0
785.0	950.0	750.0	12.5
5,792.3	10,362.5	7,050.0	

growing burden of external debt service, although domestic economic policies have played a role as well. Since 1974 almost half of the military assistance has been grant aid; and since 1979 economic aid has been a cash transfer unlinked to specific projects or commodity imports, although it must be used for nonmilitary purposes. By 1983 U.S. military assistance to Israel exceeded assistance to any other country.

The rationale for U.S. assistance has been framed in terms of promoting peace through the commitment to the security and well-being of Israel, as well as to developing confidence, maintaining a friendly relationship, and helping to maintain Israel's military edge over its hostile neighbors. It is argued that Israel must be sufficiently confident of its ability to defend itself if it is to take the risks necessary to make peace.

ECONOMIC ASSISTANCE

In Israel's early years U.S. economic assistance sought to "promote the continued peaceful development of the country economically, socially, and politically toward stability and strength."[1] Specific objectives included the development of essential industries and agriculture, an increase in industrial output and productivity, the development of natural resources, and the attraction of capital investment and private enterprise. The aid was especially important during the first years following independence because the development of a viable economy was essential. The bulk of the grants-in-aid were for refugee relief and resettlement, but they also helped to strengthen Israel's foreign-exchange position and to provide funds for the importation of basic supplies. Domestic economic expansion was further aided by the U.S. technical assistance program, while agricultural and industrial development were facilitated by Export-Import Bank loans. Purchases of U.S. agricultural surpluses helped Israel meet its domestic needs and conserved much-needed foreign exchange. American specialists advised Israel in various technical areas, and trainees were sent to the United States for specialized education.

The U.S. Operations Mission, which originally administered U .S. technical and economic assistance, dealt with a wide variety of programs and areas: agriculture, fisheries, and forestry; commerce and industry; public health and sanitation; national financial management; education and vocational training; transportation and communications; survey, development, and use of natural resources, including metallic and nonmetallic minerals, water, and power; housing; and manpower and labor. "Virtually every phase of Israel's life, directly or indirectly, was touched by the progress made in these fields."[2]

The success of the U.S. aid program was highlighted when technical assistance to Israel was terminated by mutual agreement on June 30, 1962. Fowler Hamilton, administrator of the Agency for International Development, summed up the U.S. Technical Assistance Program for Israel in these terms:

> In the eleven years since the program was started, American specialists have made important contributions to the development of effective institutions in Israel. Scores of Americans went to Israel to assist in training people in agricultural, irrigation, health, and education methods. As the economy developed, attention was shifted to industry, transportation, mineral development, and public administration. Israeli specialists were sent to the United States to study American methods and techniques. The country has made great strides in agriculture and industry. It has attained a high degree of self-sufficiency in growing food products. Its transportation system is modern, efficient, and growing. Israel continues to receive United States aid in the form of loans and surplus agricultural commodities.[3]

Immediately prior to and following the June War, U.S. economic aid was circumscribed in type and amount, and primarily took the form of sales of agricultural commodities.

In the wake of the June and October wars, however, economic assistance again became a matter of some significance, but the focus was different from that in the earlier period. Israel had achieved a substantial degree of development, and its main areas of need were the defense burden (especially the increasingly high cost of modern and sophisticated weaponry) and humanitarian problems, such as the immigration and integration of Soviet Jews. U.S. assistance focused on these two areas. Both the executive branch and Congress believed that continued economic assistance at substantial levels was essential and should be made available. Thus, for example, the joint U.S.-Israeli statement issued at the conclusion of President Nixon's visit to Israel, in June 1974, said:

> President Nixon affirmed the strong continuing support of the United States for Israel's economic development. Prime Minister Rabin expressed the gratitude of Israel for the substantial help which the United States has provided, particularly in recent years. The President and Prime Minister agreed that future economic assistance from the United

States would continue and would be the subject of long-range planning between their governments. The President affirmed that the United States, in accordance with Congressional authorization, will continue to provide substantial economic assistance for Israel at levels needed to assist Israel to offset the heavy additional costs inherent in assuring Israel's military capability for the maintenance of peace.[4]

Between 1972 and 1982 the United States provided Israel with nearly $6 billion under the Security Supporting Assistance program and through the Economic Support Fund (ESF). ESF aid to Israel has been the largest program and is provided under liberal terms. Since 1981 the program has been an all-grant transfer of dollars, provided in support of Israel's economy and to help Israel deal with its balance-of-payments problems. None of the ESF aid is tied to specific development projects.[5]

More recently, American economic assistance to Israel has focused on Security Supporting Assistance, which was initiated by the earmarking of $50 million in the fiscal 1972 Foreign Assistance Appropriations Act. This was in response to Israel's request for aid for foreign exchange and other needs related to Middle East hostilities.

Until 1975 U.S. assistance was on a grant basis; in 1976 a mix of one-third concessional loans and two-thirds grants was introduced in recognition of Israel's ability to pay for a portion of U.S. foreign aid. The 1973 and 1974 funds served primarily to bolster Israel's balance-of-payments position. The higher aid levels since 1975 were to help the Israeli economy recover from the effects of the 1973 war and to maintain a positive climate for Middle East peace, including support for the Sinai II agreement.

In support of Sinai II, the United States has provided high levels of aid to both Egypt and Israel. Aid for Israel stems in part from a separate U.S.-Israeli agreement, which states that the United States will make every effort to be fully responsive, within the limits of its resources and congressional authorization and appropriations, on an ongoing and long-term basis, to Israel's military equipment and other defense requirements, to its energy requirements, and to its economic needs.

Security Supporting Assistance to Israel has consisted of the Commodity Import Program (CIP) and a cash grant. Under the CIP the United States reimburses Israel for the foreign exchange used to purchase non-military U.S. commodities. The cash grant, introduced in fiscal 1976, is essentially unrestricted aid, although by formal agreement it is to be spent for nonmilitary commodities used within the pre-1967 boundaries of Israel. The Agency for International Development (AID) writes quarterly checks payable to Israel, and there is no requirement to account for how the funds are spent. However, Israel provides the U.S. annually with a letter stating that it will purchase from the U.S. goods equal to or greater than the value of ESF provided.

The cash grant was initially justified as helping Israel to meet the indirect costs associated with implementation of Sinai II, which included extraordinary costs necessitated by the Israeli redeployment from the Suez Canal area, increased imports of oil as a result of Israel's return of Sinai oil fields, and increased oil storage capacity in Israel. In September 1977 Congress was advised that the original Sinai-related goals had been largely accomplished. A portion of the CIP funds ($150 million in fiscal 1977) was transferred to a cash grant, and in 1978 Congress earmarked not less than $300 million of authorized Security Supporting Assistance funds as a cash grant for Israel. In May 1978 AID proposed to Congress that the CIP and the cash grant program be replaced by a cash transfer program in fiscal 1979. Israel had been receiving a mix of ESF grants and loans until fiscal 1981, when Congress began authorizing all grants, and since has followed that approach.

In addition to Security Supporting Assistance, the United States has provided aid under a number of other economic assistance programs. These have included a joint water desalinization project, a Public Law 480 (P.L. 480) food sales program, housing investment guarantees, bank and investment coverage provided through the Export-Import Bank and the Overseas Private Investment Corporation, refugee assistance (primarily to help resettle Soviet Jews in Israel), binational foundations for industrial and agricultural research, a binantional science foundation, assistance to American schools and hospitals abroad, debt relief, excess property grants, and duty-free import privileges under the generalized system of preferences.

U.S. economic aid to Israel has not been a controversial aspect of the relationship. As is clear from the data concerning the program and the nature of its evolution, the economic aid program has been accorded special status and strongly supported in Congress (as discussed in greater detail in chapter 5). Although some observers have suggested that the economic aid program might provide a useful lever to influence Israel's policies, there has been no significant effort in recent years to implement that proposal. In fact, Congress has been singularly reluctant to consider cuts in aid to Israel, and in general has often increased the aid levels beyond those proposed by the administration. This latter approach was particularly apparent during congressional consideration of the aid program in the latter part of 1982 and the early part of 1983. Despite efforts by the administration to "hold the line," congressional supporters of Israel were instrumental in raising the levels of aid provided. In the battle for Capitol Hill, Israel often has been more successful than the U.S. administrations in securing economic and military assistance at levels and under conditions more favorable than those proposed by the administration.

Various administrations have found that aid can be a useful element in its efforts to influence Israel, but in recent years it has taken the form not of proposals to cut aid, which would require concurrence of an often reluctant Congress, but suggestions that additional amounts of aid, or additional aid programs, or more lenient terms might help to reassure Israel or induce it to cooperate in a particular effort. Thus, as noted above, the Sinai II accords included an aid component, as did the Egypt-Israel peace treaty, although the more significant component was military rather than economic.

The main issue areas in the influence relationship involving aid have been in the military sector, particularly the acquisition of military equipment.

MILITARY ASSISTANCE

Military assistance, particularly arms sales, is a major component of the U.S.-Israel relationship, given the centrality of security in Israel's concerns and policymaking.[6] Arms sales are a policy instrument and provide an indication of policy direction and objectives. Prime Minister Yitzhak Rabin noted this linkage: "I served here [the United States] for five years as an ambassador. I experienced in the past some delays about decisions of selling arms. My experience shows that in the long run, when we find understanding on the basic attitudes, basic strategy, and how to cope with the problem, all other issues are solved."[7]

The United States has had a formal military assistance relationship with Israel since 1952, but did not become a major supplier of arms until after the June War. The large annual military assistance program began after the October War. Since 1974 Israel has been the recipient of more foreign military sales (FMS) assistance than any other country. FMS to Israel indicate U.S. political support and ensure Israel's security by providing military equipment for its defense needs. The military assistance relationship is unusual. Congress devotes more attention to and exerts more influence on assistance to Israel than other assistance programs. The General Accounting Office has stated: "Israel receives more FMS forgiven loans than any other recipient, more FMS loans with long term repayment periods, and its procurement of military systems has been expanded through an administration mechanism called cash flow financing."[8] Since 1974 the United States has forgiven part of the FMS loans provided to Israel, in effect making them grants. From 1976 through 1980 this amounted to about half of the FMS assistance provided. Since 1981 it has been at a somewhat lower level.

EVOLUTION OF THE MILITARY SUPPLY RELATIONSHIP

The U.S. role as arms provider has evolved from that of nonparticipant (by enacting an arms embargo in 1947) to principal supplier of modern, sophisticated military equipment to Israel since the late 1960s.

In 1947 the United States embargoed the shipment of arms to Palestine (as well as to other states in the region), in an effort to prevent conflict or, in the event of conflict, to reduce its nature and scope.[9] It refused to lift the embargo after Israel's War of Independence (1948-49), and in May 1950 joined with England and France in the tripartite declaration that sought to control the flow of arms and the development of an arms race in the Arab-Israeli zone. Although the powers stated their determination to consider future applications for arms from the states in the area on the principle that arms would be supplied, if necessary, "for the purposes of assuring their internal security and their legitimate self-defense and to permit them to play their part in the defense of the area as a whole,"[10] the United States was anxious to avoid identification as a partisan in the conflict or to become extensively involved in the area.

The tripartite declaration remained the basis of U.S. policy until the mid-1950s, when it became irrelevant, given French arms supplies to Israel and the Czech-Egyptian arms deal of 1955. The Soviet decision to supply arms to Egypt and other Arab states helped to precipitate the eventual U.S. entry into an arms supply role, particularly for Israel. The United States followed a policy of selectively supplying Middle Eastern states with limited amounts of defensive arms or of encouraging third powers (especially Western European states such as France or West Germany) to do so.

The Czech-Egyptian announcement, coupled with implacable Arab hostility, alarmed Israel, which saw the danger of conflict and a deterioration in its military position. Israel sought arms to maintain the relative military balance between itself and the Arabs, especially Egypt. Israeli Prime Minister and Foreign Minister Moshe Sharett offered the following evaluation to the Knesset on October 18, 1955: "This departure [the Czech-Egyptian arms deal] is liable to bring about a revolutionary and ominous change in Israel's security situation."[11] The generalized concern was translated into specific requests for arms from the United States, under the provisions of the tripartite declaration of 1950, with the most lenient conditions of price and credit. The United States refused, arguing that it would contribute to a regional arms race and that it preferred an arms balance.

In reality the United States sought to foster an image of nonsupplier in order to avoid identification with any of the parties to the conflict. Israel turned to alternative suppliers, including France, Canada, and England; and the United States indicated that it would not object to such sales. Dean Rusk succinctly summarized the position during those years in these words:

> We have ourselves tried not to become a principal supplier of arms in that region. But we are committed to the political independence and the territorial integrity of the states of the Middle East. And when imbalances of a major proportion occurred, we felt it was necessary for us to supply some limited military assistance to certain of the Arab countries and [to] Israel.[12]

The competition for improved armament between Israel and Egypt became a more or less permanent feature of the Arab-Israeli sector in the mid-1950s, although qualitative improvements did not become a major element until the 1960s. The U.S. reluctance to become a major arms supplier was tempered by occasional supplies of limited quantities of "purely defensive weapons" to help prevent an arms imbalance that might lead to conflict. On September 27, 1962, the United States announced the sale of Hawk missiles to Israel following the disclosure of a large shipment of Soviet arms to Egypt, Syria, and Iraq, and reports of Egyptian missiles that could reach Israeli territory. The sale was explained in the following terms:

> We also keep the arms situation in the area under constant scrutiny and may supply purely defensive weapons within an overall policy of not becoming a major supplier of arms to either side. When in the course of recent review it was established that Israel needed an improved air defense capability, the United States agreed to sell Israel the Hawk, a short-range defensive missile.[13]

The Defense Department's evaluation concluded that "the Middle Eastern balance of power would begin to tip in the Arabs' favor" and "that such an imbalance would encourage either an attack upon Israel or a 'preventive' war by Israel to destroy some of the Arab offensive power."[14] Official spokesmen hastened to point out that the United States "had no intention of becoming 'a major supplier' of weapons to the Middle East."[15]

In early 1963 Israel's anxiety was heightened by rumors of Egypt's acquisition of German scientists to aid in the establishment of a nuclear rocket capability. President Kennedy sought to reassure Israel and the Arabs, and to lessen regional tensions. In a press conference on April 3, he reiterated that the United States "has never been a supplier of military equipment directly to the Israelis."[16] Israel felt this statement to be inadequate, and Prime Minister David Ben-Gurion sought precise assurances. Kennedy obliged at a press conference on May 8, 1963, when he reiterated U.S. opposition to the threat or use of force in the Middle East and stated that the United States supported the security of both Israel and its neighbors. Tangible aid to support this perspective was not provided during the remaining months of the Kennedy administration.

During the Johnson administration the United States became more involved in the supply of military equipment to Israel (and to the moderate Arab states). When, in February 1966, the Department of State revealed that it had sold Patton tanks to Israel, it again emphasized its "established . . . policy . . . to refrain from becoming a major supplier of arms in this area while retaining the option of helping the countries of the area meet their defense requirements through occasional, selective sales."[17] The tanks were limited in number, but the sale was significant because it further involved the United States in an arms supply relationship with Israel.

By the June War the United States had emerged as a limited supplier of weapons to Israel, primarily to ensure that the complex balancing of sophisticated modern military equipment would be achieved.

At the outbreak of the 1967 War, the United States imposed an arms embargo on Israel and the Arab states that lasted until the fall. On October 24, 1967, State Department spokesman Robert J. McCloskey announced that the United States would "release selected items of military matériel" to Israel, Lebanon, Saudi Arabia, Morocco, Libya, and Tunisia.[18] Skyhawks sold to Israel in 1966 had not been delivered because of the embargo, and the announcement meant that those aircraft would now be shipped. Immediately following the war the United States sought to achieve an understanding with the Soviet Union concerning the supply of arms to the region in order to prevent an arms race from developing anew. This objective was enunciated as a part of President Johnson's Five Principles of Peace and was a subject of discussion at the Glassboro summit meeting between Johnson and Kosygin in June 1967. The failure to achieve an understanding with the Soviet Union and Israel's inability to secure jet aircraft from France intensified the pressure on the United States to become involved in the supply of arms to Israel in order to maintain the military balance in the region.

In the late 1960s the U.S. role as arms supplier to Israel became increasingly important. At the same time arms supply and the military balance in the Arab-Israeli sector became a major subject of the U.S.-Israel dialogue.

Shortly after the June War, Israel asked to buy supersonic F-4 Phantom jets, thereby providing a major test of U.S. arms-supply policy. Its request was based on the losses it had suffered during the conflict, the massive Soviet resupply of military equipment to Egypt and other Arab states, and the lack of alternative sources of supply. The United States, in order to maintain the balance, agreed to provide additional Hawk missiles and to deliver the Skyhawk A-4 subsonic fighter bombers Israel had purchased before the war,[19] but its initial response to Israel's request for Phantom jets was negative.

Prime Minister Levi Eshkol's visit to Washington in January 1968 dealt partially with the question of arms supply. In addition to reassurances of general U.S. support, Eshkol wanted tangible demonstration of this support in the form of approval to purchase arms, specifically Phantoms. At the conclusion of their meeting in Texas, Johnson and Eshkol issued a joint statement that included a reference to the arms situation:

> The President and the Prime Minister considered the implications of the pace of rearmament in the Middle East and the ways and means of coping with this situation. The President agreed to keep Israel's military defense capability under active and sympathetic examination and review in the light of all relevant factors, including the shipment of military equipment by others to the area.[20]

Johnson's decision to maintain "active and sympathetic" consideration of Israel's defense requirements was seen as a significant commitment not previously made by the United States to Israel.

Israel's campaign to secure Phantom jets gained momentum with reports of Soviet military shipments to the Arab states, and culminated in congressional pressure for the sale of the planes in the form of a sense-of-Congress resolution (section 651) attached to the foreign-aid bill:

> It is the sense of the Congress that the President should take such steps as may be necessary, as soon as practicable after the date of enactment of this section, to negotiate an agreement with the Government of Israel providing for the sale by the United States of such number of supersonic planes as may be necessary to provide Israel with an adequate deterrent force capable of preventing future Arab aggression

by offseting sophisticated weapons received by the Arab states and to replace losses suffered by Israel in the 1967 conflict.

The administration delayed responding to Israel's request and acting on the congressional declaration, in an effort to secure Soviet agreement on arms limitations, to allow for the possibility of a summit meeting, and to reduce regional tension in order to facilitate the Jarring mission. However, on October 9, 1968, President Johnson, on signing the Foreign Assistance Act of 1968, instructed Secretary of State Rusk to enter into negotiations for the sale of jet aircraft to Israel:

> I have taken note of section 651 concerning the sale of planes to Israel .
> . . . I am asking the Secretary of State to initiate negotiations with the Government of Israel and to report back to me.[21]

This decision followed a Soviet unwillingness to cooperate on arms limitations and was partly a response to a consensus expressed by Congress, the major political parties, the presidential candidates, and others. For all practical purposes, Johnson's announcement meant the sale of the jets; and negotiations were to proceed not on the principle but on such practical questions as number, cost, and delivery timetable. On December 27, 1968, the State Department announced an agreement to sell 50 Phantom F-4 jets to Israel, the delivery of which would begin before the end of 1969 and would continue until the end of 1970.

The decision to sell Phantom aircraft was a major turning point in the U.S.-Israel arms supply relationship and opened the way for ever closer ties in the years that followed. It was influenced by the French decision to tighten the embargo against military supply to Israel in the wake of its raid on Beirut International Airport in December 1968. This made Israel almost totally dependent on the United States for major purchases of modern and sophisticated military equipment.

Israel and the United States agreed on the need to maintain a military balance (which was operationally viewed as Israeli military superiority) in the Arab-Israeli sector. However, they did not always agree on when the balance was tipping against Israel or on how an imbalance might be corrected. In a national television interview on January 4, 1971, President Nixon stated:

> We have made it clear time and again that we would help to maintain the balance of power in the area, so that Israel would not be in a position that its neighbors could overwhelm them with their superior manpower or with the forces that they got from the Soviet Union.[22]

Prime Minister Golda Meir came to the United States in September 1969. She sought additional F-4 Phantom jets, A-4 Skyhawks, and Hawk missiles, as well as economic assistance to help offset the strains on Israel's economy caused by post-June War defense expenditures, and appeared reassured that the United States would be mindful of the military balance and be sympathetic to Israel's requests. Reports of additional Soviet military supplies to Arab countries and Israel's concern over Secretary of State Rogers' peace plan were the basis for Nixon's efforts to reassure Israel and its supporters in January 1970. At that time he suggested that Israel remained a friend, and that the United States would stand by its friends and provide arms to friendly governments as the need arose, should the military balance be upset. He pledged that the United States would monitor the situation in the region, particularly in light of reports of increased Soviet supply of equipment to Egypt.

The war of attrition along the Suez Canal continued, as did Soviet aid to Egypt. The United States responded cautiously, and suggested that the interim decision on Israel's request for arms would be negative. A final decision was held in abeyance, pending the results of diplomatic efforts and continued monitoring of the military balance, but it also reflected disagreement within the Nixon administration. It was suggested that the United States could provide additional or replacement aircraft promptly if the situation required it. Reports of Soviet pilots flying operational missions for Egypt increased the pressure to supply Israel.

The escalating danger impelled the United States to take an initiative in June 1970 to stop the shooting along the Suez Canal and start some form of negotiation. The United States also suggested that it would not abandon its policy of not permitting the balance of military power to shift against Israel. Nixon underscored the need to maintain Israel's military superiority in order to prevent further conflict.

The U.S. initiative raised questions about an appropriate Israeli response. In a speech to the Knesset, Mrs. Meir suggested that Israel should reject a temporary cease-fire because it would facilitate Arab preparations for resuming hostilities and because Israel's strong military position meant it did not have to accept a cease-fire on unfavorable terms. Following Nasser's acceptance of the cease-fire call, the focus was on Israel, and the United States utilized a combination of pressures and reassurances to secure a positive response. U.N. Ambassador to Israel Walworth Barbour met with Eban and Meir and delivered a personal message from Nixon, which reportedly contained a pledge that the cease-fire would not work against Israel, that the United States would maintain the military balance, and that the United States would support Israel's position of no withdrawal without peace.[23]

There were also meetings in Washington and public statements designed to help reassure Israel. Additional military equipment was provided, and some shipments under existing contracts were accelerated. In a press conference on July 30 Nixon said: "I believe that Israel can agree to the cease-fire and . . . negotiations without fear that . . . her position may be compromised or jeopardized . . . . If there's a cease-fire . . . there will be a military standstill . . . ." He reiterated the "commitment to maintaining the balance of power in the Mideast" and stated that "seventy-one Senators have endorsed that proposition in a letter to me which I received today."[24] Israel accepted the initiative, with clear references to American entreaties and pledges.

The standstill cease-fire was violated shortly after it came into effect when Egypt moved missiles into the zone and prepared additional sites. This led to further discussion and widened the confidence gap between the two states because Israel held the United States responsible for restoring the precease-fire status quo. Israel suggested that a restoration of the situation could be achieved by having the Egyptians pull back their missiles from the zone where the violations occurred. More realistically, the Israelis were testing the United States on its pledge to maintain the military balance, which had been upset by the missile movement and could be partially offset by additional military supply to Israel.

In early September the United States acknowledged the Israeli complaints and noted that it would monitor the military balance closely, to ensure that Israel's security would not be adversely affected, and would begin a continuing effort to "rectify" the breaches of the agreement. "Rectification" seemed to entail a restoration of confidence by means of additional military supply to Israel rather than a removal or rollback of the missiles by Egypt. Although Israel continued to demand a full rollback of the missiles to their precease-fire positions, it became clear during the fall of 1970 that this was unrealistic, and Israel thereafter focused its attention on the reestablishment of the military balance through arms supplies and political assurances.

Continuing discussions ultimately led to various U.S. assurances, including an apparent pledge by Nixon (contained in a note presented to Mrs. Meir on December 17 by U.S. Ambassador Barbour) to keep the arms pipeline open. The assurances apparently were sufficient to secure Israel's assent to return to the talks under U.N. negotiator Gunnar Jarring's auspices. When Mrs. Meir informed the Knesset on December 29 of the decision to return to the talks, she stressed the importance of U.S. clarifications and support, and the obtaining of "military, economic, and political conditions vital to us," including the decision to grant Israel $500 million in credits to help finance the acquisition of military equipment.

In the fall of 1971, the United States and Israel again clashed on the matter of a political settlement, and arms supply became an issue in the bilateral discussions. When Secretary of State Rogers proposed an interim Suez Canal agreement, Israel opposed the effort. Mrs. Meir detailed Israel's opposition in a speech to the Knesset on October 26, 1971, in which she noted that an important element in maintaining the cease-fire and promoting a settlement was Israel's deterrent strength. She went on to point out that while the United States had helped to maintain the military balance, "we cannot ignore the fact that in recent months there has been an interruption in the supply of planes to Israel," despite extensive Soviet arms and equipment being supplied to Egypt and Syria.

Mrs. Meir regarded the interruption in aircraft supply as upsetting the military balance and interpreted it as having political significance, in that it linked arms supply and political decisions. She stressed the importance of the aircraft: "The Government of Israel calls upon the Government of the United States to enable it to acquire the planes which are vital to Israel's security." Israel linked its willingness to participate in the interim agreement negotiations to the supply of Phantom jets, and argued that it would be at a psychological and political disadvantage without the Phantoms as long as Egypt had a certain supply of Soviet equipment.[25]

U.S. and Israeli views concerning the situation differed significantly, and the discussions continued until Mrs. Meir visited Washington in early December. The ostensible purposes were to try to restore the friendly nature of the U.S.-Israel relationship that had been negatively affected by suspicions on both sides, and to acquire the Phantom jets that had not been supplied to Israel over the preceding months. After a private meeting between Nixon and Mrs. Meir the White House press secretary said:

> The President confirmed that the United States continues to maintain an ongoing relationship with Israel of financial assistance and military supply. . . . In the context of this, it is recognized that the Israeli forces must maintain a long-term modernization program and that the United States will continue to discuss how it can help in that process.

They appeared to agree on the need for negotiations, and while it was apparently made clear that the United States would not allow the military balance to shift against Israel, there was no doubt that the current balance was in Israel's favor and thus no Phantoms were required at that time. Subsequently Mrs. Meir said that Nixon understood Israel's problems and had reassured it that he would not allow the military balance to shift against Israel.

Nevertheless, not all issues were clarified. In early January 1972, Sisco and Rabin began talks on military supply (primarily quantity and delivery timetables for Phantoms) and on the prospects for an interim settlement. The United States apparently satisfied Israel concerning the proposed negotiations, agreed to provide it with Phantom jets, and reassured it that the United States would not seek to impose its views on the substance of a settlement.[26] On February 2, 1972, Israel agreed to the U.S. proposal for indirect "proximity" talks with Egypt on the reopening of the Suez Canal. Ultimately this approach failed to generate negotiations of consequence, and the locus of decision making shifted from Rogers to Kissinger and altered the view of the linkage between arms supply and policy decisions. The State Department generally argued that withholding arms would persuade Israel to modify its position, but Kissinger believed that a secure Israel would be more flexible in negotiations.

During the Nixon administration the arms supply relationship reached significant new levels in terms of quantities, types, and value of equipment provided to Israel. Nevertheless, Israel had to justify its arms requests, and often they were granted after delays and not at the level sought. Arms sales sometimes followed disagreement concerning Israel's "need" for equipment.[27] However, the relationship was such that Israeli Ambassador Rabin was able to conclude, in 1972, that all of Israel's requests for arms essential to its defense had been granted by the United States,[28] and Golda Meir was able to say, in an address to the Knesset in October 1971:

> In addition, we have reason to assume that the principle of continuous military supply, especially of planes, is a permanent principle in the relations between our two countries.[29]

At the beginning of the second Nixon administration there was a flurry of activity concerning the Middle East, in apparent accord with Nixon's election time comment that the region would have a "very high priority." A number of leaders came to Washington early in the new administration's tenure. Golda Meir's meeting with Nixon on March 1, 1973, capped the month and reaffirmed the friendly relations of the two states while underlining their congruent perspectives concerning the regional situation. Additional arms supplies were agreed to. Between December 1971 and March 1973 the administration maintained its view that the military balance in the region had to be continued, and in their meeting Nixon assured Mrs. Meir of continued enduring U.S. support, including economic aid and military supply. The positive relations of the two states were reaffirmed and support was pledged, without the United States necessarily expecting any modifications in Israeli policy.[30]

By the October War the United States had become Israel's principal and virtually sole source of sophisticated, modern weapons systems. In testimony before the Senate Committee on Appropriations on November 5, 1973, Deputy Secretary of State Kenneth Rush said:

> But we have been the primary friend, as a nation we have been the great friend of Israel, of course, and have supplied the military equipment to her by cash sale or credit sale. Now she may buy equipment elsewhere, but we have been the primary supplier of military equipment to Israel.[31]

The U.S. arms supply role that had begun to develop slowly in the 1950s and 1960s gained substantial momentum in fiscal years 1968 through 1974. The type and sophistication of the equipment made available to Israel, as well as its value, reflected the increasingly close ties between the two states. The role was highlighted, and its significance graphically demonstrated, by American military supply to Israel during and immediately after the October War.[32]

During the October War the United States airlifted military supplies to Israel, as ordered by Nixon on October 13, 1973. The State Department spokesman announced that the United States had begun some resupply of arms to redress the military imbalance brought about by the massive Soviet airlift of military equipment to Syria and Egypt, and to replace the heavy equipment losses suffered by Israel thus far in the war. The airlift was important to Israel in both military and political-strategic terms:

> This airlift was obviously of vital importance militarily to Israel at a critical juncture, but perhaps its major significance was a political one. Its unequivocal nature, as seen by the Soviets and the Arabs, who were unaware of the hesitation and foot-dragging that had taken place in Washington for a full and fateful week of fighting, was undoubtedly a major factor in bringing about a cease-fire and in turning the United States into the central figure on the stage of the Middle East in the months subsequent to the war.[33]

On October 19 Nixon asked Congress for legislation to provide $2.2 billion in emergency security assistance to Israel, including direct military grants. Following that conflict the United States maintained its role as the principal supplier of military equipment to Israel in virtually all areas of sophisticated and modern weaponry. By the end of the summer of 1975, it was reported that the United States had either provided or agreed to provide Israel with the following major weapons systems: A-4 Skyhawk aircraft, Hawk missiles, F-4 Phantom aircraft, self-propelled howitzers, M60 tanks, M48 tanks, M107 SP 175mm long-range artillery, M113A1 armored personnel carriers, CH47 helicopters, TOW missiles, Shrike missiles, Redeye missiles, F-15 aircraft, F-16 aircraft, Lance missiles, and laser-guided bombs.[34]

The basis of that role was the concept of maintaining the military balance as a means of preventing war, assuring the security of Israel, and promoting progress toward a settlement. The joint U.S.-Israeli statement issued at the conclusion of President Nixon's visit to Israel, June 17, 1974, stated:

> Prime Minister Rabin expressed his appreciation for the United States military supplies to Israel during the October War and thereafter. The president affirmed the continuing and long-term nature of the military supply relationship between the two countries, and reiterated his view that the strengthening of Israel's ability to defend itself is essential in order to prevent further hostilities and to maintain conditions conducive to progress toward peace. An Israeli Defense Ministry delegation will soon come to Washington in order to work out the concrete details relating to long-term supplies.[35]

In an interview broadcast on NBC television and radio on January 23, 1975, President Ford said; "The State of Israel does need adequate military capability to protect its boundaries, or its territorial integrity."[36]

The overall role of the United States in Middle Eastern arms supply changed in the period following the October War. The United States became more extensively involved, not only by the supply of equipment to Israel but also by the sale of increasingly sophisticated equipment to Arab clients, and to new Arab customers such as Egypt. The overall scale of U.S. sales increased dramatically, and Saudi Arabia became the largest military customer. Military supply to Egypt developed in the wake of the 1974 disengagement agreement and the Sinai II accords.

After signing the agreements Egypt requested military assistance, and the United States supported the concept of an Egyptian shift from reliance on Soviet weaponry to reliance on Western supply. It began by providing jeeps and trucks and, in 1976, agreed to sell C-130 transport aircraft. Jordan and Saudi Arabia also secured additional American equipment, including jet fighters. Jordan was also able to secure tanks, antitank missiles, air-to-air missiles, and Hawk surface-to-air missiles. Egypt became a major recipient of American arms in the aftermath of Sadat's 1977 visit to Jerusalem, as part of the Egypt-Israel peace process.

A major watershed was the 1978 "package deal" that approved the sale to Egypt of F-5E aircraft, to Saudi Arabia of F-15 aircraft, and an increase in the number of F-15s previously pledged to Israel. This gave Egypt and Saudi Arabia access to the U.S. arsenal at sophisticated levels and in amounts that they did not previously have. However, this was soon overshadowed by the 1981 decision to allow Saudi Arabia to purchase AWACS aircraft and to enhance the capability of the previously sold F-15s. This multibillion-dollar deal was a major turning point in the U.S. role as arms provider in the Middle East, and indicates the dramatic alteration in U.S. policy on sales to the Arabs. The weapons systems were of increasing sophistication and a growing number of customers were involved.[37]

The question of arms supply to Israel and Israeli concerns about growing Arab access to the U.S. arsenal became a matter of public controversy on a number of occasions, most prominently in the case of the "package deal" and the AWACS debate. American decisions to supply substantial amounts of arms to Jordan provided a further case study of the issues involved in this U.S.-Israeli dispute. For example, in February 1982 the Israeli Knesset adopted a resolution, communicated by Begin to Reagan, in which it expressed "its profound concern at the U.S. Defense Secretary's offer to supply F-16 aircraft and improved ground-to-air I-Hawk missiles, from which the ban on their mobility will be lifted." It saw this as " a grave threat to Israel's security," given Arab hostility. Begin argued that should Jordan receive the equipment proposed, Israel "will be in direct, real and severe danger." Reagan wrote to reassure Begin:

> I want you to know that America's policy toward Israel has not changed. Our commitments will be kept. I am determined to see that Israel's qualitative technological edge is maintained and am mindful as well of your concerns with respect to quantiative factors and their impact upon Israel's security.[38]

U.S. military supply to Israel has reflected this continuing commitment (see Table 4.3).

TABLE 4.3 Select Major Military Items Delivered to Israel Under FMS, 1971-82

Aircraft
  A-4 aircraft
  F-15 aircraft
  F-16 aircraft
  F-4/RF-4 aircraft
  E2C aircraft
  AH-1G/S helicopters
  CH-53 helicopters

Ground forces
  M48 series tanks
  M60 series tanks, including M60A3
  M113A1 armored personnel carriers
  M88A1 tank recovery vehicles
  M548 cargo carriers
  M577A1 command post carriers
  M109 155mm self-propelled howitzers
  M107 175mm self-propelled guns

Surface-to-surface missile systems
  DRAGON (antitank) launchers   DRAGON missiles
  TOW (antitank) launchers   TOW missiles

Air defense systems
  I-Hawk batteries   I-Hawk missiles
  Chaparral launchers   Chaparral missiles
  M163 20mm Vulcan guns
  Redeye missiles

Air-to-air missiles
  AIM-7 Sparrow missiles
  AIM-9 Sidewinder missiles

Air-to-ground missiles
  Maverick missiles
  Standard ARM missiles
  Shrike ARM missiles

Surface-to-surface missiles
  Harpoon missiles

Source: Defense Security Assistance Agency and General Accounting Office, *U.S. Assistance to the State of Israel* (Washington, D.C.: U.S. General Accounting Office, June 24, 1983), p. 16.

MILITARY DEPENDENCE AND POLITICAL INFLUENCE

Israel's dependence on U.S. arms and financial assistance is often identified as a potential area for U.S. influence. As discussed previously, the United States has sought to modify Israeli policies through the selective granting or withholding of arms supplies. Generally, the granting of arms to induce flexibility or accommodation by providing a "guarantee" to replace the security relinquished through some significant concession has been the preferred and more successful approach. The withholding (or temporary suspension) of arms to achieve a desired political end has been utilized in a number of instances, but generally it is denied that it is linked to political and diplomatic activity. An example is the statement by Vice-President Walter Mondale in June 1977 that "we do not intend to use our military aid as pressure on Israel. If we have any differences over military aid—and we may have some—it will be on military grounds or economic grounds, but not political grounds."[39] Despite his assertion, military aid has been related to political decisions, although its provision or withholding has been justified on other, often technical, grounds.

A central question is whether the withholding or the granting of military assistance has been the more efficacious in securing the desired modifications in Israeli policy. There is substantial disagreement on this point, although the weight of evidence suggests that a forthcoming approach has had more success than sanctions. This is clear from the various instances discussed previously. Arms supply, providing reassurance to Israel, helped to secure its participation in negotiations under the Rogers initiatives and the Jarring mission, after initial complications. Israel's participation in the Sinai II accords and the Egypt-Israel peace treaty similarly was facilitated by pledges of arms supply that helped to reassure it concerning its security situation. On the other hand, the withholding of arms through the sanctions imposed by the Reagan administration between 1981 and 1983 seemed to have little effect on Israel's decisions, although the actions no doubt were weighed in Israel's policy councils.

During much of the period after the June War, the predominant perspective of U.S. administrations was that assistance to create a secure and confident Israel will result in greater concessions or policy modifications than will a policy of sanction. A contrary perspective is found in a comment reportedly made by Kissinger: "I ask Rabin to make concessions, and he says he can't because Israel is weak. So I give him more arms, and he says he doesn't need to make concessions because Israel is strong."[40] Despite Kissinger's comment, he utilized arms supply as an inducement to secure

Israeli concessions and to "bridge the gap" between the parties in the negotiating process. An example is the Sinai II negotiations, in which Kissinger's pledges with regard to military supply helped to secure Israel's assent.

Subsequent efforts have been facilitated by arms pledges that have provided assurances and modified political positions by creating confidence in the United States and in the resulting situation. This was the case in connection with the negotiations on the Camp David accords and the Egypt-Israel peace treaty. At that time the United States made pledges of military assistance to both Israel and Egypt in order to facilitate their willingness to move toward an agreement. For Egypt it marked the inauguration of a new arms supply relationship with the United States. For Israel the pledges were made partially to offset the withdrawals from positions in Sinai, and the consequent loss of significant forward military installations and diminution of Israel's strategic position.

The October War inaugurated a period of Israeli dependence on the United States for war matériel. No other country could provide or was prepared to provide Israel with the vast quantities of modern and sophisticated arms required for war (or the political and moral support necessary to negotiate peace). The United States resupplied Israel with a substantial amount of military equipment, including conventional munitions of many types, air-to-air and air-to-ground missiles, artillery, crew-served and individual weapons, and a standard range of fighter aircraft, ordnance, tanks, aircraft, radios, and other military equipment lost in action. This effort was complemented by congressional support for the resupply effort and of Israel's position, and by a presidential request for $2.2 billion in emergency security assistance for Israel.

Despite these reassuring signs, there was concern that the United States might shift away from its support of Israel and might use its leverage to achieve changes in Israel's position. Israeli concern began to develop during the war and immediately thereafter, and was symbolized by U.S. pressures on Israel to accept the initial cease-fire and to permit a relief convoy to resupply the Egyptian Third Army. There was also some concern about Kissinger's courting of the Arabs. Israel recognized the dangers inherent in its increased isolation in the international community and dependence on the United States.

Israel's uneasiness about the implications of its dependence was expressed by Defense Minister Shimon Peres in an address to graduates of the Interservice Command and Staff College on August 28, 1975, in these terms:

> There is danger in the diminishing of our nondependence. . . . The
> United States is Israel's friend—something that does not, cannot, stop
> it from sometimes attempting to inculcate in Israel stands that are more
> American than Israeli. This, at times, can be termed pressure. . . .

His suggestion was obvious:

> If there is a conclusion to be drawn from our experience, it is that we
> ought to make greater demands upon ourselves. . . . Now is the time to
> work with added energy for strengthening Israel's nondependence.
> We still have land that has not been worked and that can produce food.
> We have seas which can provide water, which can be desalinated for
> irrigation purposes, and electricity can be obtained from nuclear
> power. Our living standard is too high. In the sphere of defense we
> shall most certainly need to step up home production in all possible
> fields: planes, armored vehicles, missile boats, electronic products,
> and rockets.

Israel has sought to reduce its dependence for the weapons systems it
requires by producing necessary equipment and ammunition and by building stockpiles to avoid reliance on external sources in time of need. In the
latter case it has learned a lesson from the October War, when its supplies
were low and resupply from the United States became an important consideration in the continued military operations near the end of the war.
Clearly, both policies would help to reduce dependence and vulnerability
to influence or pressure in time of crisis. This approach has an obvious
flaw. The raw materials and some of the necessary technology for domestic
production must be secured from external sources, often the United States,
thus limiting Israel's ability to reduce its external dependence. The problem with component parts can be difficult for Israel, in that it gives the
United States a veto over the transfer of equipment to third parties and, in
the case of Israeli production with some U.S. components, over sales. A
prominent example was President Carter's veto of an Israeli sale of Kfir jets
(with U.S. engines) to Latin America. At the same time there has been U.S.
reluctance to respond affirmatively to Israel's advanced technology requests, including those that might allow it to move in the direction of limiting U.S. influence on Israel's ability to act in the defense realm.

Israel's efforts to develop its own arms industry have been impressive. An indigenous military industry has been an element of security planning since independence, and considerable resources have been invested,
with somewhat uneven results. Its basic shortcoming has been lack of resources, both natural and financial. There is the problem of economies of

scale (short production runs) and the difficulties posed by the enormous start-up costs involved in the development and production of a sophisticated weapons system.

Israel seems to have overcome many of the technological problems that plagued its arms industry in its early years, and its infrastructure has been relatively well suited to the advanced technology of a sophisticated armaments industry. The goals are multiple, and include the political aim of reducing dependence, but Israel also seeks to earn hard currency from sales abroad, to reduce the cost per item of required equipment for the Israel Defense Forces, and to ensure that those forces will have the equipment required, when it is needed, and in the desired types and quantities. In part the lessons of past embargoes (by Britain, France, and the United States) and concern about future pressures in times of political discord have helped to motivate Israel to move toward an increased arms production capability.

In the decade following the October War, Israel's arms industry made substantial progress in the quality and quantity of arms production for its own use, and increased its overseas sales dramatically in terms of numbers and diversity of customers, types of equipment, and revenues earned. Israel was, as a result, able to become self-sufficient in some areas (such as the production of small arms and some forms of missiles) and to produce a wide range of equipment. Israel's indigenous defense-manufacturing capability includes military (such as the Kfir jet) and civilian aircraft, surface-to-surface antiship missiles, air-to-air missiles, patrol boats, combat vehicles, tanks, howitzers, mortars, grenades, radar systems, communication and navigation systems, industrial and shipborne monitoring and control systems, medical electronics, microelectronics, computers and computerized communications systems, fire-control systems, security systems, air-crew and ground-crew equipment, ground-support equipment, microwave components, and small arms.

A major hindrance to Israel's efforts is its limited export capability. Israeli sales have included transport aircraft, patrol boats, antiship missiles, air-to-air missiles, automatic weapons, and Kfir fighter aircraft; however, the bulk of the exports has consisted of small arms, ammunition, communications, and electronics, as well as obsolete military equipment.[41] Although it has sold a range of products to a relatively large number of customers, it has been constrained by the technical limitations of some of its products, by the Arab-imposed boycott that threatens states dealing with Israel, by a self-imposed limitation concerning the political ideology of some prospective customers, and by U.S. limitations placed on products (such as the Kfir jet) that have U.S. components.

Despite its significant accomplishments in this area, Israel remains dependent on the United States for its most sophisticated weapons systems and for some of the advanced components of its indigenous products, a condition that is not likely to be altered in the near future.

NOTES

1. U.S. International Cooperation Administration, *Fact Sheet: Mutual Security in Action—Israel,* Department of State Publication no. 6985 (Washington, D.C.: U.S. Government Printing Office, June 1960), p. 4.

2. Bruce W. McDaniel, "American Technical Assistance and Economic Aid in Israel," *Middle Eastern Affairs* 6 (October 1955): 303-18, pp. 306-07.

3. "Mission Accomplished," *Jerusalem Post,* July 4, 1962, p. 1.

4. *Department of State Bulletin,* July 15, 1974, p. 111.

5. Much of the discussion of the aid to Israel program is drawn from U.S. General Accounting Office, *U.S. Assistance to the State of Israel* (Washington, D.C.: U.S. General Accounting Office, June 24, 1983).

6. For a more detailed discussion of Israel's security dilemma and the resultant policy, see Bernard Reich, "Israel," in Edward A. Kolodziej and Robert E. Harkavy, eds., *Security Policies of Developing States* (Lexington, Mass.: Lexington Books, 1982), pp. 203-25.

7. Interview on "Face the Nation," June 15, 1975.

8. U.S. General Accounting Office, *Assistance to the State of Israel,* p. 19.

9. On Dec. 5, 1947, the State Department announced that "the United States is discontinuing for the present [the] licensing of all shipments of arms to the troubled areas" because of "the current disorders in the Middle East." Department of State Press Release no. 949, Dec. 5, 1947. That press release, as well as a background note for the press issued on Dec. 10, 1947, showed that between 1945 and Oct. 1947 no arms, no ammunition, and no nonmilitary war surplus were transferred to Palestine, although some was made available to several of the neighboring Arab states.

10. *Department of State Bulletin,* June 5, 1950, p. 886.

11. J. C. Hurewitz, *Diplomacy in the Near and Middle East,* Vol. II, *A Documentary Record: 1914-1956* (Princeton, N.J.: D. Van Nostrand, 1956), p. 409.

12. *Department of State Bulletin,* Aug. 7, 1967, p. 160.

13. Mimeographed policy brief issued by the Department of State, April 1963.

14. *New York Times,* Sept. 27, 1962.

15. *New York Times,* Sept. 28, 1962.

16. *New York Times,* Apr. 4, 1963.

17. *New York Times,* Feb. 6, 1966.

18. *Department of State Bulletin,* Nov. 13, 1967, p. 652.

19. See *New York Times,* July 7, 1968.

20. *Department of State Bulletin,* Feb. 5, 1968, p. 174.

21. *Department of State Bulletin,* Oct. 28, 1968, p. 452.

22. *Weekly Compilation of Presidential Documents,* Jan. 11, 1971, p. 39. See also Nixon's interview on Jan. 2, 1972, in *Weekly Compilation of Presidential Documents,* Jan. 10, 1972, p. 22.

23. *Washington Post* and *Jerusalem Post,* July 26, 1970. *Davar,* Aug. 2, 1970, provides further elaboration on these points. See also Nixon's press conference on July 30, 1970.

24. *Weekly Compilation of Presidential Documents,* Aug. 3, 1970, p. 999.

25. See *New York Times* and *Jerusalem Post,* Nov. 2, 1971. Initially the United States stressed that Israel continued to hold a military edge, and thus did not need the supplies. Secretary of State Rogers, in an interview published in *U.S. News and World Report,* Nov. 22, 1971, said: "Up to now, the military balance has not shifted. And a review is in train in light of the recent Soviet-Egyptian communiqué. . . . Now, the Soviet Union in the last four or five months has operated with some restraint as far a shipments are concerned. . . . In the last four months, as I said, their shipments have been very moderate" (p. 34). This assessment conflicted with Israel's. Ambassador Rabin stated: "Israel has not accepted this evaluation either from the military or from the political point of view." Quoted in *Jerusalem Post,* Nov. 16, 1971. On Nov. 18 State Department spokesman Charles Bray noted that the Soviet Union had supplied Egypt with medium bombers equipped with air-to-ground missiles in the past two weeks. Bray said that earlier U.S. statements were based on information as of Nov. 1 and that the United States "obviously will be assessing the implications of this development" on the balance of arms in the region. *New York Times,* Nov. 19, 1971.

26. See Nixon's comments during a national television interview on Jan. 2, 1972, in *Weekly Compilation of Presidential Documents,* Jan. 10, 1972, esp. p. 22. See also the comments by Rogers in an ABC TV news interview taped on Jan. 4, in *Department of State Bulletin,* January 24, 1972, p. 91. It was subsequently reported that the United States had agreed to sell F-4 Phantom and A-4 Skyhawk aircraft to Israel over a period of two or three

years. The long-term commitment involved in this reported arrangement, as well as an earlier "agreement in principle" whereby the United States would provide Israel with technical assistance in the manufacture of defense equipment in order to help Israel become more self-sufficient in producing major weapons, became widely known in mid-January. See *Jerusalem Post,* Jan. 16, 1972: *Washington Post,* Jan. 15, 1972; *New York Times* and *Washington Evening Star,* Jan. 14, 1972.

27. For example, in the fall of 1971 there was the continuing U.S. refusal to provide Israel with requested Phantom jets. At the same time Israel was concerned about a U.S. press campaign describing Israeli military prowess, which it believed was inspired by the State Department in an effort to minimize Israel's request for arms.

28. *Jerusalem Post,* Apr. 20, 1972.

29. Golda Meir's Knesset address, Oct. 26, 1971; excerpts in *Jerusalem Post,* Oct. 27, 1971, p. 5.

30. White House Press Secretary Ron Ziegler in *Washington Evening Star,* Mar. 2, 1974. William Beecher reported in *New York Times,* Mar. 14, 1973, that the United States would permit Israel to buy 24 additional Phantoms and 24 additional Skyhawks after current agreements ran out, and that the United States would provide technical assistance to Israel for the production of its own version of the Mirage aircraft. Economic aid agreements were also reached.

31. U.S. Senate, Subcommittee of the Committee on Appropriations, *Hearings, Emergency Military Assistance: Cambodia, Israel—Emergency Disaster Assistance: Nicaragua, Pakistan, Sahelian Africa,* 93rd Cong., 1st sess. (Washington, D.C.: U.S. Government Printing Office, 1973), p. 16.

32. For details on the airlift and U.S. supply during the war, see U.S. General Accounting Office, *Airlift Operations of the Military Airlift Command During the 1973 Middle East War*—Report to the Congress by the Comptroller General of the United States, April 16, 1975" (Washington, D.C.: U.S. Government Printing Office, 1975).

33. Chaim Herzog, *The War of Atonement* (Jerusalem: Steimatzky's Agency, 1975), p. 277.

34. International Institute for Strategic Studies, *The Military Balance* (various issues 1967-76); *Aviation Week and Space Technology,* Sept. 15, 1975; *Washington Post,* Sept. 15, 1975.

35. *Weekly Compilation of Presidential Documents,* June 24, 1974, p. 639.

36. *Department of State Bulletin,* Feb. 17, 1975, p. 221.

37. U.S. arms supply policy during the Carter and Reagan administrations is discussed in detail in chapters 2 and 3.

38. Texts of letters in *New York Times,* Feb. 17, 1982.

39. Text in *New York Times,* June 18, 1977.

40. Edward R. F. Sheehan, *The Arabs, Israelis, and Kissinger: A Secret History of American Diplomacy in the Middle East* (New York: Reader's Digest Press, 1976), p. 199.

41. U.S. General Accounting Office, *U.S. Assistance to the State of Israel,* p. 49.

5

EXPLAINING THE RELATIONSHIP

The U.S.-Israel special relationship is multifaceted and complex, and the efforts to influence its course have been substantial. Explaining it requires consideration of the numerous unique components of the links between these two states.

THE U.S. NATIONAL INTEREST AND THE ISRAEL COMPONENT

The U.S. national interest, as interpreted by successive administrations, lies in its continued independent existence, survival, and security with its institutions and values safeguarded, and with the welfare of its people enhanced. There is an "American ideology" that seeks democratic institutions, with morality and principles as guidelines of policy, and with liberty and human rights for its own people and for others. "Making the world safe for democracy" is an operational imperative because the United States cannot maintain its existence in isolation; it requires a world conducive to its unique political experiment. The United States imposes on itself constraints in foreign policy that reflect this special conception—a moral dimension that limits the methods and techniques employed.

The evolution of the U.S. national interest in the Middle East has been slow. However, since World War II, and especially in the Nixon, Carter, and Reagan administrations, the area has had an unusually central position in U.S. foreign policy, and has been given high priority and substantial attention by senior officials, sometimes to the virtual exclusion of other concerns, such as at Camp David in September 1978. Increasingly U.S. economic and military aid has had its largest segments allocated to states of the Middle East. It has been an important focal point of private activity, both philanthropic and commercial, for more than a century.

U.S. interests and concerns in the Middle East can be cataloged with substantial agreement, although debate surrounds their priority. Preventing Soviet dominance (and the expansion of Soviet power and influence in the area); assuring the flow of oil at reasonable prices, particularly to U.S. friends and allies; assuring access to regional markets, as a means of recycling the petrodollars earned by the regional states through the sale of oil; and the security and prosperity of Israel are at the core.[1] The United States has increasingly seen it as "in its interest" to resolve the Arab-Israeli conflict, because of its concern about the potential of superpower conflict (perhaps at the nuclear level), because the security and well-being of Israel are closely linked to it, and because it would improve the U.S. position in the region and help to promote its other interests.

There is general agreement that Israel is an important interest and that no other state in the Middle East is identified in quite the same way, despite some disagreement as to whether this should be the case. Although the United States continues to see other states as having a particular significance at various times, none has achieved the status, over an extended period, of the special position accorded to Israel. Successive administrations and congresses have reaffirmed that link. Recognition of the interest is widespread and essentially beyond the realm of debate, even by observers, such as George Ball, who are regarded by Israel as hostile to it:

> First of all, one of our interests in the Middle East is the carrying out of a rather deep emotional commitment to the Israeli people to permit them to achieve their objective of a national home. Now this goes back a long way. . . . From a strictly strategic position, apart from the intellectual and emotional basis for our commitment, the fact that we had made it not formally and in treaty form, but in a dozen different ways, means that we should sustain it. It is not in the American interest to engage in a reversal of alliances, or to indicate that we abandon our friends. Israel is established as a friend of the United States.[2]

In his highly controversial article "How to Save Israel in Spite of Herself," Ball wrote:

> Most Americans approach the problems of the Middle East with a pro-Israel bias—and rightly so. . . . Not only must Americans admire

Israel, there can be no doubt that we have an interest in, and special responsibility for, that valiant nation. . . . The question is no longer whether the United States should contribute to assuring Israel's survival and prosperity; that goes without saying.[3]

Support of Israel is "in the national interest," and the United States is served by closer relations with it. There is an ideological concern and a political-strategic value in the relationship. Minority Leader of the House Gerald Ford said in 1969: "I firmly believe that the fate of Israel is linked to the national security interests of the United States. I therefore cannot conceive of a situation in which the U.S. Administration will sell Israel down the Nile."[4] Israel is seen as a like-image state whose survival is crucial to the ideological prospering of the United States. This perspective goes beyond the more general concern for all similar states, to one associated particularly with Israel:

It is unthinkable that the international community could stand idly by . . . if Israel were in danger of destruction. The moral and political convulsion which such an event would engender is beyond calculation. It could spell the end not only of the Atlantic alliance, but of liberal civilization as we know it.[5]

The ideological/emotional interest is buttressed by a perspective that regards Israel as a political-strategic asset. Israel has been supportive of U.S. policy in the United Nations and in other world forums. In a study prepared by the U.S. mission to the United Nations, Israel was the most reliable supporter of U.S. policies in that body. In the 37th U.N. General Assembly, Israel voted with the United States 86.2 percent of the time, more than any other state. This voting behavior suggested a parallelism between Israeli and U.S. policies on various international issues.

Tangible national security advantages also have been identified, including the view that Israel is a reliable bulwark against Soviet penetration and domination of the Middle East, and against radical Arab expansion. The former view has been articulated by Senator Henry Jackson and by other, more conservative, anti-Soviet members of Congress. The Reagan administration has seen Israel in this way, as evidenced by the memorandum of understanding on strategic cooperation (1981), which focused on the Soviet threat, and by the statements of Secretary of Defense Weinberger identifying the strategic value of Israel. In a speech on May 13, 1983, he said that the Soviet Union was actively seeking to undermine moderate and Western-oriented regimes in the Middle East, and that its military power posed a grave threat to U.S. interests in the region: "We know that the Soviets would dearly love control over the Middle East's resources and strategic chokepoints, but Israel stands determinedly in their way." In the 1960s Israel reduced the ability of Egypt to pursue President Nasser's expansionist efforts in the Arabian Peninsula and the Persian Gulf. This was understood by some of the threatened Arab states and by the Shah of Iran, who regarded Israel as a reliable, if essentially covert, ally in the effort to curb radical Arab expansion in the region.

Israel's strategic value became a component of the U.S. interest primarily after 1967, when specific contributions could be identified. Israel's positions in Sinai and along the Suez Canal prevented Soviet use of the canal to shorten its supply lines to the Indian Ocean and Southeast Asia. Israel provided the United States with valuable military information and intelligence as captured Soviet equipment facilitated U.S. countermeasures against similar weaponry in Vietnam, and Israeli experience with U.S. equipment helped in the modification of designs and tactics. Israeli military installations could prove valuable to the United States in various military situations.

The 1970 civil war in Jordan, between the forces of King Hussein and the PLO, and the threatened intervention of Syria on behalf of the Palestinians, demonstrated the strategic value of Israel. Israel was able to take actions that the United States could not because of political and military constraints; it thus acted on behalf of the United States in support of King Hussein. The United States reacted to the crisis with a highly visible response, including the movement of Sixth Fleet ships toward the eastern Mediterranean, the positioning of evacuation aircraft, and the alerting of military units in the United States and Western Europe.

The matter was discussed during a previously scheduled visit of Prime Minister Meir to Washington; and Israel's highly visible military actions became an element in U.S. policy. Israel mobilized its forces, ostentatiously moved tanks to the Golan Heights, and alerted the air force. There was close coordination between the Israeli embassy in Washington and the White House, as well as at other levels and in other locations. The possibility of Israeli intervention was a factor in the Syrian withdrawal from Jordanian territory, which permitted Hussein's forces to deal effectively with the threat and to terminate the Palestinian role in his kingdom. Israel served its own interests and those of the United States.

President Reagan has articulated a precise perspective of Israel's value:

. . . our own position would be weaker without the political and military assets Israel provides. . . . The fall of Iran has increased Israel's value as perhaps the only remaining strategic asset in the region on which the United States can truly rely. . . . Israel has the democratic will, national cohesion, technological capacity and military fiber to stand forth as America's trusted ally.[6]

During the campaign for the presidency, Reagan said, in a speech to B'nai B'rith on September 3, 1980: ". . . the touchstone of our relationship with Israel is that a secure, strong Israel is in America's self-interest. Israel is a major strategic asset to America."

Various commentators have argued that peace, stability, and security in the Middle East and U.S. interests can be preserved by a strong Israel receiving U.S. arms and economic assistance, as well as diplomatic and political support. In this view Israel represents a solid foothold for the West in the region, and serves as a proxy by acting as a countervailing factor to the Soviet presence in some of the Arab states. More precisely, it has been suggested that Israel serves as a defender of the oil riches of the Middle East and provides a base for American military operations to protect or, in other scenarios, to act against the Persian Gulf oil fields.

This subject, often discussed in Washington in the mid-1970s, was again prominent in the early 1980s, in the wake of the Soviet invasion of Afghanistan and the consequent renewed concern about a potential Soviet drive toward the Persian Gulf and the Arabian Peninsula. The Carter Doctrine and Reagan's "strategic consensus" recognized this potential threat, and the latter envisaged an Israeli role. In the Nixon administration, with its Nixon Doctrine, Israel's high-quality security and defense capability, and its stress on the need for American equipment and assistance, but not personnel, became elements in gaining U.S. support.

U.S. credibility is at stake. Israel is perceived by the Arab world and much of the international community as benefiting from a U.S. security commitment. U.S. actions that might be interpreted as backing away from that obligation would undermine the credibility of the United States as an ally. If the United States were to "abandon" Israel, its role in other, and lesser, relationships would be open to question. Continued support for Israel, at a time when U.S. dependability as an ally is questioned, helps to reassure other U.S. allies and to ensure the credibility of the United States.

THE U.S. COMPONENT OF ISRAEL'S NATIONAL INTEREST

The centrality of the United States in Israel's perception of its national interest has evolved over time, and may be ascribed to changing regional and international circumstances, as well as to bilateral factors.

Upon independence, Israel sought positive relations with both West and East, especially the United States and the Soviet Union. This was not a naive assumption based on an idealistic hope, but an assessment of Israel's needs and its perception of the policies of the superpowers. Although there were strong factors propelling Israel toward the West, initially it was not an obvious approach. Superpower support for the establishment of the Jewish state, and an apparent competition between them for closer links with it, suggested that avoidance of a choice might be possible. This initial euphoria and the nonalignment policy it spawned, faded as the Soviet and, to a lesser degree, U.S. perceptions of their regional positions, particularly with regard to the Arab-Israeli conflict, were altered. Almost inexorably Israel moved into a position of alignment with the West and estrangement from the East, and into a clear linkage with the United States.

Israel's policy of nonidentification was debated extensively in the Knesset toward the end of 1951. Prime Minister David Ben-Gurion justified Israel's moves toward the West but suggested that there could not be complete identification between Israel and the United States. He differentiated between the type of relations Israel could establish with Western states and those possible with the Soviet Union and the Communist bloc. Formal governmental relations were the extent of links possible with Communist states, but in the Western world, and especially the United States, ties could be established on both governmental and people-to-people levels. In a prophetic observation he noted that in the case of the United States, Israel could deal with the people, the press, the legislators, and the executive; this facilitated the relationship and made it possible to effect changes in governmental policy.

This shift to the West led, by the late 1960s, to the United States' becoming the single most significant element in Israeli calculations. By the late 1970s the United States had assumed an unrivaled position in the national interest calculations of Israel and had become virtually indispensable as a source of economic and military assistance, as well as of political and diplomatic support.

THE DOMESTIC U.S. FACTOR IN
U.S.-ISRAEL RELATIONS

Those critical of U.S. Middle East policy, particularly toward Israel and the Arab-Israeli conflict, have often ascribed the policy to the existence of a substantial and influential American Jewish lobby exerting inordinate influence on the government to the detriment of U.S. interests in the region and beyond. This perspective often quotes President Truman: ". . . I have to answer to hundreds of thousands who are anxious for the success of Zionism; I do not have hundreds of thousands of Arabs among my constituents."[7] The State Department records of the meeting at which Truman reportedly made the statement make no mention of this comment.[8]

Truman's support of the creation, independence, recognition, and development of the Jewish state generally has been explained by the fact that he had succumbed to domestic political pressures because of the size and importance of the Jewish lobby, and to the advice and influence of pro-Zionist advisers, such as Clark Clifford and David Niles. Truman helped to perpetuate this view with statements, in his memoirs and elsewhere, that "the White House . . . was subjected to a constant barrage. I do not think I ever had as much pressure and propaganda aimed at the White House as I had in this instance."[9] Elsewhere he commented: "Well, there'd never been anything like it before, and there wasn't after."[10]

Generally, the response to this pressure is attributed to the need to secure political support and votes in crucial constituencies, in order to ensure election or reelection to office. Truman's support of Israel in 1947-48 is often linked to his quest for votes to defeat Thomas Dewey for the presidency. The New York Jewish vote was seen as virtually indispensable, yet Truman did not win New York in 1948, although he defeated Dewey. In the case of Israel, Truman acknowledged the pressures but seemed to be genuinely motivated by additional considerations: "My purpose was then and later to help bring about the redemption of the pledge of the Balfour Declaration and the rescue of at least some of the victims of Nazism."[11] This threat of concern and commitment runs through his approach to the issue.

Other decision makers have reported on, or complained about, Zionist influence. John Foster Dulles, for example, has been quoted as saying: "I am aware how almost impossible it is in this country to carry out a foreign policy not approved by the Jews." He also complained about the "terrific control the Jews have over the news media and the barrage which the Jews have built up on congressmen."[12]

There are numerous examples of the success of the Israel lobby, but few are as prominent as the letter of 76 senators to the president in 1975. Following the failure of the spring 1975 Kissinger shuttle, the Ford-Kissinger team undertook a "reassessment" of U.S. Middle East policy and more than three-quarters of the member of the Senate wrote to Ford in support of continued aid for Israel. Subsequently, Senator Charles Mathias, Jr., wrote that "seventy-six of us promptly affixed our signatures although no hearings had been held, no debate conducted, nor had the Administration been invited to present its views." One of his colleagues said that "the pressure was just too great. I caved."[13] Senator Mathias elaborated:

> . . . American Presidents, and to an even greater degree Senators and representatives, have been subjected to recurrent pressures from what has come to be known as the Israel lobby. For the most part they have been responsive, and for reasons not always related either to personal conviction or careful reflection on the national interest.[14]

This illustrates the limits of U.S. influence because of a factor unique to the bilateral relationship with Israel—the existence of strong support for Israel in the legislative branch that can act as a check on the executive branch. In this particular instance the *New York Times* reported from Jerusalem: "The letter, *in the view of the Israeli leadership,* demonstrates that there is a limit to the political leverage the Ford administration can apply against Israel in the course of its current reassessment of Middle East policy."[15]

In democratic systems foreign policy is influenced by domestic politics—public opinion, political participation, and voting behavior all have an effect.

The Israel lobby enjoys a number of advantages in its efforts to secure its objectives. Its operational environment has generally been sympathetic rather than hostile. Hyman H. Bookbinder, the Washington representative of the American Jewish Committee and an important member of the Israel lobby, described it succinctly in these terms:

> The greatest single thing going for American support for Israel is the fact that our American leaders—the President, Cabinet officials, Senators, Congressmen, national security advisers—have for 30 years consistently *said* it is in America's interest. I do not contend that the great majority of Americans have themselves studied this issue carefully, know where the West Bank is, [or have] come to their own con-

clusion. They have accepted a national verdict. That verdict has been that Israel's security is in America's interest.[16]

There is a widespread fund of goodwill toward Israel that is not restricted to the Jewish community, which favored the establishment and consolidation of a Jewish state in Palestine and favors the continued existence, integrity, and security of Israel. At the same time pro-Arab forces have to operate in an environment that provides no mass support.

PERCEPTIONS OF ISRAEL: THE BASIS OF WIDESPREAD SUPPORT

Underlying much of the support, and providing Israel with an ability to influence U.S. decisions, is the basic U.S. perception of Israel and the Middle East.[17] Israel is seen as the type of state ("like-image"), with a similarity of outlook and generally progressive in nature, that the United States would like to see exist worldwide. President Ford, in a White House toast to Prime Minister Rabin in September 1974, said:

> The American people have a great deal of understanding and sympathy and dedication to the same kind of ideals that are representative of Israel. And, therefore, I think we in America have a certain rapport and understanding with the people of Israel. . . . We have mutual aims and objectives. We have the kind of relationship that I think, if expanded worldwide, would be beneficial to all mankind.[18]

In a similar vein former Israeli Foreign Minister Abba Eban identified a basic harmony of the two states: "harmony in democratic values, harmony of historic roots, harmony in spiritual memories, harmony of ideals, and, I am convinced, a profound, underlying harmony of interests in this hard and dangerous world."[19]

There is an element of cultural identity that sees Israel as a "Western" state in a sea of feudal, Oriental entities and as a perpetuator of the Judeo-Christian heritage. It is perceived as sharing the concept of individual freedom and the right of all individuals to live in peace. It is seen as a free, open, and democratic society—a "showplace of democracy"—pursuing peace. It is characterized as a brave, gallant, and young state that provides a model of courage and tenacity. Its people have been praised for their sacrifice, mettle, industriousness, dedication, determination, and spirit. Israel is seen as having achieved substantial progress, despite its precarious existence, and as worthy of emulation.

There is a historical affinity and similarity of national experience, which includes the immigrant and pioneering nature of the two states and their commitments to democracy. The U.S. experience in striving to escape persecution and establish an independent national homeland has a parallel in a Jewish state in Palestine that appears to reaffirm these ideals through absorption and integration of immigrants in distress. There has been a corresponding dedication to the values of pioneering—the United States placed a premium on the pioneers who heeded the call to "go west," and Israel places a similar value on the settlers who moved to the frontiers to develop those areas.

There is a general understanding of Jewish history and the advantages of the biblical connection. Israel fits into the historical-religious collective memory of Americans. President Truman expressed it well when he said, ". . . that is one part of the world that has always interested me, partly because of its Biblical background . . . ."[20] However,

> it wasn't just the Biblical part about Palestine that interested me. The whole history of that area of the world is just about the most complicated and most interesting of any area anywhere . . . . And the Arabs have just never seemed to take any interest in developing it. I have always thought that the Jews would, and of course, they have.[21]

The perception is also influenced by a religious factor (discussed in more detail below) that perceives Israel as fulfilling the biblical prophecy that the Jews would return to the promised land. This perception, nurtured in America's Bible Belt fundamentalist Christian areas, is further reinforced by "Sunday-school stories" linking the Jews to the Holy Land. In response to the historical persecution of the Jews, particularly the Holocaust and the destruction of large numbers of Jews in Europe during World War II, there was an effort to provide for the saving of the remnant of world Jewry through the maintenance of a sanctuary, which also helped to assuage a "guilt element." There is also the feeling of moral responsibility deriving from the U.S. involvement in the creation of the state in 1947 and 1948 and from the commitment to the Balfour Declaration after World War I, the latter playing a role in Truman's decision to support and recognize the creation of Israel. Further, there is the sympathy that derived from the "underdog" image that Israel had in relation to the Arab states during much of the early decades of the Arab-Israeli conflict.

This positive perception of Israel has been complemented by a generally negative image of the Arabs, although there has been some modification of this image in recent years, particularly with regard to Sadat and Egypt.

PUBLIC OPINION AND THE MEDIA

Public opinion affects foreign policy decisions, and interest groups gain influence when it appears that public opinion supports their positions. Gauging public opinion is difficult and imprecise, although polls provide a useful measure. In general, public support for Israel has been substantial. Informed Americans have consistently been far more willing to declare support and sympathy for Israel than for the Arab states, and continue to endorse Israel's existence, integrity, and security. This also has been reflected in views on issues of specific concern to Israel. (See Table 5.1.)

In general, sympathy for Israel has remained fairly constant over time, although there was an increase during and immediately after the 1967 and 1973 wars and in reaction to the completion of the Israeli withdrawal from Sinai in April 1982. The 1982 war showed a different trend. Polls taken soon after the start of hostilities showed that pro-Israel sympathies were unchanged and Americans appeared to be somewhat sympathetic to the Israeli incursion, despite disapproval of specific actions. On July 2, 1982, the Gallup Poll stated: "Although almost as many Americans disapprove as approve of Israel's incursion into Lebanon, the Israeli action appears not to have altered Americans' basic loyalties in the Middle East." The Harris Survey reported similar findings in August: "Israel has lost some backing in this country, but it is still viewed as a close ally or as friendly to the United States by an overwhelming majority."

The massacre at Shatila and Sabra and related developments in September seem to have had a significant effect; many Americans appeared to hold Israel at least partially responsible for those events. A poll conducted by Gallup and reported in *Newsweek* on October 4, 1982 showed that U.S. sympathies were about evenly divided between Israel and the Arab states. This was the first time ever that Israel was not heavily favored, and much of the change seemed to be related to the massacres. In response to the question "Compared with a year ago, would you say you are more sympathetic or less sympathetic to the Israeli position?" 51 percent of a national sample and 36 percent of an American Jewish sample responded that they were less sympathetic. At the same time 39 percent said they were more sympathetic to the Palestinian position.

TABLE 5.1 American Sympathies (percent)

Question: Have you heard or read about the situation in the Middle East? [If yes] In the Middle East situation are your sympathies more with Israel or more with the Arab nations?

Gallup Poll Responses

Date	Israel	Arab States	Neither	No Opinion
June 1967	56	4	25	15
January 1969	50	5	28	17
March 1970	44	3	32	21
October 6-8, 1973	47	6	22	25
October 19-22, 1973	48	6	21	25
December 7-10, 1973	54	8	24	14
January 1975	44	8	24	24
April 1975	37	8	24	31
June 3-6, 1977	44	8	28	20
October 14-17, 1977	46	11	21	22
February 1978	33	14	28	25
April/May 1978	44	10	33	13
September 22-25, 1978	42	12	29	17
November 10-13, 1978	39	13	30	18
January 5-8, 1979	42	15	29	14
July 1981	49	10	20	21
January 8-11, 1982	49	14	23	14
April 30-May 3, 1982	51	12	26	11
June 11-14, 1982	52	10	29	9
July 11-14, 1982	41	12	31	16
September 22-23, 1982	32	28	21	19
January 21-30, 1983	49	12	22	17

ABC/*Washington Post* Poll Responses

	2/25-3/2 1983	1/18-22 1983	9/24-26 1982	8/17 1982	3/3-9 1982
Israel	52	47	48	52	55
Arab nations	16	17	27	18	18
Neither/both	13	15	12	16	13
Don't know	19	21	13	14	14

Sources: Connie de Boer, "The Polls: Attitudes Toward the Arab-Israeli Conflict," *Public Opinion Quarterly* 47 (1983): 121-31, p. 123; Alvin Richman, "American Attitudes Toward the Middle East Since Israel's Invasion of Lebanon," paper presented at the AAPOR meeting, Buck Hill Falls Inn, May 1983, table 4.

Nevertheless, the fundamental, long-standing U.S. sympathy for and support of Israel has not diminished. Specific events have caused changes, generally transitory, in popular opinion on Israel or on its policies or leaders, but apparently have not affected the base of support. Thus, after the 1977 election that brought Menachem Begin to power, there began to appear a distinction between support for Israel and support for the policies and government of Israel. Specific disappointments with Begin's policies were not translated into lack of sympathy for Israel.

However, in the summer of 1982, elements in U.S. opinion seemed to hold Israel accountable for the policies of Begin and Sharon in Lebanon. Americans were chagrined by the casualties and losses resulting from the war and the "aggressiveness" of Israeli actions, but there remained a base of support for Israeli actions against the PLO, given a general negative perception of that body. This view began to shift with Israel's siege and bombing of Beirut, with Israel's opposition to the Reagan initiative, and, most significantly, with the Shatila and Sabra massacre. Extensive U.S. media coverage, particularly on network television, of the Israeli actions in Beirut led to negative conclusions and affected Israel's standing in U.S. eyes. By late September sympathies had changed—support for Israel was down and sympathy for the Arabs was up—dramatically.

The immediate response to events and the narrowing of the sympathy gap between Israel and the Arabs and between Israel and the Palestinians proved to be, as often in the past, short-term. An ABC/*Washington Post* poll conducted in February-March 1983 found that pro-Arab sympathy had declined considerably from the high point just after the massacre, and pro-Israel sympathy virtually had returned to its prewar level. By the first anniversary of the war, and particularly after the release of the report of the Kahan Commission, the polls showed a rebounding of sympathy to its prewar, premassacre levels.[22]

The media have also played an important role. In general, the U.S. media widely report news concerning Israel[23] and, over the years, have portrayed a positive (sometimes very positive) image of Israel, although there has been some modification in recent years.[24] Respect for and positive views of Egypt and Egyptians (especially Sadat) increased after Sadat's 1977 peace initiative. Begin was at a severe disadvantage because Sadat had learned the value and importance of the communications media, and exploited them skillfully. His statements to the media were short and simple, he avoided the negative (he did not use the word "no"), and he repeatedly stressed his desire for peace. Begin conveyed the image of a lawyer stressing minute legalistic points, rather than that of a statesman matching Sadat's grand vision of peace. Sadat and Egypt benefited from the image and also from the action, an approach to peace, which was widely endorsed in the United States.

Editorials have tended to favor Israel over the Arabs and to support Israel, particularly in the major publications and cities.[25] Despite the increased coverage of the Arab world since the 1973 war and the accompanying oil crisis, the orientation toward, and overall positive image of, Israel rather than the Arabs continues. This has tended to reinforce existing perspectives and proclivities, is reflected in public opinion, and has been instrumental in Israel's efforts to retain congressional support.

CONGRESS AND ISRAEL

Congress has been, and continues to be, an important element of support for Israel, and provides a unique factor of influence for Israel in its relations with the United States. Congress has often provided support for Israel in its efforts to influence the administration to act in Israel's favor and to undermine executive branch pressures on Israel.

Congressional support for Israel has been strong, as indicated in numerous resolutions, votes, statements, cosponsors of resolutions, public statements, letters for public release, and other factors. Generally, resolutions and statements favorable to Israel have had substantial numbers of cosponsors. On issues of importance, positions favorable to Israel have been consistently successful in the House and the Senate, although voting support has varied over time and with the specific issue at hand. The support is widespread, and not confined to representatives coming from Jewish population centers—it includes Republicans and Democrats, conservatives and liberals, although the reasons for support vary from individual to individual, from group to group, and from issue to issue.

The extent of support for pro-Israel actions led Senator J. William Fulbright to suggest, in 1973, that "the Israelis control the policy in the Congress and the Senate. . . . On every test on anything the Israelis are interested in the Senate . . . the Israelis have 75 to 80 votes."[26] The Fulbright view appears exaggerated, especially in recent years and when the matter is of crucial concern to the president and he is willing to put his prestige on the line, as in the 1978 and 1981 debates on arms sales to Arab states. However, pro-Israel strength is such that at times the administration has utilized it to assist in securing passage of other legislation. Aid for Greece in the days of the junta was argued on the ground that support of Israel required facilities in Greece, and aid to Cambodia was combined with legislation providing aid to Israel in order to facilitate congressional approval.

Foreign aid (economic and military assistance) has become a measure of congressional support for Israel. Israel has been the beneficiary of significant congressional efforts to increase its levels of aid. One study, focusing on the Nixon and Ford administrations, concluded that during that period "Congress consistently favored assistance to Israel, overwhelmingly approving every measure specifically proposing aid to Israel which reached the floor of either house and defeating all motions designed to cut aid."[27] Throughout that period "an average of about 80 percent of the Senate and 86 percent of the House cast votes favorable to Israel [on aid issues]."[28] Congress was more favorable to Israel than the executive branch, and generally expressed its support by increasing assistance levels beyond those requested by the executive branch. The increases for Israel in the fiscal years 1970 to 1977 were nearly 9 percent more than the amounts requested by the administration.

In addition to increasing the amounts of aid, various other devices favored Israel. These included lenient repayment terms and the conversion of loans to grants. Congress at times initiated new foreign aid programs to Israel's benefit, such as providing funds for the resettlement of Soviet Jews in Israel. Congress has also earmarked specific funds to reduce administration discretion and has included prohibitions in the aid bills to prevent assistance to others that might prove harmful to Israel. Beyond the aid programs themselves Congress has often used legislative measures and other, more indirect means to influence administration policy on Israel's behalf. Thus, there have been letters and statements and "sense of Congress" resolutions as well as committee hearings and reports designed to influence the administration and the public.

Support for Israel has also been reflected in careful scrutiny of Arab states' appropriations, which are sometimes reduced and often granted with conditions. Military sales to the Arab sales have been subjected to substantial discussion and often have been approved after significant and sometimes embarrassing (to the Arab states) debate—such as the AWACS decision in 1981. Congress has passed legislation governing businesses and their compliance with the Arab boycott of Israel, and their compliance with various racial and religious restrictions on the employment of Americans on projects in or with the Arab world.

JEWS AND POLITICS

There is a widespread view that Israel's success with Congress, and with the executive branch, over an extended period is a function of its success in the U.S. political system—which, in turn, is attributed to Jewish politicians, Jewish votes, and Jewish money. Generally, observers have exaggerated the role and effect of each of these factors.

Jews have not been very disproportionately represented among senior elected officials of the United States. There has not been a Jewish president or vice-president. Historically, Jewish membership in Congress has been approximately proportional (3-4 percent) to the Jewish population of the United States, but this has increased slightly in recent years. In the 93rd Congress, for example, there were only three Jewish senators and about twelve Jewish congressmen. In the 94th Congress there were 23 Jews; twenty in the House and three in the Senate. The 98th Congress, which convened in January 1983, had a record number of Jewish members: eight senators and thirty congressmen.

The "Jewish vote" has been seen as a factor resulting from the concentration of the American Jewish community in the northeastern section of the country, especially in states with large blocs of electoral votes that could be critical in influencing the outcome of a close presidential election. This is significant, since Jews tend to be politically active, thus gaining something of a multiplier effect for their votes and exerting an influence out of proportion to their numbers. The "Jewish vote" tends to have an influence—whether in reality, when it is actually cast, or in perception, when the office seeker modifies or tailors his position to gain or maintain the identified "vote."

Jewish money is often regarded as a potent factor in the effort to gain influence. Jews have been important among the financial backers of prominent political candidates, especially Democrats, and among the fundraisers of the major parties. Although this factor has been modified in recent years as a result of campaign reforms, Jewish donations to political causes have been out of proportion to population percentages and to wealth. The 1982 congressional election provides an illustration of the means by which American Jews have sought to influence elections. Numerous political action committees (PACs) were established, and helped to provide substantial funding to favored candidates, with some focus on members of committees that approve aid to the Middle East.

The political effect of Jewish PAC money is difficult to gauge, but the concentration on a single foreign-policy issue, rather than a number of diffuse subjects, apparently gives the funding more weight. Some money was used to help defeat Representative Paul Findley of Illinois, long regarded as hostile to Israel and favorable to the PLO, to elect or defeat members of the House Foreign Affairs Committee and the House Appropriations Committee's Foreign Operations Subcommittee, and to elect or reelect various senators on such committees as the Senate Appropriations Committee. National PACs provided campaign contributions to various congressional friends of Israel. The activities of these PACs were summarized thus:

> According to Federal Election Commission records, 31 Jewish PACs that were active in the 1981-82 congressional campaigns contributed a total of $1,676,016. Of that, $966,695, or 58%, went to Senate races. And 74% of the money was bet on incumbents like Sen. Mitchell, who drew money from 28 of the groups—all of them based outside of Maine.[29]

The Jewish PACs form something of a network and work closely together in determining which candidates they will support and which they will oppose. They work to ensure that Congress will be generous to Israel in its aid allocations.

THE AMERICAN JEWISH COMMUNITY AND ISRAEL

The role of the American Jewish community is broad: It includes a political effort to influence policy, and its seeks to create a bridge between the Jewish communities of Israel and the United States and to extend it to the broader U.S. society. By numerous connections, ranging from tourism to philanthropy, the bridge has been established and maintained. This social-cultural-human connection has involved a steady flow of Americans to Israel, to participate in all aspects of Israel's life and to facilitate the cultural exchange between the two states, and from Israel to the United States of emissaries from various institutions, to provide a "people to people" connection that facilitates other links and enhances the policy climate.

> The "secret weapon" of ethnic interest groups is neitehr money nor technique . . . but the ability to galvanize for specific political objectives the strong emotional bonds of large numbers of Americans to their cultural or ancestral homes. . . . "We do it out of a very, very passionate commitment."[30]

The American Jewish community is unified and motivated to work in Israel's behalf. The special relationship between it and Israel was ably described by the foreign minister of Israel, Moshe Sharett, to the annual convention of Hadassah in 1951 in these terms:

> I suggest that the presence in America of five million Jews, the responsibility which Israel feels toward them on the one hand, and their deep attachment to Israel on the other hand, do provide such an ultimate assurance [of maintaining American sympathy and friendship]. As long as the bond between Israel and American Jewry persists—for all the differences which may arise from time to time on this or that political decision or course of policy between the government of Israel and the government of the United States—there can never be a rupture between the two countries, because Israel will never turn its back on American Jewry and because, so we believe, American Jewry will never turn its back on Israel.

Menachem Begin has stated:

> No one will frighten the large and free Jewish community of the United States. No one will succeed in deterring them with anti-Semitic propaganda. They will stand by our side. This is the land of their forefathers, and they have a right and a duty to support it.[31]

The American Jewish community, the world's largest and most influential, numbers about 5.7 million, roughly 2.5 percent of the population of the United States. Geographically, Jews live in every state, with the largest proportion concentrated in the northeast. In 1982 New York State recorded 1.87 million Jews, or 10.6 percent of its population, while Arkansas, Idaho, Mississippi, Montana, South Dakota, and Wyoming each estimated that Jews accounted for 0.1 percent of their total populations. Wyoming had but 310 Jews and Idaho 505. The northeast had 54.3 percent of all Jews, the north central region 12.2 percent, the south 17.2 percent, and the west 16.3 percent.[32] The Jewish community is highly urbanized. There is a heavy concentration of Jews in states with large numbers of electoral votes.

The American Jewish community is generally better educated, has a higher social status, is more engaged in philanthropic activity, and is more heavily involved in political action than the American population in general. It is well organized, it is concerned, and it is committed on the issue of Israel. Major American Jewish organizations are characterized by large memberships, well-trained professional staffs, substantial financing, and effective programming and communications. They form a highly organized bureaucratic network and are connected in a number of national organizations. There are local and national organizations and umbrella groups that link the units. These factors create an ability to mobilize Jewish responses to issues of concern and interest in an organized, substantial, and rapid way.

The increasing centrality of Israel for the American Jewish community is a significant development. In a major study of the American Jewish community, Daniel Elazar argued that ". . . Israel has become the crucial operative element in shaping organized Jewish life today."[33]

America's Jewish organizations were not created because of Israel and have numerous other concerns, many of which have involved Jewish communities for centuries. There is a multiplicity of American Jewish organizations, reflecting the heterogeneous character of the population they represent, that deal with virtually every conceivable area of activity and interest. The creation of Israel provided an additional focal point that has increasingly gained attention—serving as a religious focus for some and as a secular focus for others. American Jewish leaders dote on their Israeli activities; fund-raising for Israel is often the centerpiece of local and national Jewish activity.

Although the centrality of Israel in American Jewish life developed over time, Zionism is at the focus of Judaism. The Bible, Jewish writings, and the Jewish religion focus on Zion and Jerusalem. Zionism as a religious or spiritual movement has deep roots in Jewish history and tradition, but the political component is of more recent origin. Political Zionism called for the creation of a Jewish homeland in Palestine, and derived its inspiration from the ideals of nationalism and the practices of anti-Semitism in nineteenth-century Europe. The leadership of the movement remained primarily European until World War II, when it shifted to the United States. The Biltmore Conference of May 1942 marked the turning point because the meeting was held in the United States and was called specifically for the creation of a "sovereign Jewish commonwealth" in Palestine. The Holocaust lent credence and urgency to the Zionist efforts, and American Jews became more significant in the movement and more active on its behalf.

The role of a Jewish state was hotly debated prior to Israel's independence, and three diverse perspectives—Zionist, anti-Zionist, and non-Zionist—were represented in the Jewish community. The anti-Zionist element, small and weak, opposed the identification of Israel and American Jewry, and the Zionist approach to Israel. The non-Zionists consisted of those organizations whose primary focus is cultural, social, religious, fraternal, or service, and for whom Israel has been *a* concern and not *the* concern. This group is composed of the largest and best-known of the American Jewish organizations. Originally noncommittal with regard to a Jewish state, after Israel's independence they adopted some form of program focusing on it and tend to engage in public relations activities for Israel. The Zionist organizations were established with Israel as their focus, and their basic purpose is to secure political, moral, and material support for it. Promotion of the security and well-being of Israel remains their raison d'être.

The June War of 1967 altered the role of Israel in American Jewish thinking and action, and the distinctions among the organizations became blurred. Israel became a more central concern, and support for it intensified. Confronted, they believed, with the possibility of the destruction of Israel, American Jews suddenly became aware of the intensity of their feeling and their commitment to the survival and well-being of the Jewish state. While one might argue that Israel's survival was never at stake, the fact remains that many in Israel and in the American Jewish community believed that it might have been. For them the war again evoked historical Jewish concerns with survival and the memories of the Holocaust. The result was an end to the ambivalence within the American Jewish community. After the war and the Israeli victory, the interdependence and linkage of Israeli and Diaspora (especially American) Jewry became more obvious, each recognizing the significance of the other. The 1973 war intensified many of the feelings generated by the June War. The attack on Israel on Yom Kippur—the Day of Atonement—reaffirmed much of the Jewish concern for and commitment to Israel.

In recent years there have been modifications in the Jewish community's approach to the question of Israel. Much has been written, impressionistically, about the nature and views of the American Jewish community and its relationship to Israel, especially since the accession of the Begin government to power in 1977. A study commissioned by the American Jewish Committee provides some specific data.[34] American Jews have reservations about the traditional Zionist view that all Jews should settle in Israel, and overwhelmingly seem content to remain in the United States.

> However, reservations about classical Zionism do not inhibit deep, passionate, and widespread concern for Israel. Fully 83 per cent [of the survey group] agree that "if Israel were destroyed, I would feel as if I had suffered one of the greatest personal tragedies in my life." The deep caring for Israel emerges in other findings as well.[35]

The study also notes that "consistent with other studies, more than nine Jews out of ten (94 per cent) regard themselves as 'very pro-Israel' (44 per cent) or 'pro-Israel' (50 per cent); almost all the rest are 'neutral.'[36]

These findings tend to confirm many of the generalizations that have been advanced over the years about the American Jewish community and its relationship to Israel. The Jewish community remains strongly supportive of Israel, although there are some areas where it differs with the policies of the Jewish state. The American Jewish Committee's survey suggests:

> They [American Jews] may be developing yet another distinction between concern for Israel and support for Israeli government policy. The vast majority of respondents are convinced that the Palestinians and the PLO seek to destroy Israel. They line up with the majority of Israeli political leaders in rejecting (by 74 to 18 per cent) negotiations with the PLO. By a smaller, though still lopsided majority (64 to 11, with 25 per cent undecided), they fear that an independent Palestinian state on the West Bank of the Jordan "would probably be used as a launching pad to endanger Israel." At the same time, the respondents divide over whether Israel should permanently annex territories occupied in the Six Day War. By a small majority (42 to 28, with fully 30 per cent undecided), the sample prefer annexation to an independent Palestinian state; the many "undecideds" reveal considerable difficulty with this question. Even more telling, the respondents split evenly (41 to 41, with 18 per cent undecided) over whether Israel should trade occupied territory for assurances of peace. Clearly, annexationist policies are less popular among American Jews than are actions taken to defend Israel against perceived Palestinian threats. A summary question asked the respondents to characterize "Israel's policies in its dispute with the Arabs." Almost a quarter (23 per cent) emerge as "doves"; they believe Israel's policies are "too hawkish." Almost all the other respondents (74 per cent) think Israel's policies area "about right."[37]

A concluding observation, drawn from the study, is important in assessing the role of the American Jewish community in providing support for Israel. American Jewish alienation from Israel,

> at least at this point, is limited to disagreement with Israeli policy; there is no general disillusionment with Israel. Significantly, the greatest disenchantment is found among Jews who are far removed from organized Jewish life. The more committed Jews find far less to

fault in Israeli policies. As of now, hard-core critics of Israeli policy form only a small but noticeable minority of American Jews.[38]

The Israel-oriented American Jewish organizations serve two broad-scale purposes: fund raising and educational/public relations/political activity.

American Jewry has materially aided the establishment, development, and consolidation of Israel through outright philanthropic gifts and the purchase of Israel bonds. The major American Jewish organization that secures philanthropic contributions for Israel and for American Jewish needs is the United Jewish Appeal (UJA), established in 1939. It channels aid to Israel primarily through the United Israel Appeal. There are also substantial contributions that go directly to specific charities or programs in Israel, such as hospitals, schools, and research institutions, without involving the UJA. These private funds are provided for charitable institutions and are largely tax-deductible. Supplementing the purely philanthropic activity is the Israel Bonds Organization, whose purpose is investment rather than donation, and which provides Israel with a significant amount of foreign exchange each year.

The political and public relations activities have been extensive and have involved the American Jewish community in cultural, social, educational, public relations, and political activities on behalf of Israel in the United States.

THE ISRAEL LOBBY

The American Jewish community and the Israel lobby are well organized to perform the tasks on behalf of Israel that they have set for themselves. Although the American Jewish community is well organized and highly structured, it is highly complex, and not monolithic or hierarchical, and no one organization or individual represents American Jewry, despite the claim of several to do so. When the issue is Israel-oriented, the American Israel Public Affairs Committee (AIPAC) and the Conference of Presidents of Major American Jewish Organizations (the Conference) are at the focal point, although others, such as the American Jewish Committee, often pursue their own course.

The Israel lobby has an influential role in the formation of attitudes and the formulation of policies concerning Israel and the Middle East. It functions within the parameters of the U.S. political system and is composed of diverse organizations whose activities and concerns relating to Israel range from cultural, educational, and religious to philanthropic, financial, and political.

Although there are other national and umbrella Jewish organizations in the United States, AIPAC and the Conference are the major coordinating bodies in terms of the lobbying efforts for Israel in the United States.

At the core is AIPAC, the only officially registered lobbying organization established for the purpose of influencing legislation on Capitol Hill to improve U.S.-Israel relations. It is registered under the lobbying law. Its officially stated purpose is to maintain and improve the friendship and goodwill between the United States and Israel. AIPAC is a small but not insignificant organization. By 1983 it had a staff of about 30 (both lobbyists and support personnel) and a budget of about $1.5 million contributed by American donors and not tax-deductible. With more than 15,000 members nationwide, it is the focal point of the American Jewish community's efforts to deal with Israel-oriented issues, as it is of the broader lobby that extends beyond the Jewish community. It concentrates on direct work with Congress.

AIPAC is a single-purpose organization. Its framework is the U.S. national interest and, while it is concerned about Israel's view and the Israel embassy is a natural "ally," it operates independently. Its activities include informing members of Congress about Israel and informing its membership (and the broader Jewish community) about congressional activity and U.S. policy concerning Israel and the Middle East. It carefully monitors how members of Congress act on Middle Eastern issues, and seeks to mobilize its members and others to ensure that members of Congress maintain a posture supportive of Israel and the U.S.-Israel relationship. I. L. Kenen, the founder and long-time (1954-1975) head of AIPAC, has described its approach as multifaceted, but: "Our technique was always to rouse the constituents to mobilize the Members of Congress to press the Administration that this or that policy was what the American people wanted."[39]

One observer has noted AIPAC's "ability to order up batches of telegrams and letters by state and congressional district to impress key Members of Congress at the right time and to produce background documents, voting records and analyses on issues affecting Israel within hours."[40] It can influence votes through rewards for members of Congress in the form of positive statements and support in their home districts, particularly at election time. It has also been able to castigate members of Congress whose positions it finds unhelpful, which often will work to the disadvantage of the member at election time.[41]

The Conference is a coordinating body of various major Jewish organizations with diverse concerns—fraternal matters, community relations, religious themes, philanthropic activity, and Zionist concerns. Originally created in 1955 to present a consensus perspective of the major American Jewish organizations and to prevent the overlapping of response on matters affecting Israel, it had a minor role until the June War because there were relatively few organizations anxious to act with regard to Israel. With the "Zionization" of the American Jewish community in 1967, and with the growing links between the communities and the increased need for coordination of the various groups, the Conference became a more significant organization. It became a mechanism for contact and consultation between Israel and American Jewry at the most senior levels.

The Conference is composed of 34 organizations and has a rotating presidency. It is not a single-purpose organization, and Israel is but one element of its concern, as it is for the many organizations that have joined to create it. There are numerous issues on the agenda (such as civil rights, social welfare programs, and unemployment) and religious issues or those with religious overtones often divide the members. Generally the organizations derive their income from tax-deductible sources and do not engage in direct lobbying. However, they inform their memberships about issues of concern, and thus have an indirect effect. Also, while their focus of activity may lie elsewhere and they are, at times, at odds with each other on various issues, support for Israel is a common denominator.

The Conference seeks to develop a consensus, when possible, on issues of major concern to the Jewish community. The members discuss and consult, and seek to coordinate their activities, but to decide and to act they must be unanimous; they speak out as a group only when they reach a consensus. They seek to present this American Jewish perspective to the White House and the State Department and to their memberships for their information and, often, for their action. Often political action is recommended, and may take the form of communications to the White House or other executive agencies. The Conference and its components also seek to interpret Israel to the U.S. body politic (and to explain the United States to Israeli officials).[42]

The Conference concentrates its activities in the executive branch, much as AIPAC devotes its primary efforts to the legislative branch.

The lobbying process gets an assist from its "client"—the government of Israel—in a number of ways. Clearly it is in the interest of the government of Israel in Jerusalem (and its embassy in Washington) to maintain close contact with the various groups lobbying on its behalf and with Congress, which is so important to it, in addition to the traditional and ordinary linkages with the executive branch. There are connections to the Conference and to AIPAC, as well as to other Jewish organizations and prominent Americans, Jewish and non-Jewish, who might serve Israel's cause and promote its views. Senior Israeli officials (including the prime minister, the minister of defense, and the minister of foreign affairs, as well as other cabinet ministers, members of the Knesset, and numerous officials) visit Washington, New York, and other U.S. cities frequently. During these visits there is often a pilgrimage to Capitol Hill for meetings, formal and informal, with members of Congress, particularly those on key committees.

Members of Congress often are as anxious to meet with the visiting Israelis as the Israelis are to meet with them. The Israelis also visit and consult with prominent American Jewish figures and with the Conference. Often these meetings serve not only to inform the American Jewish leadership and the pro-Israel elements on the U.S. scene of Israel's views, but also to give Israel's leadership a perspective on the United States. These meetings, especially if they are large and public, can be "used" as a means of influencing Congress and the executive branch by demonstrating the extent of popular support for Israel.

The precise role and success of the Jewish community and Israel interest group in influencing the nature of U.S. policy toward Israel is impossible to measure, but it is clear that the United States has extensive ties with Israel, some of which partly reflect the efforts of these groups and the individuals that compose them.

Although no precise judgment is possible, the success and failure of the Israel lobby has been highlighted by events in recent years: the 1975 letter of 76 senators to President Ford endorsing aid to Israel, the 1978 vote by a Senate majority that did not prevent the Carter administration's sale of F-15 jets to Saudi Arabia, and the 1981 vote not to prevent the sale of AWACS to Saudi Arabia. The first was an important achievement, the other two debatable "failures." U.S. military and economic aid has been the most tangible accomplishment. In more general terms the effectiveness of the Israel lobby was evaluated thus by Congressman Benjamin Rosenthal:

> I'd say that with or without them, the same things would have occurred. The U.S. and Israel would still be strong allies and the politics in the Middle East would still be a mess. For the most part, the lobbyists are just mimeograph operators, pushing out piles of information, moving papers around.[43]

An official of the executive branch with extensive Middle East involvement offered a similar perspective: "You have to try hard to think of specific things that would have turned out differently without the Jewish Lobby. A lot of things that came to pass were in our interest anyway, and an internal decision would have produced the same result that the lobby argued for. Maybe not precisely the way they wanted it, but close enough."[44] Senator Mathias has described the "operating successes" of the lobby in these terms:

> More important . . . has been the success of the Jewish organizations in maintaining solid congressional support for a high level of military and economic aid to Israel. This is not to suggest that Congress supports Israel for no better reason than fear of the Israel lobby; on the contrary, I know of few members of either house of Congress who do not believe deeply and strongly that support of Israel is both a moral duty and a national interest of the United States. It is rather to suggest that, as a result of the activities of the lobby, congressional conviction has been measurably reinforced by the knowledge that political sanctions will be applied to any who fail to deliver.[45]

Mathias sums up the work of the Jewish community and the lobby well:

> In the case of the Middle East there seems little doubt that, but for the efforts of American Jews, our military and economic aid to Israel would've been less than it is, although I remain convinced that, even if there were no Israel lobby, the American people would remain solidly committed to Israel's survival.[46]

JEWISH INFLUENCE ON ISRAEL

It is generally assumed that the U.S. Jewish community and the Israel lobby work in a unidirectional manner to influence U.S. policy toward Israel, without any corresponding activity to influence Israel's decisions. This is inaccurate. The U.S. Jewish community, and particularly its leadership, plays a role in influencing Israeli policy toward the United States and toward issues in Israel and the Middle East, and elsewhere, of interest and concern to the United States. The reasons for this are manifold but flow logically from the many interests and concerns of the U.S. Jewish community.

The U.S. Jewish community's role in attempting to influence Israel's policies is generally the result of a decision that it is important to effect a change in the Israeli position because the U.S. Jewish leadership believes that it will be in the best interests of Israel and/or of the American or worldwide Jewish community. Or the U.S. government may seek to modify Israeli policies and to utilize the American Jewish leadership to assist in this effort, knowingly or otherwise. This latter role helps to account for the significant links between most administrations and the American Jewish community, particularly its leadership. Often the connection has taken the form of a formal or informal White House liaison to the Jewish community. There have been numerous "briefings" and meetings with the American Jewish leadership to inform, mollify, influence, cajole, and, rarely, to confront with regard to U.S. policy in the Middle East or U.S.-Israel relations. How successful this process has been in generating changes in the views of the American Jewish leadership and, thereby, in effecting modifications in Israel's policies remains unclear.

The American Jewish leadership informs Israel's leadership concerning the situation in the United States and plays a role in generating change in Israel's thinking and policy. Howard Squadron, a prominent American Jewish leader, has described the American Jewish community's dual influence role in these terms:

> I have tried, and others have tried, to explain to American officials the perception in Israel of events and to explain to Israeli officials the perception of the administration and the State Department of events.[47]

Needless to say, these explanations are designed to develop greater understanding and rapport, and probably affect policy decisions.

Having noted that there is an effort to be involved in the process of policy formulation and the links between the United States and Israel, it must be said that the influence is limited, often indirect, and personal rather than institutional, and lacks the major channels of influence one might expect to find in areas affecting public policy.

The American Jewish community, and Diaspora Jewry more generally,

> exercises very little influence over Israeli public policy. It is not true to suggest that it exercises no influence. . . . But it is fair to say that in the sum total of factors that constitute influences on the sum total of Israeli policies, Diaspora influence is slight.[48]

This is somewhat surprising, given the fact that the Diaspora, especially the American Jewish community, has enormous resources that can be brought to bear on Israel. The reasons for this lack of influence can be traced, to a great extent, to a lack of effort and desire to exert such infleunce. Israel is not seen as an appropriate target for the American Jewish community in its efforts to modify policies. At the same time Israel has not provided a legitimate role for non-Israeli Jewish involvement in the Israeli decision-making process, nor are there official channels for the expression of political views or influence by non-Israelis within the Israeli political structure.

The American Jewish community is not organized to express its political views or positions in the Israeli political system. If non-Israeli Jews wish to influence the Israeli decision-making process, they have few channels through which to try to present their views. There are the Jewish Agency and the World Zionist Organization, but these are somewhat tangential to the main Israeli political institutions. They deal with the Israeli system, but are not a part of it with direct access to cabinet or Knesset decision making. Other Jewish organizations, even the most prominent, must rely on informal and indirect channels in their efforts to affect Israeli decisions. At the same time, leading Israeli decision makers in the prime minister's office and in the Foreign Ministry, and to a lesser degree in the Knesset, are sensitive to the counsel and concerns of the American Jewish leadership. However, these mechanisms are ad hoc and outside the primary political institutions of the Israeli system.

Do they influence Israeli decisions? While it is impossible to determine with certainty the extent of influence, clearly no Israeli leader will ignore the collective wisdom of the American Jewish leadership when it makes its views known on issues affecting the course of the U.S.-Israel relationship, given the importance of the American Jewish community to Israel. At the same time, Israelis have been careful to emphasize that they alone must bear the responsibility for the decisions that affect Israel's future, particularly on matters of national security and vital national interest.

NON-JEWISH SUPPORTERS

American Jewish supporters of Israel, and Israel itself, have long realized the need for Christian support if Israel is to flourish, just as that support was essential to ensure the establishment of the state. The ability of pro-Israel groups to form coalitions with other domestic elements and to secure endorsements from such diverse sources as prominent public figures, black leaders, scholars, and entertainers has been a positive element.

The U.S. religious heritage, overwhelmingly Christian, helps to secure a religious interest in and link to the land and people of Israel. Father Robert Drinan has described it in these terms:

There is . . . a profound bond between the Christians of America and the Jews of Israel. This bond goes back to the fact that the original pilgrims who came to America from Europe did so because they were persecuted for religious or political reasons in their fatherland. Because of the similarity of the origin of immigration to Israel, Christians in America have a profound, if unconscious, affinity for the hundreds of thousands of Jews who have gone to Israel since the holocaust.[49]

The original settlers of the United States brought their religious identity and concerns with them, and the Old Testament served as a guide to both history and daily life. The religious faith of the Pilgrims later became a factor in support for Israel throughout the U.S. Christian, and especially fundamentalist, community. Hebrew was a significant language of study in U.S. colleges and universities in their early days, and there was a religious and spiritual connection with the land of the Bible and its inhabitants—universally seen as Jews, not Arabs.

Christian support for Israel has varied in intensity and in source since the debates in the 1940s over the creation of the Jewish state. In recent years the evangelical movement has become increasingly significant, although there have been concerns in the American Jewish community about the ˙˙ ˙kage in view of evangelical positions on significant U.S. social questions. Other, more traditional and mainstream Christian groups have provided support over a more extended period. The American Christian Palestine Committee and similar groups have been influential. The National Christian Leadership Conference for Israel brings various fundamentalist groups together in support of Israel.

Within the U.S. Christian community ". . . the *most influential and vocal* elements of the Religious Right are the greatest champions of Israel outside the Jewish community itself."[50] The religious Right "is composed of evangelical and fundamentalist Christians, estimated at between thirty to fifty million."[51]

The basis for this strong pro-Israel perspective lies in their approach to the Bible.

According to their interpretation of scripture, it is essential that the Jews be regathered in the Holy Land before Christ will come again. Only after the establishment of a new Israeli nation can the drama of the "end days" begin. It commences with a seven-year period of great tribulations, during which the anti-Christ temporarily rules the world and ends with the catastrophic Battle of Armaggedon (in Israel). Before humankind completely destroys itself in this bloody battle, Christ returns to save the faithful Bible believers and to usher in the millennium.[52]

Given this perspective, Israel's establishment provided "proof" that biblical prophecies were being fulfilled. Begin's accession to power seemed to comport well with the values of this group, since he was seen as representing "deep religious convictions, militaristic policies, patriotic fervor, and economic conservatism. . . ."[53] Thus, strong support for Israel under his leadership seemed logical and appropriate.

At the same time there has been a growing trend among some Christian groups—such as the National Council of Churches—to espouse the Palestinian (often the PLO) cause and to question the legitimacy of Israel.[54]

U.S. political leaders, including the president, have been influenced by religious factors. Wilson and Truman identified such a component in their decision making, and even the noted "politician" Lyndon Johnson seemed to be affected, as he told B'nai B'rith in September 1968:

> Most, if not all of you, have very deep ties with the land and with the people of Israel, as I do, for my Christian faith sprang from yours. The Bible stories are woven into my childhood memories as the gallant struggle of modern Jews to be free of persecution is also woven into our souls.

These perspectives add to the overall positive image of Israel and facilitate adoption of policies favorable to Israel.

THE NATURE OF THE COMMITMENT

In a press conference on May 12, 1977, President Jimmy Carter said:

> We have a special relationship with Israel. It's absolutely crucial that no one in our country or around the world ever doubt that our No. 1 commitment in the Middle East is to protect the right of Israel to exist, to exist permanently, and to exist in peace. It's a special relationship.[55]

Israel's special relationship with the United States, based on substantial positive perception and sentiment evident in public opinion and official statements, and manifest in political-diplomatic support and military and economic assistance, has not been enshrined in a legally binding commitment joining the two states in a formal alliance. Despite the substantial links that have developed, the widespread belief in the existence of the commitment, and the assurances contained in various specific agreements, such as Sinai II and the letters attached to the Camp David accords and the Egypt-Israel peace treaty, the exact nature and extent of the U.S. commitment to Israel remains imprecise.

Israel has no mutual security treaty with the United States, nor is it a member of any alliance system requiring the United States to take up arms automatically on its behalf. It has been assumed that the United States would come to Israel's assistance should it be gravely threatened, a perception that has become particularly apparent in times of crisis, especially during the June War of 1967. Despite this perception and the general "feeling" in Washington and elsewhere that the United States would take action if required, there is no assurance that this would be the case. The exact role of the United States in support of Israel, beyond diplomatic and political action and military and economic assistance, is unclear.

The commitment has taken the generalized form of presidential statements rather than formal documents. U.S. statements of policy have reaffirmed the U.S. interest and concern in supporting the political independence and territorial integrity of Middle Eastern states, including Israel. They do not, however, commit the United States to specific actions in particular circumstances.

In April 1969 the Senate Foreign Relations Committee summarized the U.S. commitment to Israel in these terms:

> Consider, for example, the widely held view that the United States is committed to the defense of Israel even though we have no security treaty with that country. The source of this alleged commitment is in fact nothing more than a long series of executive policy declarations, including: President Truman's declaration of support for the independence of Israel in 1948; the British-French-American tripartite declaration of 1950 pledging opposition to the violation of frontiers or armistice lines in the Middle East; President Eisenhower's statement of January 1957 pledging American support for the integrity and independence of Middle Eastern nations; Secretary of State Dulles's assertion of February 1957 that the United States regarded the Gulf of Aqaba as an international waterway; President Kennedy's press conference of March 1963 pledging American opposition to any act of aggression in the Middle East; and President Johnson's statements of February 1964 indicating American support for the territorial integrity and political independence of all Middle Eastern countries.

All of these declarations are executive policy statements; not one is based on a treaty ratified by the Senate. The only treaty commitment the United States has in the Middle East is as a signatory to the United Nations Charter. . . . It is not the committee's position that the United States ought not to come to the support of Israel should it be the victim of aggression. It is the committee's position that, should so significant an obligation be incurred, it ought to be the result of a treaty or other appropriate legislative instrumentality.[56]

More recently the arrangement has been codified in a specific document on two occasions, the Sinai II accords of 1975 and the memorandum of understanding on strategic cooperation of 1981, although commitments made in the Egypt-Israel peace process and other "memoranda" have been significant.

Sinai II, particularly the bilateral U.S.-Israel memoranda, placed the U.S. role on a more precise footing by articulating several aspects of the relationship. They reflected much of past practice and the specific requirements of the particular situation. The arrangements dealt with a number of themes, including U.S. support for Israel's security:

> In view of the long-standing United States commitment to the survival and security of Israel, the United States Government will view with particular gravity threats to Israel's security or sovereignty by a world power. In support of this objective, the United States Government will in the event of such threat consult promptly with the government of Israel with respect to what support, diplomatic or otherwise, or assistance it can lend to Israel in accordance with its constitutional practices.

The pledged response was similar to that contained in the main U.S. alliance treaties, and focused on the Soviet threat. There were other pledges focusing on specific elements in the relationship, including the role of the PLO, and the U.S. role in the Security Council and its use of the veto power to prevent alterations in the agreement by Security Council resolutions. Additional assurances on economic and military assistance were also provided. But, despite the codification aspects of the Sinai II assurances, they did not provide a formal and legally binding commitment for U.S. military action.

Over the years a U.S. commitment to Israel has developed that is essentially unwritten but widely perceived as a policy reality in the United States, in Israel, and in much of the remainder of the world, including the

Arab world. The commitment is not formalized, except for some components, and centers on the survival of Israel against implacable enemies. The Soviet threat is central. Israeli decision makers have long believed that the United States would not permit major Soviet military action against Israel and would act to deter the Soviet Union from significant involvement in conflict in the Middle East against Israel.

In October 1968 Deputy Prime Minister Yigal Allon said in the Knesset: "Israel is isolated when she has to defend herself against the aggression of the Arabs, but I have solid grounds to say that when it concerns military intervention by the Soviet Union against Israel she will not be isolated."[57] Other Israeli leaders have articulated this theme on other occasions. The U.S. agreement in the Sinai II accords to consult with Israel in the face of threats to Israel's "security or sovereignty by a world power" appears to be consistent with this view, as were the provisions of the memorandum of understanding of 1981. Although Israeli leaders continue to feel reasonably confident about the U.S. role against Soviet machinations, they are not certain about the nature and extent of U.S. actions in support of its position. While they believe that the United States would ensure Israel's security and integrity, they have not interpreted the commitment too broadly and have not been precise as to the form it might take.

Israeli leaders continue to be interested in military and economic assistance as the primary tangible expression of U.S. commitment. They have been particularly cautious about potential U.S. participation in conflict, and they do not want Americans fighting in or for Israel. The dangers inherent in such participation have been recognized, and this judgment appears validated by the experiences of the United States in overseas military involvements. The Israelis are concerned about possible situations analogous to Vietnam, and see this in the debate in the United States in 1983 concerning Central America and the American presence in Lebanon. Defense Minister Moshe Dayan expressed this view in an interview on CBS Television's "60 Minutes" on April 13, 1971:

> Believe me, one of the things that I really, really don't want is to have any American commitment that will make the American fighting for Israel. . . . Because I want your friendship and I want—you will not be friendly for us if you will have to fight for us. I would like you to sell us arms, to help us in the political field. I don't want you to fight for us, because once you will be getting killed for us, you won't like us very much. You won't like us.

In March 1978 Begin said: "We don't want even one American soldier to fight our battles. . . . We can sustain our independence. From time to time we need some tools. . . ."[58]

Understanding the nature of the commitment is difficult. Israel stands in a unique position and holds a place in U.S. concern and policy occupied by few other states. It is complex and multifaceted, and has become more so in recent years. Israel is not merely a friendly state or even an "ally," nor is the relationship always positive.

The idea of a formal treaty guarantee for Israel by the United States has been raised on several occasions, but the prevailing sentiment appears to be that it is neither necessary nor desirable. Nevertheless, when Menachem Begin presented his new cabinet for approval to the Knesset in August 1981, he stated that he was prepared to recommend that Israel enter into a formal alliance with the United States:

> True, no written and signed alliance exists between us. I have been asked more than once by American statesmen whether we would wish or be prepared to sign with their country a written defense pact. I have answered them consistently: "If you make such a proposal to us I shall recommend to my colleagues in Government to sign such an agreement." We, on our part, cannot assume the initiative on a matter of this kind in case we be refused. It is proper that the mighty power take the initiative, no country, including a small one, wants to court refusal. And this is my answer again today to such questions put to me in the past, and which may be asked in the future. The truth is that an unwritten alliance, too, which often is no less important than a signed one, determines the relations between peoples on matters of a common stand, especially in times of crisis.

This despite the fact that more narrow accords, such as the memorandum of understanding on strategic cooperation, have been sought and consummated. Although the United States has incurred no legally binding commitment requiring it to come to Israel's assistance in the event of conflict, it is clear that there is general support for the commitment to Israel. This tends to render a formal document superfluous and perhaps undesirable. The critical factor is not the formal requirement, but the perception of it and the willingness to act in support of perceived obligations. In the final analysis the commitment of the United States to Israel will reflect the nature of the relationship at any particular time.

THE FUTURE OF THE RELATIONSHIP: CONSENSUS AND DISCORD

The United States and Israel have established a special relationship replete with broad areas of agreement and numerous examples of discord over nearly four decades. The two states have worked together in many spheres. Broad agreement and understanding and a generalized commitment to peace exist, and specific questions and issues have consistently been approached within that framework. It is with regard to the specifics, especially the tactics and techniques to be employed in efforts to achieve the broad objectives, that the relationship has often had its episodes of disagreement, and that each has been particularly active in its efforts to influence the actions of the other. A combination of agreement on broad goals and discord on specifics is likely to characterize the U.S.-Israel relationship in the future, and will likely increase their efforts to influence each other's policies.

The two states maintain general agreement on broad policy goals. The policy consensus—the commonality of interest—includes the need to prevent war, both regional and that involving the superpowers, the need to resolve the Arab-Israeli conflict, and the need to maintain Israel's existence and security and to help provide for its economic well-being. There has been a remarkable degree of parallelism and congruence between the two states, but there also have been episodes of noncongruence of policy that have led to efforts by one party or the other, or both operating simultaneously, to influence the nature and direction of the policy of the other.

There was, is, and will be a divergence that derives from a difference of perspective and overall policy environment. The United States has broader concerns resulting from its global responsibilities, while Israel's perspective is conditioned by its more restricted environment and lesser responsibilities. Israel's horizon is more narrowly defined, and essentially limited to the survival of the state and a concern for Jewish communities and individuals that goes beyond the frontiers of the Jewish state, such as the Falashas of Ethiopia and the Jews of the Soviet Union.

The linkage of the two states reached new levels between the 1967 and 1973 wars, when there was an exclusivity in the relationship as a result of the war, the ruptures of relations between the United States and some Arab states, the general agreement on the need for a settlement, and the intrusion of the Soviet Union. However, this exclusivity gave way to a period in which U.S.-Arab relations gradually improved during the Nixon (after 1973), Ford, Carter, and early Reagan years.

Since the October War there has been an incremental change in the U.S. presence and role in the region—ties with both Israel and the Arab states have increased. At the same time the United States began a process of establishing links that presaged a substantial and multifaceted relationship that has grown to encompass complex economic interrelationships including technical and economic assistance, and agreements on investment and political and strategic consultation (and some cooperation), as well as economic assistance and military assistance and sales. In the Reagan administration, with its initial Persian Gulf-Southwest Asia focus and its concept of strategic consensus, the relationship with some of the Arab states, especially Saudi Arabia, gained new centrality.

Israel's concern with the altering relationships and the improved American links with the Arab states did not become a major public issue until early 1976, when proposed U.S. military sales to Saudi Arabia and Egypt became open knowledge. Israel opposed the sales, while the United States saw them as important for regional stability and peace, and for an improved relationship with the Arab states. U.S. plans to sell Egypt six C-130 military transport aircraft became a matter of major controversy. It was seen by the United States as an important boost for Sadat, to encourage his moderation and move away from the Soviet relationship, and as not affecting, deleteriously, the U.S.-Israel relationship. This raised the issue rather clearly, and foreshadowed the arms sales controversies of 1978 and 1981.

Despite the generally positive nature of the relationship between the United States and Israel since 1948, Israelis tend to recall a series of negative episodes.[59] They highlight the 1947 arms embargo and the subsequent refusal to provide military equipment or other assistance during the War of Independence and much of the subsequent period, Dulles' aid suspensions and general unfriendliness, U.S. actions in connection with the Sinai War of 1956 and Israel's subsequent withdrawal from Sinai and the Gaza Strip, and the disappointing lack of action by the United States, just prior to the June War, in support of its 1957 pledge concerning freedom of passage for Israeli shipping in the Strait of Tiran.

In 1967 Israel decided that the United States would not act unilaterally and that multilateral action would not succeed. Israel determined its need to act alone and estimated that the United States would not object to, or seek to prevent, its action. Thus, when Israel finally decided to go to war, it did not consult or inform the United States. With the outbreak of hostilities the U.S. response, especially that of the president, was favorable to Israel, reflecting a sense of relief at Israel's accomplishments and the obvious fact that U.S. involvement would not be necessary even to consider. Clearly, the danger of a superpower confrontation was reduced.

There has been a divergence on methods and techniques to be employed as well as discord on specific issues, including the appropriate form of response to Arab terrorism, the value of great-power efforts to resolve the conflict, the appropriateness and timing of face-to-face and direct Arab-Israeli negotiations, and the provision of essential military supplies (types, quantities, and timing). During the 1967 war there was a clash over Israel's attack on the U.S. intelligence ship *Liberty,* which resulted in casualties. In May 1968 there was disagreement over Israel's control of the islands of Tiran and Sanafir. The two nations have disagreed on the matter of reprisals by Israel in response to Arab actions, and on the limits placed on the refugees from the West Bank in the wake of the June War. They have come into major disagreement concerning the occupied territories, their status, and Israel's role there, including the building of settlements. They have argued over Israel's desire for significant changes in the pre-June War armistice lines, in contrast with the U.S. desire that there be "insubstantial alterations" or "minor modifications."

In many respects the issue of Jerusalem has highlighted the areas of discord. The United States has not recognized unilateral action affecting the status of the city. Jerusalem has been a matter of particular sensitivity because of its unique character and its significance to Judaism as well as to other major faiths, especially Islam. The United States has supported the partition plan designation of Jerusalem as a separate entity, and has stressed the international character of the city while refusing to recognize unilateral actions by any state affecting its future. The United States will not move its embassy to Jerusalem and maintains it in Tel Aviv, thus illustrating the differing perspectives of the two states. These perspectives have placed them in conflicting positions virtually continuously since 1947, especially since the Israeli declaration of Jerusalem as the capital of the state and the reunification of the city during the 1967 war.

The two states will continue to hold divergent views on the several elements of the Palestinian issue, particularly the West Bank's future, the rights of the Palestinians, and the potential creation of a Palestinian homeland, entity, or state. These differences have become increasingly obvious in the Carter and Reagan administrations, particularly during the autonomy negotiations. The two states have differed over the construction of settlements in the territories and whether they are legal or obstacles to peace.

There have been personality clashes. Senior U.S. and Israeli officials have not always been compatible, and this has affected the tenor of the relationship. This was particularly evident in the relations between Carter and Begin. In the Reagan administration mutual dislike and mistrust extended further—the United States was unhappy with Begin and Sharon, while Israel had strong anxieties about Weinberger and his policies.

There have been disagreements concerning the nature of the situation in the region, often focusing on alternative intelligence estimates of the threat. These differences have involved data, analyses, and policy results.

In an interview in 1969, Prime Minister Golda Meir summarized the situation well with a comment that is likely to remain accurate for some time to come:

> We have been very fortunate that there is a basic friendship to Israel and this doesn't change with the administration. There have been problems at various times since the state of Israel was established, and every once in a while we don't see eye to eye as to how the problem should be solved. But underlying these differences of opinion there is always the consciousness we carry with us that basically there is a deep friendship, understanding, and concern for the existence of Israel.[60]

The consensus on major issues does not ensure agreement on all aspects or specifics of each problem. As the dialogue has increasingly dealt with details, rather than broad areas of agreement, there have been disturbances in the relationship. Israel and the United States understand that this is inevitable, but seek to minimize the areas of discord. This has been recognized by Israel, as indicated in the following observation by Golda Meir:

> There is one thing we must be clear on. We don't suppose for one moment that the Americans would knowingly do anything to hurt us, or that they would agree to or suggest anything they knew was injurious. But from here on, differences of opinion begin because we can agree that no matter how great is our friendship, there is no possibility of absolute identity between us and what others see as our security need.[61]

Strains in the relationship are probably inevitable, given the extensive nature of the issues considered in the dialogue. During these discussions and in an effort to achieve mutually-identified goals, each of the parties is likely to try to influence the policies of the other, as they have over the previous decades.

Israeli Foreign Minister Shamir described the situation in these terms:

Our relations with the United States are of a special character. Between our two nations there is a deep friendship, based on common values and identical interests. At the same time, differences between our two countries crop up occasionally, chiefly on the subject of our borders and how to defend our security. These differences of opinion are natural; they stem from changing conditions, and they express our independence and our separate needs. . . . Israel is a difficult ally, but a faithful and reliable one. We are certain that what we have in common with the United States is permanent and deep, while our disagreements are ephemeral. The permanent will overcome the ephemeral.[62]

CONCLUDING OBSERVATIONS

Generalizations about the complex nature of the relations between states are always difficult. Nevertheless, some overall observations may be useful, as much for what they cannot tell us as for the details they can provide on the nature of the U.S.-Israel relationship.

Power differentials resulting from differences in size or resource base do not always translate directly into influence. A great or greater power does not always have influence over a small or lesser power at all times simply as a function of the power calculus. Former Senator J. William Fulbright commented: "The United States, because of its enormous financial and undeviating political support for Israel, is generally regarded abroad as being responsible for Israeli policy and as the only power which has the capacity to influence that policy."[63] The U.S.-Israel relationship belies that fact, since it is obvious that the massive differences in "power" have not been translated into obvious differences in influence. Influence is often a function of time and issue. A power may be able to exert influence on a specific matter at one time and not at another, and sometimes on one matter but not on another at a particular time. The nature and centrality of the issue under consideration may well set the limits of outside influence. Israel may yield on peripheral matters but not on core concerns.

Influence is not unidirectional. Each actor in a bilateral relationship will seek to influence the activity of the other, often at the same time. This will act to counter the behavior of the adversary and thereby to limit its influence. Much of the time the relationship is one of mutual influence, and this has been particularly true in the dealings of the United States and Israel. There are countervailing or balancing influences. The influence efforts are not exerted by one side without an effort of the other to resist it or to try to reduce its effects through a countervailing effort. Thus, while the United States may try to alter Israeli policies through various means, Israel will seek to alter the American approach through the techniques and means available to it. This effort may follow similar channels or utilize similar methods. For example, the American Jewish community and especially its organized leadership may well be utilized by the U.S. administration to try to prevail upon Israel to modify its policies, while Israel and its supporters may seek to use the same mechanism, at the same time, to modify the approach of the U.S. administration.

The influence relationship is affected by nontangible as well as tangible factors, which makes their identification more difficult. At the same time, and particularly in the U.S.-Israel influence relationship, states are not the sole actors. Private groups and individuals are often involved, and sometimes mobilized, in the effort to influence, and are appealed to as part of the process. This is especially characteristic of the relations of the United States and Israel, in which the Jewish connection and the special perception of Israel in the Judeo-Christian heritage have played an important role.

There are definite limits on the relationship, particularly the goals sought and the methods used to achieve them, beyond which neither side will go. Neither will "push" for goals that are seen as beyond the pale of the relationship, and neither will refuse to comply with "reasonable" requests for action or "inaction." The United States will not push Israel beyond certain parameters, and Israel will not risk losing U.S. support by refusing to respond when essential. The general unwillingness of Israel to lose U.S. support suggests an important area of influence, particularly when this element is combined with the use of personal prestige as a form of pressure. In the bilateral relationship the personal prestige of a senior U.S. official has been a significant factor affecting Israeli decisions. The examples are numerous, but it might be useful to recall that after the initial failure of the Kissinger shuttle, Israel "could not say no" to Kissinger in the renewed attempt that led to the Sinai II agreement, or to Carter at Camp David. In 1983 Israel could not refuse to accede to an Israel-Lebanon agreement that Shultz came to the region to negotiate. In these instances the United States was also sensitive to the limits of Israeli policy modifications.

The United States has sought to create pressure through circumstances that force modifications in the policies of the parties to a negotiation. High visibility at high-level negotiation, such as Camp David and the March 1979 Carter shuttle, combined personal prestige with high drama at the summit. Failure would have been dramatic and obvious, to the detriment of all parties but particularly the one perceived as being at fault. Placing the blame thus becomes a mechanism for influencing the outcome. It was suggested that Israel might be blamed for the failure, with all the obvious negative consequences for the relationship and its tangible components, such as military assistance and economic aid. The threat of a negative judgment by the Congress and U.S. public opinion is a particularly significant tool in the U.S.-Israel relationship, given the significance of Congress and public opinion for the continued support of Israel by the United States, and was "threatened" by Carter on several occasions. The threats of unfavorable public opinion often had an Israeli counter, in that Begin suggested that he too was prepared to take his case to the U.S. people and Congress.

There are the usual limits on policy and decisions, but there are also self-imposed limits (there is a difference between won't and can't) in the dealings of states. These limits apply to the U.S.-Israel relationship. There are limits to concessions that are possible, despite extensive pressures that might be employed. Israel will not "give in" on certain points even under extensive pressure, and U.S. efforts to influence changes in Israeli positions generally are cognizant of the limits beyond which they will achieve little, if any, policy modification. Core values and elements identified as matters of vital national interest are not susceptible to modification through influence. Israeli Foreign Minister Shamir has commented:

> . . . on the fundamental life-and-death issues—such as security, Jerusalem, the 1967 borders, the danger of a Palestinian state—we have no choice but to stand by our position firmly, strongly and clearly—even against our great friend the United States.[64]

There is a base that undergirds this perspective, and there is care, on both sides, not to undermine the identified foundations of the relationship. Even those Americans seen by Israelis as essentially hostile identify a foundation of consequence. What form does this base take? Zbigniew Brzezinski has identified it in these terms:

> The relationship between the United States and Israel is genuinely organic and moral in character. I put that above any formal ties of alliance or treaties. There are such direct personal links between America and Israel, and there is such a sense of moral identification with Israel because of what has happened in the last 40 years that this relationship is as strong as ever and as enduring as ever.[65]

Finally, it must be recognized that Israeli decision makers do not respond well to direct pressures. Resentment and defiance characterize their response to perceptions that they are being pressured. Begin summed it up when he told the Knesset, as Carter sat on the dais, in March 1979: "No, it is not true that you came to bring pressure on us. I may add that if pressure had been exerted on us, we would have rejected it."[66] Pressure is seen as an unacceptable interference in Israel's sovereign decision-making process, and hence counterproductive when utilized, as numerous examples have shown. Israel will not rely on the "wisdom" or the "guarantees" of others on matters of vital national interest, and overt efforts to exert such influence are doomed to failure. Because of this sensitivity, and because U.S. decision makers have understood it, the United States often has pursued the path of reassurance, indicating it would not use pressure to generate changes in Israeli policies, and providing tangible evidence of its support through military and economic aid and political and diplomatic action.

Reassurance has become a significant tool utilized by the United States in the influence relationship. American economic and military aid has played an important role in bridging the gap between the parties in negotiations, and has been particularly effective in inducing Israeli concessions, as in the Sinai II accords and the Egypt-Israel peace treaty. In the latter instance Israel's agreement to withdraw from the Eitam and Etzion air bases in Sinai was closely linked to the U.S. pledge to assist in the construction of new and sophisticated air bases in Israel's Negev. Israel's decision to withdraw from the Sinai oil fields was facilitated by the American commitment to meet Israel's oil needs if alternative sources were not available. American guarantees of the basic treaty were also important inducements to the parties to reach agreement. Reassuring Israel may also take less tangible forms, such as indicating sensitivity to its concerns and restating the commitment to its survival and security. Kissinger has suggested: "Israel is more likely [to negotiate] . . . if it feels compassion on our side, maybe even affection, rather than unremitting pressure. . . . America must . . . treat Israel compassionately and seriously."[67]

As these concluding words are being written, the United States is approaching its quadrennial presidential election season with a hiatus in the peace process and a positive aura for the special relationship with Israel. This mimics past patterns but also reflects the reality of the situation in the fall of 1983, when there was no clear and obvious mechanism for a breakthrough in the peace process. However, the process will resume, given its centrality to both the United States and Israel, and the issues will be contentious, given the positions of the parties. Periodic crises will emerge and will be characterized, as their predecessors have been, as "the worst ever" and reflective of "the nadir" of the relationship. Observers are continually predicting "inevitable collisions" and "confrontations" in the relationship.

However, given the strong ties linking the United States and Israel in the special relationship, the storms of the future will be weathered, as those of the past have been. The relationship has survived the poor personal relations of Carter and Begin, and the Weinberger onslaught as seen by Israel, as well as significant substantive disagreements, such as those surrounding the war in Lebanon, the AWACS debate, the Reagan initiative, and the massacre at Sabra and Shatila. Its resilience is noteworthy. The special relationship will continue with its particular patterns of intercourse and influence between the United States and Israel.

NOTES

1. On U.S. interests in the Middle East, see Bernard Reich, "United States Interests in the Middle East," in Haim Shaked and Itamar Rabinovich, eds., *The Middle East and the United States: Perceptions and Policies* (New Brunswick, N.J., and London: Transaction Books, 1980), pp. 53-92; and Seth P. Tillman, *The United States in the Middle East: Interests and Obstacles* (Bloomington: Indiana University Press, 1982)

2. "American Policy on Trial: An Interview with George Ball," *Journal of Palestine Studies* 7 (Spring 1978): 17-30, p. 20.

3. George W. Ball, "How to Save Israel in Spite of Herself," *Foreign Affairs* 55 (Apr. 1977): 453-71.

4. *National Jewish Monthly,* June 1969, pp. 10, 12.

5. Eugene V. Rostow, "The American Stake in Israel," *Commentary* 63 (Apr. 1977): 32-46, p. 46.

6. Ronald Reagan, "Recognizing the Israeli Asset," *Washington Post,* Aug. 15, 1979.

7. William A. Eddy, *F.D.R. Meets Ibn Saud* (New York: American Friends of the Middle East, 1954), p. 37.

8. See *Foreign Relations of the United States, Diplomatic Papers, 1945,* vol. VIII, *The Near East and Africa* (Washington, D.C.: U.S. Government Printing Office, 1969), pp. 10-18.

9. Harry S. Truman, *Memoirs, Vol. II: Years of Trial and Hope* (Garden City, N.Y.: Doubleday, 1956), p. 158.

10. Merle Miller, *Plain Speaking: An Oral Biography of Harry S. Truman* (New York: Berkley and G. P. Putnam's Sons, 1973), p. 216.

11. Truman, *Memoirs,* vol. II, p. 157.

12. Quoted in Donald Neff, *Warriors at Suez: Eisenhower Takes America into the Middle East* (New York: Linden Press/Simon and Schuster, 1981), p. 433.

13. Charles McC. Mathias, Jr., "Ethnic Groups and Foreign Policy," *Foreign Affairs,* 59 (Summer 1981): 975-98, p. 993.

14. Ibid., pp. 992-93.

15. *New York Times,* May 27, 1975. Emphasis added.

16. William J. Lanouette, "The Many Faces of the Jewish Lobby in America," *National Journal,* 10 (May 13, 1978); 748-56, p. 749.

17. Richard H. Curtiss, *A Changing Image: American Perceptions of the Arab-Israeli Dispute* (Washington, D.C.: American Educational Trust, 1982), provides an interesting approach to this subject.

18. White House press release, Sept. 12, 1974.

19. Abba Eban, *Near East Report,* Apr. 23, 1975, p. 72.

20. Miller, *Plain Speaking,* p. 214.

21. Ibid., p. 215.

22. A very useful contribution to this subject is Alvin Richman, "American Attitudes Toward the Middle East Since Israel's Invasion of Lebanon," paper presented at the AAPOR meeting, Buck Hill Falls Inn, May 1983.

23. See, for example, James F. Larson, "International Affairs Coverage on U.S. Evening Network News, 1972-1979," in William C. Adams, ed., *Television Coverage of International Affairs* (Norwood, N.J.: ABLEX Publishing Corp., 1982), pp. 15-41.

24. See William C. Adams, ed., *Television Coverage of the Middle East* (Norwood, N.J.: ABLEX Publishing Corp., 1981), esp. chs. 1, 4, 5.

25. See S. Robert Lichter, "Media Support for Israel: A Survey of Leading Journalists," in Adams, ed., *Television Coverage of the Middle East,* pp. 40-52. Robert H . Trice, "The American Elite Press and the Arab-Israeli Conflict," *Middle East Journal* 33 (Summer 1979): 304-25, explores the role of the elite press in the period from 1966 to 1974.

26. Interview on "Face the Nation," Oct. 7, 1973.

27. Marvin C. Feuerwerger, *Congress and Israel: Foreign Aid Decision-Making in the House of Representatives, 1969-1976* (Westport, Conn.: Greenwood Press, 1979), p. 28.

28. Ibid.

29. John J. Fialka, "Jewish Groups Increase Donations, Target Them Precisely," *Wall Street Journal,* Aug. 3, 1983.

30. Mathias, "Ethnic Groups and Foreign Policy," p. 996.

31. *New York Times,* Dec. 21, 1981.

32. *American Jewish Year Book 1983* (New York: American Jewish Committee; Philadelphia: Jewish Publication Society of America, 1983), pp. 130-31.

33. Daniel Elazar, *Community and Polity: The Organizational Dynamics of American Jewry* (Philadelphia: Jewish Publication Society of America, 1976), p. 79.

34. Steven Martin Cohen, "The 1981-1982 National Survey of American Jews," in *American Jewish Year Book 1983* (New York: American Jewish Committee; Philadelphia: Jewish Publication Society of America, 1983), pp. 89-110. A popularized version is Steven M. Cohen, "What American Jews Believe: An Eye-opening Report on a Recent Survey of Attitudes Toward Israel," *Moment* 7 (July-Aug. 1982): 23-27.

35. Cohen, "The 1981-1982 National Survey . . . ," p. 95.

36. Ibid.

37. Ibid., pp. 95, 97; see also Table 3, pp. 96-97.

38. Ibid., p. 98.

39. Lanouette, "The Many Faces of the Jewish Lobby . . . ," p. 751.

40. Ibid.

41. For a detailed historical account of AIPAC's efforts for Israel, see I. L. Kenen, *Israel's Defense Line: Her Friends and Foes in Washington* (Buffalo, N.Y.: Prometheus Books, 1981).

42. For a sense of how the American Jewish community acts in the event of a crisis affecting Israel, see Elazar, *Community and Polity,* "Appendix A: The American Jewish Community's Response to the Yom Kippur War: A Case Study in Organization Dynamics," pp. 341-77.

43. Quoted in Lanouette, "The Many Faces of the Jewish Lobby . . . ," p. 756.

44. Ibid.

45. Mathias, "Ethnic Groups and Foreign Policy," p. 993.

46. Ibid., p. 997.

47. Interview on ABC TV, "Nightline," Sept. 9, 1981.

48. Charles S. Liebman, *Pressure Without Sanctions: The Influence of World Jewry on Israeli Policy* (Rutherford, N.J.: Fairleigh Dickinson University Press; London: Associated University Presses, 1977), p. 232.

49. Robert F. Drinan, *Honor the Promise: America's Commitment to Israel* (Garden City, N.Y.: Doubleday and Co., 1977), p. 3.

50. Ruth W. Mouly, "Israel: Darling of the Religious Right," *The Humanist* 42 (May/June 1982): 5-11, p. 6.

51. Ibid.

52. Ibid.

53. Ibid.

54. For a detailed account of American liberal Protestantism and Israel, see Hertzel Fishman, *American Protestantism and a Jewish State* (Detroit: Wayne State University Press, 1973).

55. *New York Times,* May 13, 1977.

56. U.S. Senate, Committee on Foreign Relations, *Report, National Commitments,* 91st Cong., 1st sess., Apr. 16, 1969, pp. 26-27.

57. Quoted in *New York Times,* Oct. 31, 1968.

58. *New York Times,* Mar. 24, 1978.

59. Mordechai Gazit, "America and Israel," *Partisan Review* 49 (1982): 363-70, provides an interesting perspective by a distinguished Israeli diplomat.

60. Interview in *U.S. News and World Report,* Sept. 22, 1969, p. 54.

61. Interview in *Washington Post,* Aug. 7, 1969.

62. Shamir speech to the Knesset, Sept. 8, 1982.

63. J. William Fulbright, "Foreword," in Seth P. Tillman, *The United States in the Middle East: Interests and Obstacles* (Bloomington: Indiana University Press, 1982), p. ix.

64. Shamir speech to the Knesset, Sept. 8, 1982.

65. "The World According to Brzezinski," James Reston interview of Zbigniew Brzezinski, *New York Times Magazine*, Dec. 31, 1978, p. 11.

66. *New York Times*, Mar. 13, 1979.

67. Kissinger interview, *The Economist*, Nov. 13, 1982, p. 30.

SELECTED BIBLIOGRAPHY

The U.S.-Israel relationship has been the subject of extensive writings by academics, journalists, and observers, and many of the participants have published their memoirs. There are statements, speeches, parliamentary debates, official publications, and numerous other materials made available by officials and others involved. This abundance of material both facilitates and complicates the effort to research, analyze, and write about the special relationship. Despite the large quantity of material available in numerous languages, some aspects of the relations are barely considered and much of the material is contradictory. This is particularly true of the memoirs of many of the participants.

The bibliography listed below is designed to suggest some of the materials that may further elucidate the themes contained in this work or offer alternative interpretations of the subjects under consideration.

Dean Acheson, *Present at the Creation: My Years in the State Department* (New York: Norton, 1969).

Gil Carl AlRoy, *The Kissinger Experience: American Policy in the Middle East* (New York: Horizon Press, 1975).

Michael Brecher, *Decisions in Israel's Foreign Policy* (New Haven, Conn.: Yale University Press, 1975).

————, *The Foreign Policy System of Israel: Setting, Images, Process* (New Haven, Conn.: Yale University Press, 1972).

John C. Campbell, *Defense of the Middle East: Problems of American Policy,* rev. ed. (New York: Praeger, 1960).

Naomi W. Cohen, *American Jews and the Zionist Idea* (New York: Ktav Publishing House, 1975).

Robert F. Drinan, *Honor the Promise: America's Commitment to Israel* (Garden City, N.Y.: Doubleday, 1977).

Daniel J. Elazar, *Community and Polity: The Organizational Dynamics of American Jewry* (Philadelphia: Jewish Publication Society of America, 1976).

Walter Eytan, *The First Ten Years: A Diplomatic History of Israel* (New York: Simon and Schuster, 1958).

Herbert Feis, *The Birth of Israel: The Tousled Diplomatic Bed* (New York: Norton, 1969).

Marvin C. Feuerwerger, *Congress and Israel: Foreign Aid Decision-making in the House of Representatives, 1969-1976* (Westport, Conn.: Greenwood Press, 1979).

Reuben Fink, ed., *America and Palestine: The Attitude of Official America and of the American People Toward the Rebuilding of Palestine as a Free and Democratic Jewish Commonwealth* (New York: American Zionist Emergency Council, 1944).

Lawrence H. Fuchs, *The Political Behavior of American Jews* (Glencoe, Ill.: Free Press, 1956).

Eitan Haber, Zeev Schiff, and Ehud Yaari, *The Year of the Dove* (New York: Bantam Books, 1979).

Samuel Halperin, *The Political World of American Zionism* (Detroit: Wayne State University Press, 1961).

J. C. Hurewitz, *Middle East Dilemmas: The Background of United States Policy* (New York: Harper, 1953).

Stephen D. Isaacs, *Jews and American Politics* (Garden City, N.Y.: Doubleday, 1974).

Marvin Kalb and Bernard Kalb, *Kissinger* (Boston: Little, Brown, 1974).

Abraham J. Karp, *To Give Life: The UJA in the Shaping of the American Jewish Community* (New York: Schocken Books, 1981).

I. L. Kenen, *Israel's Defense Line: Her Friends and Foes in Washington* (Buffalo, N.Y.: Prometheus Books, 1981).

Henry Kissinger, *White House Years* (Boston and Toronto: Little, Brown, 1979).

Charles S. Liebman, *Pressure Without Sanctions: The Influence of World Jewry on Israeli Policy* (Rutherford, N.J.: Fairleigh Dickinson University Press; London: Associated University Presses, 1977).

James G. McDonald, *My Mission in Israel, 1948-1951* (New York: Simon and Schuster, 1951).

David Pollock, *The Politics of Pressure: American Arms and Israeli Policy Since the Six Day War* (Westport, Conn.: Greenwood Press, 1982).

William B. Quandt, *Decade of Decisions: American Policy Toward the Arab-Israeli Conflict, 1967-1976* (Berkeley: University of California Press, 1977).

Bernard Reich, *Quest for Peace: United States-Israel Relations and the Arab-Israeli Conflict* (New Brunswick, N.J.: Transaction Books, 1977).

Nadav Safran, *Israel: The Embattled Ally* (Cambridge, Mass.: Belknap Press of Harvard University Press, 1981).

———, *From War to War: The Arab-Israeli Confrontation, 1948-1967* (Cambridge, Mass.: Harvard University Press, 1963).

Mohammed K. Shadid, *The United States and the Palestinians* (London: Croom Helm, 1981).

Haim Shaked and Itamar Rabinovich, eds., *The Middle East and the United States: Perceptions and Policies* (New Brunswick, N.J.: Transaction Books, 1980).

Harvey Sicherman, *Broker or Advocate? The U.S. Role in the Arab-Israeli Dispute, 1973-1978* (Philadelphia: Foreign Policy Research Institute, 1978).

Robert Silverberg, *If I Forget Thee O Jerusalem: American Jews and the State of Israel* (New York: William Morrow and Co., 1970).

Seth P. Tillman, *The United States in the Middle East: Interests and Obstacles* (Bloomington: Indiana University Press, 1982).

Melvin I. Urofsky, *We Are One! American Jewry and Israel* (Garden City, N.Y.: Anchor Press/Doubleday, 1978).

Evan M. Wilson, *Decision on Palestine: How the U.S. Came to Recognize Israel* (Stanford, Calif.: Hoover Institution Press, 1979).

A NOTE ON CURRENT MEMOIRS

Many of the participants in the relationship have written memoirs that provide interesting, although not always fully accurate, accounts of the substance and methods of the relationship. These are important sources, and while many could be cited, I have chosen to focus on those of more recent vintage that offer differing perspectives and recollections of events. They therefore tell us a good deal about what happened, how these two states interacted, and—often—why. They are recommended as much for their substance as for their ability to provide insight into varying interpretations of contemporary events.

American Perspectives

Zbigniew Brzezinski, *Power and Principle: Memoirs of the National Security Adviser, 1977-1981* (New York: Farrar, Straus, Giroux, 1983).

Jimmy Carter, *Keeping Faith: Memoirs of a President* (Toronto, New York, London, Sydney: Bantam Books, 1982).

Cyrus Vance, *Hard Choices: Critical Years in America's Foreign Policy* (New York: Simon and Schuster, 1983).

Israeli Perspectives

Moshe Dayan, *Breakthrough: A Personal Account of the Egypt-Israel Peace Negotiations* (New York: Alfred A. Knopf, 1981).

Ezer Weizman, *The Battle for Peace* (Toronto, New York, London: Bantam Books, 1981).

Hassan, King of Morocco, 107
Hawk Missile, 9, 156, 158, 160, 165, 167
Holocaust, 2, 186, 195, 196
Humphrey, Hubert H., 17
Hussein (King of Jordan), 48, 79, 121, 124, 126, 128, 129, 130, 132, 136; opposition to Camp David Process, 79, 80, 121
Hussein-McMahon correspondence, 1

interim agreement (*see* Rogers Plan C)
Iran, 92, 180; revolution in, 75, 79, 83, 92, 94, 110; holding of American hostages, 75, 88
Iraq, 79, 100; Israeli raid on nuclear reactor, 96, 97-100, 101, 102, 103, 138
Israel: air force, 25, 117; Arab boycott of, 191; defense forces, 30, 61, 78, 102, 112, 117, 134, 137, 171; independence, 1, 4, 182; Labor party, 48, 64, 90, 95, 108, 114, 124; oil supply, 28, 47, 50, 73; policy of non-identification, 182; withdrawal from occupied territories, 11, 13, 15, 16, 17, 18, 23, 31, 32, 45, 50, 56, 58, 79, 103, 213
Israel arms industry, 171, 172
Israel Bonds, 145, 198
Israel-Lebanon Agreement, May 1983, 133, 134, 135, 136, 137, 138; negotiations, 127, 133
Israel lobby (*see also* Jewish lobby), 76, 106, 184, 198-202
Israel-Egypt disengagement of forces, 32, 35, 166
Israel-Syria disengagement of forces (1974), 32

Jackson, Henry M., 54, 179
Jarring mission, 15, 16, 17, 19, 20, 21, 26, 27, 159, 161, 168
Jerusalem, 16, 17, 23, 24, 66, 69, 76, 77, 79, 88, 104, 107, 123, 213
Jerusalem "Basic Law" (May 1980), 77
Jewish Agency, 204
Jewish homeland in Palestine, 2, 195
Jewish lobby (*see also* Israel lobby), 106, 183, 202
Jewish vote, 183, 192, 194
Jews, political role (*see* American Jewish community), 183, 192, 194
Johnson, Joseph E., 9
Johnson, Lyndon B., 9, 10, 12, 13, 14, 15, 16, 157, 158, 159, 206
Johnston, Eric, 6
Jordan, 23, 32, 36, 44, 53, 58, 68, 69, 72, 74, 79, 89, 90, 121, 131, 132, 137, 138, 180
Jordan River development schemes, 6
Judea and Samaria (*see* West Bank)
June War (1967), 9, 10, 11, 12, 13, 14, 18, 37, 45, 50, 154, 157, 158, 160, 168, 188, 196, 207, 211, 212, 213

Kadum, 51
Kahan Commission, 126
Kenen, I. L., 199
Kennedy, John F., 8, 9, 157
Kfir Jets, 47, 50, 170, 171, 172
Khalil, Mustafa, 70, 71
Khartoum Arab summit (1967), 13
Kilometer 101 meetings, 31
Kimche, David, 112, 134
Kirkpatrick, Jeane, 100

ABOUT THE AUTHOR

Bernard Reich is Professor of Political Science and International Affairs and former Chairman of the Department of Political Science at the George Washington University in Washington, D.C. where he specializes in Middle East politics.

Dr. Reich was a Fulbright Research Scholar in Egypt in 1965 and a National Science Foundation Postdoctoral Fellow in Israel in 1971-72. He has served as a consultant to various U.S. government agencies and corporations on Middle Eastern affairs and lectures regularly on these subjects both in the United States and abroad.

His numerous publications include *Government and Politics of the Middle East and North Africa* and *Quest for Peace* as well as articles and monographs on United States Middle East policy and Israeli politics and foreign policy.